DIVIDING REALITY

DIVIDING REALITY

Eli Hirsch

New York   Oxford
OXFORD UNIVERSITY PRESS

Oxford University Press

Oxford   New York

Athens   Auckland   Bangkok   Bogota   Bombay   Buenos Aires
Calcutta   Cape Town   Dar es Salaam   Delhi   Florence   Hong Kong
Istanbul   Karachi   Kuala Lumpur   Madras   Madrid   Melbourne
Mexico City   Nairobi   Paris   Singapore   Taipei   Tokyo   Toronto

and associated companies in
Berlin   Ibadan

Copyright © 1993 by Eli Hirsch

First published in 1993 by Oxford University Press, Inc.
198 Madison Avenue, New York, New York 10016

First issued as an Oxford University Press paperback, 1997.

Oxford is a registered trademark of Oxford University Press, Inc.

Library of Congress Cataloging-in-Publication Data

Hirsch, Eli
Dividing reality / Eli Hirsch.
p.   cm.   Includes bibliographical references and index.
ISBN 0-19-505754-6   ISBN 0-19-511142-7 (pbk.)
1. Division (Philosophy)   I. Title.
B390.H57   1993   111—dc20   92-36251

1 3 5 7 9 8 6 4 2

Printed in the United States of America
on acid-free paper

To my wife Pam
and my daughters Dena and Suzanna

Preface

This book deals with a certain philosophical question that I call the division problem. Roughly, the question is why it seems reasonable for us to have words that classify and individuate in ordinary ways rather than other ways. The question may be viewed as Kantian in its general orientation but, in its specific content, I venture to suggest at the end of chapter 1 that the division problem is in a sense a "new problem." This is a somewhat awkward remark for an author to make. I make it because I have often found in the past that people react to the division problem by confusing it with a number of other problems that have been widely discussed in the literature, such as the problem of projectibility, or various issues of ontology. I am therefore obliged to state forthrightly that the problem I am trying to get at is distinct from these. If any other author has seriously addressed the division problem, I am not aware of it. The reader must judge, of course, whether this problem has the significance I assign to it.

I can try to give a prefatory inkling of what I think is the essential novelty of the division problem. The problem is about the rational basis for the ordinary classificatory and individuative functions of general words. In an important sense I am asking a question about (part of) the *lexicon* of languages, about the rational basis for having certain kinds of general words (or morphemes) rather than others. I am asking, for instance, whether there is any reason why we ought to have a word for green things rather than a word for things that are either green or circular. Philosophers from Aristotle to Locke to Kripke and Putnam have said many things about the standard functions of general words in a language—about the standard classificatory and individuative roles of words—but have scarcely addressed the question whether there are any good reasons why a language ought to have words that function in those standard ways. Why have philosophers generally not concerned themselves with this question?

My impression is that there are two perplexingly contradictory impulses at work here. On the one hand, some philosophers may immediately assume, prior to any serious examination of the matter, that there can be no philosophically important constraints on the lexical features of languages, that these features are either arbitrary or at best reflect some trivial pragmatic facts of little philosophical interest. I think that this assumption will seem intuitively plausible only insofar as one ignores central cases, as if one ignores the air we breathe and concludes that gases are not important to us. Of course, there are many peripheral features of a language's lexicon which do seem arbitrary and unimportant, but the most central features seem to reflect fundamental constraints on the structure of language and thought. That seems, at any rate, to be the intuitive judgment when one considers the sorts of examples that I will introduce in the first chapter. Intuitively, it is plausible to suppose that the range of permissible lexicons is severely restricted by important philosophical considerations.

But there may be an opposite impulse at work in rendering the division problem inconspicuous to philosophers. It may be felt that, at least with respect to the most central lexical features of languages, the relevant constraints are indeed important but are so obvious and so compelling that there is no need to belabor them. I am confident, however, that this book will show, if nothing else, that there is nothing *obvious* to be said on this topic. The nature of the constraints on lexicons is a fundamental question for philosophy.

The general structure of the book is as follows: In chapter 1, I introduce the division problem and try to give a preliminary idea of some of its implications. Chapter 2 relates the problem to certain questions about projectibility, similarity, and ostensive definitions. In chapters 3 and 4, two kinds of "reality's joints" are discussed: "natural properties" in the former chapter and "natural things" in the latter. Chapter 3 also explores certain connections between the division problem and the nature of explanation, and chapter 4 connects the problem to questions about semantic compositionality and the inscrutability of reference. In chapter 5, I formulate and criticize a number of pragmatist reactions to the problem. Readers who, after completing chapter 1, are thoroughly convinced that the only sensible response to the division problem is pragmatic might want to jump directly to chapter 5, most of which is independent of the intermediary chapters, and afterward return to chapter 2. (But, other things being equal, it would be preferable to read the book straight through.) Chapter 6 presents a certain theory of propositional structure and relates this to claims that some concepts necessarily depend on others. I take the material in this chapter to provide the basis for the most serious response to the division problem. This response is explored further in chapter 7, which also relates the division problem to issues of ontology. The three appendices contain somewhat more technical or narrowly focused material related, respectively, to chapters 2, 3, and 6.

No one who writes a philosophy book can be consciously aware of more than a small minority of the major presuppositions that shape the work, but it may be worth trying to state one or two that are especially important. Throughout this book I presuppose the intelligibility of the notions of a priority and (metaphysical) necessity. In this respect, I presuppose at least the most general epistemological and metaphysical framework of Saul Kripke's *Naming and Necessity* (1980). At the very outset I formulate the division problem in terms of the notion of a priori necessary equivalence, and in all that follows I make frequent use of the notions of a priority and necessity. Nowhere in the book are these notions challenged or even carefully explained. This may be viewed as a limitation of the book but should not be viewed as a mistake or oversight. Even in philosophy, there must be some division of labor. I presuppose here a framework that has been widely influential and that I regard as correct. Of course, this framework ought to be critically evaluated, but not by me in this book. I have sometimes considered whether the issues discussed here could be reframed, say, by substituting some Quinean notion of paraphrase for a priori necessary equivalence. I think this could be done at least to a significant extent, but I have not attempted to pursue it. It should be understood that while the Kripkean notions of a priority and necessity are what I require to pose the division problem, later chapters in the book may perhaps imply that, in order to solve the problem, other traditional notions are required, such as propositional structure or synonymy.

A second presupposition is of a methodological sort, something roughly to the following effect: Philosophical problems and questions are valuable in their own right, even if no definite solution to them seems forthcoming. Let me explain why I am saying this. The division problem exemplifies a pattern that is quite common in philosophy. We start out with an intuitive judgment and then find that this judgment is hard to clarify and defend. If the judgment is about something of philosophical significance, we have a philosophical problem. The problem of the external world and the problem of induction can readily be seen as exemplifying this pattern. The relevant intuitive judgment in the case of the division problem is that there are rational constraints on how the words of a language ought to classify and individuate. That this is our strong intuition can be brought out by reflecting on the kinds of examples that I present throughout chapter 1. It seems obvious that the intuition concerns something of philosophical importance. And we will find that it is hard to clarify or defend the intuition. So we have here a philosophical problem, the division problem. Any problem of this general sort admits of two kinds of responses: A "straight" solution attempts to clarify and defend the relevant intuition; a "skeptical" solution rejects the intuition. (See Kripke 1982, pp. 66–67.) Someone who adopts a skeptical solution to the division problem is called a "relativist" in this book.

Many of the sections in this book do not deal directly with the division problem but deal with various ancillary issues, such as natural properties and things, the inscrutability of reference, the structure of propositions, the nature of ontology, and the projectibility of terms. With regard to these matters I often attempt to defend a definite position or theory. But as regards the division problem itself, I wind up taking no definite stand. To a large extent my discussions are negative, attempting to show that various tempting answers to the problem are unsatisfactory. In the final two chapters (and in the third appendix) I develop, as far as I am able, a theory which I regard as the only real hope for a straight solution to the problem. But, for the reasons given in the last chapter, I do not see how to work out this theory successfully. Nevertheless, the strength of the initial intuitions about the problem, especially when buttressed by considerations that come out of the last two chapters, make the skeptical, relativist response to the problem seem unacceptable to me.

This book, therefore, does not offer a definite answer to the central question it raises. It strikes me that a mathematician who spent ten years working on an intuitive theorem but could neither prove it nor disprove it would probably not write a book on the topic. I assume, however, that finding out and highlighting what we do not understand has been an essential part of philosophy going back to Socrates. I accept Thomas Nagel's judgment that in philosophy "one should trust problems over solutions," and the best one can do is "try to maintain a desire for answers, a tolerance for long periods without any" and "an unwillingness to brush aside unexplained intuitions" (Nagel 1979, pp. x, xxi.) I would be content if this book succeeds in both presenting the division problem and discouraging quick or glib responses to it.

It scarcely needs saying that, even if the problem I am here addressing is in some ways novel, virtually all of the ideas that I apply to it are derived in one way or another from other people. I am indebted to the work of Sydney Shoemaker, among other reasons because the germ of the division problem was planted in my mind a number of years ago when reading his "Comments on Chisholm" (Shoemaker 1969, especially pp. 117–25). David Lewis's writings on natural properties and related matters affect almost every page of chapters 3 and 4. A number of key formulations, especially in chapter 6, are adapted from George Bealer's *Quality and Concept* (1982).

Several philosophers commented on drafts of this book, and I want to express my debt to them. George Bealer, Georges Dicker, and Jerry Samet gave me extensive comments on various portions of the book, which led to fundamental revisions. I thank James van Cleve for commenting on almost all of the penultimate draft. I am also grateful for help with particular chapters provided by Alan Berger, Peter Unger, and David Wong.

Portions of this book were written while I held a National Endowment for the Humanities grant, for which I am grateful.

Brookline, Mass.   E. H.
January 1992

Contents

DIVIDING REALITY

1

The Division Problem

1. Introduction to the Problem

Our language divides up reality in a certain way, though we can apparently describe an indefinite number of other ways this might be done. This fact may not in itself be seen as generating a philosophical problem, for it may merely suggest the need for an empirical explanation, in terms of psychology or sociology, of why our division practices are as they are. A philosophical problem is generated, however, by certain *normative* intuitions which we seem to have about these practices. Intuitively, it seems that there are good reasons why we ought to have essentially the division practices we do have; it seems that it would be in some sense incorrect or irrational for us to employ a language that divides reality in some way significantly different from our ordinary way. The philosophical problem is to explain what these normative intuitions amount to, and to determine whether they can be properly defended. What, if anything, makes our division practices more correct or rational than various alternative practices we seem able to describe? This is what I am calling the division problem.

In this opening chapter I will make a preliminary pass through a number of aspects of the division problem which will be explored more fully in the course of the book. My immediate aim is to establish the point that we do have the problem-generating intuitions and that some of these appear indeed to be extremely strong and deep intuitions.

The notion of "language dividing up reality" has a number of important philosophical associations but, at least to begin with, I want to adopt a highly austere interpretation of the notion. When I say that our language divides up reality in a certain way, rather than other describable ways, I simply mean that the *single words* of our language denote (the members of) certain classes of things rather than others.[1] Evidently, in this sense, even actual languages differ somewhat in how they divide reality. The relevant normative intuitions, however, arise most vividly, not when we compare actual languages, but when we compare a given actual language, such as English, to certain imagined languages that are radically different from it. The following is the sort of example to which I will often appeal in this book. We have in English a word that denotes the class of green things, but we do not have a word that denotes the class of things that are either green or circular. We can describe an alternative language in which the situation is exactly the opposite. This language contains a word, say "gricular," that applies to anything just in case it is either green or circular but contains no word that applies to anything just in case it is green. To generalize the example, let us suppose that in this language *many* ordinary words are replaced in the same manner. In this example, we have a strikingly radical departure from the way that English divides up reality.

In order to develop the example further, let me fix some terminology. *Throughout this book I will use "equivalent" simpliciter to mean "a priori necessarily equivalent."* Hence, two sentences are equivalent if someone who understands both of them can know a priori that they hold true in exactly the same possible situations, and two terms are equivalent if someone who understands both of them can know a priori that they apply to exactly the same things in every possible situation.[2] If two languages are such that for any sentence in one there is an equivalent sentence in the other, then there seems to be an obvious sense in which the two languages have the *same descriptive content.*

I want to assume that "gricular," in the imagined alternative language, is equivalent to the English expression "green or circular." If we simply replaced "green" by "gricular" and left everything else the same, we might not have any term that is equivalent to "green." ("Gricular and not circular" is equivalent to "green and not circular," not to "green.")[3] So the alternative language so construed might not have the same descriptive content as English. The sort of example that seems more interesting is one in which two languages divide up reality differently

---

[1]I will follow Quine in assuming that a general word denotes (applies to, is true of) particular things; for example, "green" denotes all and only green things. (See Quine 1972, p. 80.) In a derivative sense, however, it will often be convenient to express this by saying that "green" denotes the class of green things (i.e., all and only members of that class).

[2]As stated in the Preface, I assume throughout this book the notions of a priority and necessity in roughly the sense explained in Kripke 1980. I have discussed these notions in Hirsch 1986. I assume that the notion of "equivalence" formulated in the text can be understood in a manner that does not beg any substantive questions about whether semantical knowledge can be said to be a priori.

[3]I do not want to consider at this point more complicated possibilities for defining "green" in terms of "gricular" (cf. appendix 3.2).

despite having the same descriptive content. This is the sort of example that I want to focus on.

We can accordingly elaborate our previous example by imagining that both "green" and "circular" are eliminated and replaced by the three words "gricular," "grincular," and "ngricular" that apply, respectively, to things that are either green or circular, things that are either green or not circular, and things that are either not green or circular. Then "green" and "circular" are equivalent, respectively, to "gricular and grincular" and "gricular and ngricular." The Gricular language now divides up reality differently from English though it has the same descriptive content as English.

Two points must be understood about this example. First, I am imagining that "gricular" is an unambiguous word that applies univocally to anything that is either green or circular. Ambiguous words or homonyms are of course prevalent in ordinary language, but that has nothing to do with how our language divides up reality in the relevant sense. As I use the term "word" throughout this book, it means "word *taken in a particular sense*." If this is a departure from correct usage (it seems controversial whether it is), let this be accepted as a kind of abbreviatory stipulation. I would not say, therefore, that there is a word of English (i.e., "bank") that denotes anything that is either a certain kind of financial institution or a certain kind of shore of a water body. In the sense that concerns me, that is *not* the way English divides up reality.

The second point is that one must not imagine that "gricular," "grincular," and "ngricular" occur only in the context of the two expressions "gricular and grincular" or "gricular and ngricular." If that were so, one might count the two expressions as semantically indivisible words, and the distinction between the Gricular language and ordinary language would collapse. We are to imagine instead that "gricular," "grincular," and "ngricular" have the typical syntactic and semantic independence of ordinary words, so that speakers of the Gricular language would accept such sentences as "Tomatoes and peppers are two kinds of gricular vegetables," and "None of those blocks is ngricular."[4]

What is our intuition about the Gricular language (bearing in mind that in this language many words function like "gricular," "grincular," and "ngricular")? It seems clear that our intuitive judgment is that this language is in some sense absurd and that we have compellingly good reasons to favor our ordinary language over it. The division problem, as applied to this case, is to explain what these good reasons are.

Our intuition may be that the Gricular language would be an absurd language for *us*, in our particular context, or that it would be an absurd

---

[4]In general, I intend to rely on the ordinary intuitive notion of a "word (taken in a particular sense)." My assumption is that various complex issues discussed, e.g., in morphology, will not be critical to this discussion.

language for *anyone*, in any imaginable context. This distinction will be looked into later. In general, it is the former context that will be pre-supposed, for this is the context that most obviously elicits the prob-lem-generating intuitions. If we imagine that speakers of the Gricular language are relevantly like us in their beliefs and motives, certainly it seems intuitively absurd that they should employ such a language. The problem is to explain why this would be absurd.

That this question is not easy to answer must emerge in subsequent discussions throughout this book. However, the prima facie difficulty can immediately be appreciated. The word "gricular" does denote certain things; sentences containing the word do often express truths; indeed, if the word is surrounded by others of the same sort (e.g., "grincular" and "ngricular"), the expressible truths seem to be equivalent to the ones we ordinarily express. Why, then, is the language absurd?

In general, the division problem is to explain what good reasons there may be to favor ordinary languages over various imaginary *strange lan-guages*, where a strange language is one that divides up reality in ways that intuitively strike us as absurd. A strange language such as the Gricular language serves to illustrate the intuitive idea that there are strong nor-mative constraints on our division practices. It should be emphasized that this need not imply that there are no reasonable alternatives to the prac-tices we have. On the contrary, it seems immediately plausible to sup-pose that the way our language divides reality is arbitrary in certain respects, in the sense that it would not be unreasonable for us to have a language that is different in these respects. But the intuitive idea, which the strange languages help to make vivid, is that there are definite limits on what can constitute a reasonable alternative to our ordinary division practices. The division problem is to understand what the nature of these limits might be.

Since I intend to explore the division problem from a number of dif-ferent angles in the course of this book, it is essential that the reader not assume that certain substantive matters have already been settled. We have, I said, the intuition that there are rational constraints on our division practices, constraints that are violated by the Gricular language. I do not assume that this intuition must be correct. Even if it is correct, we may have no definite idea at the outset of how to formulate the in-tuitive constraints on division practices. Certainly we can think of many examples with respect to which it seems unclear whether (or to what extent) the supposed constraints are violated. It may not even be clear at the outset what general sort of "irrationality" we are dealing with when we judge intuitively that a strange language is irrational or absurd. Is it that speakers of such a language will be led to reason fallaciously about certain things? Is it that their language is in some sense rooted in some factual, or perhaps metaphysical, error? Or is it rather that a strange lan-guage like the Gricular language would have to be impractical in some way? Might there be some other, perhaps idiosyncratic way in which such

languages are absurd? And might it be that some examples of strangeness are absurd in one way whereas others are absurd in quite different
ways? I want all of these questions to be open at this stage of the discussion. They are indeed all part and parcel of what I mean by the division problem.

Summarily put, the division problem is this: Can we clarify and justify our intuition that there are rational constraints on how the words of
a language ought to divide up reality (with special attention to constraints
on languages having the same descriptive content as ours)?

2. Classificatory and Individuative Strangeness

It will be useful to draw some preliminary distinctions between different
kinds of strange languages. One essential distinction is between *classificatory* strangeness and *individuative* strangeness.

a. Individuative Strangeness and Ontological Commitment

The Gricular language classifies ordinary things in strange ways, but we
can also imagine languages that, in a sense, divide up the world into
strange things. One way to describe such languages is by specifying
strange transtemporal identity conditions for things, that is, strange truth-
conditions for sentences of the form "There exists something that is A
at t_1 and (that same thing is) B at t_2." As an example, let me specify the
strange identity conditions that operate in the imaginary language called
Contacti.[5] In this language the identity through time of things is partly
determined by their contact relations. The language contains, for
example, the word "ctable" (corresponding to the English word "table")
such that the history of a single "ctable" combines what we would ordinarily regard as stages of one table, followed by stages of a second table
with which the first is exclusively in contact, followed by stages of the
first table after exclusive contact is broken off. Hence, it is a principle of
"ctable identity" that during an interval when two "ctables" come into
contact exclusively with each other (i.e., with each other but with no
other "ctables"), they temporarily exchange all of their characteristics
(including their spatial positions).[6] There is evidently a certain symmetry in the relationship between tables and ctables, for the history of a
single table combines what is regarded in Contacti as stages of one ctable,
followed by stages of a second ctable with which the first is exclusively
in contact, followed by stages of the first ctable after exclusive contact is

---

[5]This example (with a slight notational difference) is discussed in Hirsch 1982, chapter
10.

[6]But note that if one regards it as possible that, under some special circumstances, ordinary
tables might exchange all of their characteristics when they come into contact, then in those
circumstances ctables would *not* exchange their characteristics. I leave it open whether this
qualification is necessary; if it is, let it be assumed.

broken off. It appears, then, that Contacti has the same descriptive content as English.[7]

We may imagine Contacti generalized to include many other bizarre individuals such as "cpersons" and "cdogs" whose identities depend in a correlative fashion upon their contact relations. The division problem, as regards this example, is to explain why it would seem absurd for us to operate with such a language.

Some readers will immediately want to object that my characterization of Contacti presupposes a disputable commitment to the existence of such entities as ctables and cdogs. This objection is based on a misunderstanding, however. What I intended to do in characterizing Contacti was to stipulate the truth-conditions for Contacti identity sentences, that is, the conditions under which the sentences would count as true.[8] No disputable ontological commitment is required for that stipulation. Indeed, one might convey the truth-conditions more graphically— and obviously without any disputable ontological commitments—by drawing a picture. (See Figure 1.1.) In the picture, the unbroken arrows represent our ordinary identity sentences and the broken arrows represent the Contacti identity sentences. We imagine that at one o'clock two dogs come into contact with each other (and with no other dogs). In the pictured situation, what one would say in Contacti is "A cdog was brown and to the left at twelve o'clock and (that same cdog) was white and to the right at one o'clock and (that same cdog) was brown and to the left again at two o'clock."

My stipulation of the truth-conditions for Contacti sentences is not intended to foreclose every question of detail that could be raised about Contacti. Such questions are unimportant if they merely suggest the possibility of describing slightly different versions of this intuitively bizarre

---

[7]For example, the Contacti sentence "There exists a ctable that is first brown and then white" is equivalent to the complex English sentence "There exists a table that either is first brown while not exclusively in contact with another table and is then white while not exclusively in contact with another table, or is first exclusively in contact with a brown table and is then exclusively in contact with a white table, or is first exclusively in contact with a brown table and is then white while not exclusively in contact with another table, or is first brown while not exclusively in contact with another table and is then exclusively in contact with a white table." The English sentence "There exists a table that is first brown and then white" is equivalent to a correspondingly complex Contacti sentence.

It will be noted that, for the sake of brevity, I use expressions of the form "two F-things are exclusively in contact with each other" (or "an F-thing is exclusively in contact with another F-thing") to imply that the two F-things are in contact with each other and neither is in contact with a third F-thing (of course, they may be in contact with various other things).

[8]We know the truth-conditions of sentences in the relevant sense if we know, with respect to every context in which they might be uttered, what their truth-values are with respect to every possible situation. Note that (at least with respect to the sort of examples under consideration) sentences have the same truth-conditions in this sense if and only if they are equivalent.

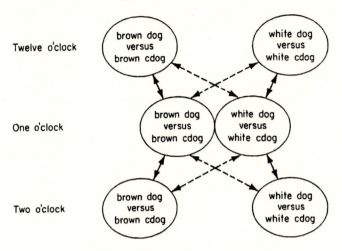

Figure 1.1 English versus Contacti.

form of language. One question that perhaps should be briefly addressed relates to statements about identity through possible worlds. How might such statements operate in Contacti? The simplest way to try to answer this question is by analogy to how statements about identity through time operate. Contact relations can be stipulated to determine the transworld identity of a ctable in much the way that they were stipulated to determine the transtemporal identity of a ctable. (For example, a table at one time constitutes the same ctable as another table at a second time if some third table is exclusively in contact with both the first table at the first time and the second table at the second time; likewise, a table in some actual situation might be said to constitute the same ctable as another table in some counterfactual situation if some third table is exclusively in contact with both the first table in the actual situation and the second table in the counterfactual situation.)[9]

Let me mention another question about Contacti. In order for Contacti to have the same descriptive content as English, it must be the case that any sentence in one language is equivalent to some sentence in the other. This seems to imply that if Cfido is the cdog that sometimes coincides with, and sometimes is in contact with, the dog Fido, then Contacti sentences containing "Cfido" are a priori necessarily equivalent to English sentences containing "Fido." The claim of necessary equivalence seems fairly straightforward, but there may be a problem

---

[9]In ordinary language, statements about transtemporal and transworld identity seem to be closely connected in various ways (cf. Kripke 1980, pp. 112–115); the stipulation sketched in the text would transfer many of these connections to Contacti.

about the claim of a priori equivalence. One can interpret the rules of Contacti to imply that necessarily Fido exists if and only if Cfido does.[10] There is, however, a general problem in determining when sentences containing different proper names can be a priori equivalent. Nevertheless, I think it is plausible to assume that sentences of English containing names are a priori equivalent to sentences of Contacti containing names. If this assumption is not acceptable, I would need to modify my earlier characterization of what it means for two languages to have "the same descriptive content" by requiring that corresponding sentences containing names be only necessarily equivalent (rather than equivalent *simpliciter*).[11] Evidently, there could be nothing in this modification to diminish the force of the division problem (or to suggest, in particular, why ordinary sentences containing names are better than Contacti sentences containing names).

Let me generalize the point just made. Perhaps there are other problems with the assumption that sentences of the various strange languages under consideration can be a priori equivalent (and not just necessarily equivalent) to ordinary sentences.[12] If so, we can always retreat to the weaker assumption that the sentences can at least be necessarily equivalent. This may somewhat affect the intuitive vividness of the division problem, but the problem is certainly not removed. (Having said this, I will continue to assume that sentences of the strange languages can be both a priori and necessarily equivalent to ordinary sentences.)

b. The Believer and the Disbeliever

I have pointed out that to explain Contacti, in the sense of explaining the truth-conditions of its sentences, does not require any disputable ontological commitments. Something more must be said, however, about the notion of "individuative strangeness." There are two obvious kinds of positions that one can adopt toward the strange Contacti descriptions of "ctables": One may believe that there exist strange things (entities, objects) answering to such descriptions or that there do not exist any such strange things. That is, the believer affirms, and the disbeliever denies, that there exist objects which are just like tables except that they

---

[10]Given the stated rules of transtemporal identity for Contacti, Fido persists at a given time if and only if Cfido does, for Fido and Cfido coincide unless they are in contact. One can interpret transworld identity in Contacti in the same spirit. If one has trouble seeing this, it is clear in any case that we could arrange for a strange language to have this effect.

[11]As stipulated earlier, "equivalent" *simpliciter* means "a priori necessarily equivalent." Hence, "necessarily equivalent" and "a priori equivalent" express weaker relations than "equivalent."

[12]On some views, certain general terms are semantically akin to proper names, in which case the problem mentioned in the last paragraph may arise with respect to some general terms.

exchange their qualities and spatial relations when they come into exclusive contact with each other.[13]

I assume that, according to the believer, many ordinary English words characterizing the qualities and relations of things (e.g., "red," "to the left of") apply, in their ordinary senses, to ctables. The disbeliever, however, holds that, since the strange things do not exist, no such English words denote any strange things. Indeed, since on the disbeliever's position there are no strange things answering to the strange Contacti descriptions, it seems there are no things to be denoted by the word "ctable" in Contacti. What may apparently be concluded, on this position, is that, while the sentences of Contacti have certain specified truth-conditions, many key words of Contacti fail to denote anything.[14]

Since, on the believer's position, even English contains many words that denote the strange things, in what sense, one may wonder, can Contacti be said to be intuitively absurd? The believer may point out, however, that though English has many words that denote ctables, none of these words is *individuative*, where a word is individuative if it can typically be combined with a demonstrative to single out something. One cannot single out a ctable in English by pointing in a certain direction and saying "that F," unless "F" is an enormously complicated expression (specifying conditions of transtemporal and perhaps transworld identity). What seems intuitively absurd about Contacti, the believer might say, is that it contains the individuative word "ctable" geared to singling out ctables.

I said before that in a case of classificatory strangeness we have a word like "gricular" that classifies ordinary things in strange ways. But on the believer's position, "gricular" (like "green") also denotes strange things. So what we should say more cautiously is that in classificatory strangeness we have a word that strangely classifies ordinary things and perhaps also strange things. In individuative strangeness, by contrast, we have a word that denotes *only* strange things.[15] So the believer can also say that Contacti seems to be an absurd language because it seems absurd to have a word that denotes only strange things such as cdogs or ctables.

The notion of "individuative strangeness" is harder to get clear about on the disbeliever's position. Since I am inclined to be a certain kind of disbeliever (for reasons that I will eventually explain in section 7.2.e), I must take pains to make the notion clear on this position. The difficulty

---

[13]Variations of these positions will be introduced in section 4.1.a.

[14]Other options for the disbeliever will be considered in sections 4.2.a and 4.2.b One option is that, for the disbeliever, the word "ctable" functions in Contacti to denote certain set-theoretical constructions. Let us ignore that kind of complication for the time being.

[15]Even a ctable that never comes into contact with another ctable is a strange thing, because it has the potentiality to suffer the strange transformations if it did come into contact with another ctable (cf. section 2.4.a).

is that if there are no things that undergo the strange Contacti transformations, how can one say that Contacti "divides up reality into strange things" such as ctables? Surely one cannot coherently suppose that to imagine a strange language is to imagine things coming into existence that do not in fact exist. How, then, can there be "individuative strangeness"?

Part of the answer to this question can be given in negative terms. If, on the disbeliever's position (as earlier construed), strange Contacti words like "ctable" fail to denote anything, it seems at least to follow that such words *do not* "divide up reality into ordinary things." This is, if not "individuative strangeness," at least the *absence* of "individuative ordinariness." But something more positive than this should be said too, for I think that, even on the disbeliever's position, there is an important sense in which Contacti "divides up reality into strange things."

Even if we are disbelievers, we should, I think, accept the following proposition:

> In Contacti, the word "ctable" *ostensibly denotes*—behaves *as if* it denotes— strange things that are like tables except for exchanging their characteristics whenever they come into or go out of exclusive contact with each other.[16]

This proposition can be understood as expressing an analogy between the contribution made by the word "ctable" to the truth-conditions of Contacti sentences and the contribution made by ordinary words like "table" to the truth-conditions of ordinary sentences. The analogy rests primarily, I think, on the formal or syntactic point that the ordinary formal logic of existence and identity (as expressed in quantification theory, for example) applies to Contacti sentences. (For example, the truth of a Contacti sentence of the form "*a* is a ctable that is *F*" entails the truth of a Contacti sentence of the form "There exists a ctable that is *F*.") There is, in addition, a substantive analogy between the epistemological activity that we can call in English "tracking (the history of) an object" and the activity that could be called by that expression in Contacti. To track an object in the ordinary sense involves taking account of the spatial, qualitative, and causal connections between objects presented at different times. (This remark leaves open the question whether there are a priori necessary "criteria of identity" for objects.) Much the same holds in Contacti.

---

[16]There is a partial analogy to Quine's remarks about "virtual classes" in Quine 1969c, pp. 15–21: "The virtual theory . . . talks much *as if* there were classes, but explains this talk without assuming them" (p. 20, my emphasis). From the point of view of the disbeliever, ctables are merely "virtual objects." The analogy is only partial because, whereas the theory of virtual classes cannot accommodate any semblance of (non-substitutional) quantification over virtual classes, disbelievers can explain in terms of their ontology the ostensible quantification in Contacti over the strange things, i.e., they can describe the truth-conditions of Contacti sentences which make such ostensible quantifications come out true.

The proposition that "ctable" in Contacti behaves as if it denotes some strange things seems to me quite irresistible. And there is no good motive to resist it. I am not proposing to introduce "ostensible denotation" ("as if denotation") as a rigorous technical notion. It merely marks an analogy that anyone might be expected to appreciate. And it is this analogy that (on the disbeliever's position) explains what it might mean to say that Contacti "divides up reality into strange things."

If, on the disbeliever's position, the strange individuative words do not denote, but only behave as if they denote, this may be held to present some form of semantic difficulty for the strange individuative languages. I will consider a "semantic argument" against individuative strangeness later (see section 4.2). Let us simply note at present that it is not immediately obvious what such an argument will amount to. Since Contacti appears to have the same descriptive content as English, the problem is to explain how the former language would be rendered absurd in virtue of its containing words like "ctable" and "cdog" which fail to (really) denote.

c. The Hybrid Meta-Language

Of course if we accept the disbeliever's position, we still cannot say such things as "There exist some strange things that are ostensibly denoted by the words of Contacti" because, on this position, we do not believe that any such things exist. But I am now about to alter this situation in a way that I am afraid some readers may find perplexing. So it will be necessary to try to dispel this perplexity.

It seems natural when teaching a language to combine words of the language being taught with words of the language in which it is taught, as in "This fruit is a *pomme*." It is especially tempting to mix languages in this fashion when one is attempting to critically examine another language. I have already succumbed to this temptation to a limited extent because I have occasionally used (rather than merely mentioned) the words "gricular" and "ctable." I now want to make this policy explicit and to apply it extensively. In discussing various strange languages throughout this book, I am often going to employ a kind of hybrid meta-language that combines English with relevant fragments of the strange languages under consideration. Hence, when talking about Contacti, I will say in this meta-language such things as "There exist exactly as many tables as ctables." In the meta-language, this expresses a non-controversial truth.

Since I am now saying (in my meta-language) that there exist ctables, can I also say that these things are denoted by "ctable" in Contacti or must I limit myself to saying (in deference to the disbeliever's position) that they are ostensibly denoted by "ctable"? I will assume that it is all right to say the first thing. Since the strange things exist (as I now say),

there seems to be no significant difference between saying that they are
denoted by a word and saying that they are only ostensibly denoted. (If
this is not acceptable, let "denotes" in all that follows be replaced by
"ostensibly denotes," where denotation is taken to be a special case of
ostensible denotation.)

Is there some ontological duplicity going on here? Have I in effect
abandoned the disbeliever's position? But one does not abandon a position merely by adopting a language. I assume that I have properly
introduced Contacti. I am therefore entitled to adopt it. The virtue of
the meta-language is that it will enable me, at various stages of discussion in this book, to put aside the ontological issue dividing the believer
and disbeliever while I attend to various other issues. In considering the
strange individuative languages, I want to be able to assess such claims
as the following:

> Ctables are not similar to each other in the way that tables are.
>
> The stages of ctables are not causally connected in the way that the
> stages of tables are.
>
> Ctables are not important to us in the way that tables are.

These claims suggest such principles as:

> The general words of a language ought to denote things that are
> similar to each other.
>
> The general words of a language ought to denote things whose stages
> are causally connected.
>
> The general words of a language ought to denote things that are
> important to us.

The hybrid meta-language serves the purpose of allowing such claims
and principles to be expressed in an intuitive fashion, without immediately
getting involved in the ontological issues dividing the believer and disbeliever. I assume that even disbelievers could express these claims and
principles in (what they regard as) plain English, without appealing to
the hybrid meta-language, but this might be harder to do. For instance,
the first claim might be recast roughly as follows:

> Whereas English sentences of the form "Something is a table at place p
> throughout time t" are true only if similar conditions obtain at the specified
> places and times, it is not the case that Contacti sentences of the form "Some-
> thing is a ctable at place p throughout time t" are true only if similar condi-
> tions obtain at the specified places and times.

I assume that in some such manner the intended import of the various
claims and principles can be captured regardless of one's specific
ontological commitments. There is therefore no harm in expressing them
more neatly and intuitively in the hybrid meta-language. In attempting

to assess these claims and principles, ontological niceties can be temporarily waived.

There will, indeed, be contexts of discussion in this book in which it will be necessary to carefully address the ontological issues dividing the believer and the disbeliever. In principle, this could be done in the hybrid language in various ways, for example, by asking whether the English sentence "There are no entities that exchange their characteristics when they touch" is true, or whether the strange entities exist *in the English sense*. In such ontological contexts, however, since it is the plain English sense of words that concerns us, we might as well consider the hybrid language to be suspended. Let it indeed be stipulated that when our aim is to address fine points of ontology, we will drop the hybrid meta-language and revert to plain English. In general, I expect the reader to have no difficulty in discerning from the context whether the hybrid language has been suspended for the space of a particular ontological discussion.[17]

In short, I intend to be ontologically casual in this book except in those places where ontology itself is the issue. The hybrid language is a device for ontological casualness, and this device will naturally be dropped wherever ontological strictness seems required.[18]

d. Individuative Strangeness without Classificatory Strangeness

We should now consider the following question. We know that a case of classificatory strangeness need not be a case of individuative strangeness. But must a case of individuative strangeness be a case of classificatory strangeness? I suggest that the proper answer is no. I suggest that we should look at the matter like this. We have a word "*F*" that denotes a certain class of things including the thing *a*. This is a case of classificatory strangeness only if it strikes us as absurd that, *given* the thing *a*, we should have had a word with the denotation of "*F*." If we are given the ctable *a*, it does not strike us as at all absurd that we should have had a word with the denotation of "ctable." What strikes us as absurd is that we should be given such a thing (i.e., that any word, or any individuative word, should denote it), but once such a thing is given it seems not strange but completely inevitable that we should classify it as a ctable. In this sense, the word "ctable" classifies intuitively strange things in an intuitively ordinary way.

---

[17]For instance, if I say, "The disbeliever holds that there are no things that exchange their properties when they touch," I obviously mean to imply that the disbeliever holds (speaking plain English) that there are no things that exchange their properties when they touch.

[18]Another way to view ontological casualness is this: For ease of exposition, we pretend that the believer's position is correct—except, of course, where that position is the point at issue.

3. Strange Languages and Strange Thoughts

A question that inevitably arises when one reflects upon the strange languages is how to imagine the *thinking* of the people who speak these languages. Do they think just the way we do but merely talk strangely or do they think in a strange way too? A related question is whether expressions in the strange languages *mean the same* as any ordinary expressions. There are a number of very hard issues here, and some of these may eventually need to be seriously addressed if the division problem is to be properly treated.[19] At this point, I will only make a few preliminary remarks with the aim of giving a sense of some of the problem's ramifications. My general suggestion in this section is that the strange languages can plausibly be imagined as having a deep effect on thinking and meaning

a. Strong and Weak Versions of Strangeness

Let us first note a certain distinction between two ways in which a strange language can be developed. As I stated earlier, I am primarily interested in examining strange languages that have the same descriptive content as English. Accordingly, I stipulated that in the Gricular language the words "green" and "circular" are replaced by "gricular," "grincular," and "ngricular." But there is, of course, a more trivial way to achieve sameness of descriptive content: we can stipulate that "gricular" (with or without the other two strange words) is *added* to the words of English. Let me say that the first version of the Gricular language is "strong" and the second "weak." In general, a weak version of a strange language adds certain strange words to English whereas a strong version replaces some English words with strange words. The weak version of Contacti contains both "table" and "ctable," but the strong version contains only "ctable."

b. Thinking in a Strange Language

I think that many readers will find it immediately plausible to suppose that speakers of a strange language would have to think in a strange way. This supposition may seem especially plausible for strong strange languages. I am here making a certain tacit assumption. Obviously people would not need to think differently from us if their primary language was English but on some special occasions they haltingly spoke a strange language. Let me stipulate that the strange languages under consideration are always to be imagined as the *primary* or, to make things simple, the *only* language these people speak.

Whether it really is plausible to suppose that speaking a strange language would have to affect how people think depends on one's general

---

[19]Many of these issues will be more fully discussed in chapters 6 and 7.

view about the relationship between language and thinking. The question may be raised whether thinking takes place within a language, and to this there are the following possible replies: always, sometimes, never. For those who believe that thinking is at least sometimes in a language, another question is whether this language is the public language in which communication takes place, and to this again there are the possible replies: always, sometimes, never. This gives us a number of different permutations answering to different positions. Let me first comment on how the two most extreme positions relate to the strange languages, and afterwards I will say something about the intermediary positions. One extreme is that thinking is never in a language, and the other is that thinking must always be in a public language. Let me call these, respectively, the extreme anti-language view and the extreme public language view.

A proponent of the first extreme would appear to have no reason to suppose that people who speak the strange languages must think differently from the way we do. (I mean to ignore in this discussion thinking *about* language; I am always referring to thinking about non-linguistic matters.) Indeed, on this view, it is not immediately clear what can even be meant by "thinking in a strange way," since this cannot mean "thinking in a strange language." I doubt that many people will find this view plausible; the connection between language and thinking seems closer than the view allows. But the main point I want to stress now is that the extreme anti-language view clearly does not solve, or dissolve, the division problem. Let it be supposed that the strange speakers think (not in a language) just the way we do. It would still strike us as utterly absurd, perhaps *especially* absurd given their presumed ordinary thinking, that they should speak the strange languages. The problem remains to explain why this is absurd.

The extreme public language view clearly seems to require us to say that speakers of the strong Gricular language think differently from us. If, when we think the sentence "It's green," they think the sentence "It's gricular and it's grincular," there is certainly a difference between their thinking and ours, at least in some important sense. However, this point need not carry over to the weak Gricular language. It remains possible that speakers of the weak Gricular language think in the part of their language that coincides with English. Even when they utter (or hear) "It's gricular and grincular," they may be thinking the sentence "It's green."

Many of the intermediary views allow that people's thinking might take place in a language of thought different from their public language. Knowledge of people's (only) public language would then not imply, or at least not guarantee, anything about their thinking. The division problem would still apply to thinking, for we may imagine that the strange languages being described are languages of thought. If it strikes us as intuitively absurd to imagine such languages being spoken, it will strike us as equally or more absurd to imagine such language entering into thinking. At a much later stage, I will want to consider the suggestion that the kinds of constraints on classification and individuation that apply to thinking are different from those that apply to the public language. Until then, however, the "languages" I refer to can be taken either as public languages or languages of thought. Moreover, in considering examples of strange languages, it should be understood, unless otherwise stated, that any feature of classificatory or individuative strangeness under discussion applies to both the public language and the language of thought.[20]

c. *Synonymy and Strangeness*

Does "gricular" mean the same as "green or circular"? What I had stipulated is that these terms are equivalent, that is, that it is a priori necessary that something is gricular if and only if it is green or circular. Obviously, equivalence does not entail synonymy or sameness of meaning, at least not in any full-blooded sense. For example, expressions that are equivalent because of complicated truth-functional connections would not generally be regarded as meaning the same.

If we are considering the weak Gricular language, it is easy to imagine a case in which it would seem clearly correct to say that "gricular" means the same as "green or circular." Imagine that typical speakers of the weak Gricular language learn "gricular" only after they have already learned "green" and "circular" and that they learn "gricular" by being given the definition: "'gricular' means 'green or circular.'" In this case, it certainly seems that "gricular" means the same as "green or circular."

Even if "gricular" is learned ostensively in the weak Gricular language, there may be strong reasons to judge that "gricular" means the same as "green or circular." Suppose, first, that the typical speaker learns "gricular" ostensively only after having already learned "green" and "circular"; second, that the typical speaker finds it immediately obvious that "gricular" can apply to something if and only if "green or circular" applies to it (but does not find it equally obvious that "green" can apply to something if and only if "gricular and grincular" applies to it); and, third, that the typical speaker will *say* that "gricular" means the same as "green or circular" (but not that "green" means the same as "gricular and grincular"). These three conditions would provide strong reasons for saying that in this language "gricular" does indeed mean the same as "green or circular" (rather than that "green" means the same as "gricular and grincular").

If none of these conditions obtained, then we would apparently have good reason for saying that synonymy does not hold between "gricular"

---

[20]I take it that the notion of "deep semantic structure," found in some literature, is closely related to the language of thought. The point just made in the text should then be applied also to deep semantic structure: We should imagine that the strange languages are strange even at the level of deep semantic structure (if there is such a level).

and "green or circular." And if only two of the conditions obtained, it would be less determinate whether synonymy holds, or, alternatively put, the degree of synonymy would be less. It seems unlikely that the synonymy relationship can be made so exact as to exclude many borderline cases. Of the three conditions, I would suppose that the second is the most fundamental, at least as a necessary condition. It seems that in many typical examples, expressions are synonymous only to the extent that it is immediately and irresistibly obvious to those who understand them that they must stand or fall together.[21]

Hence, in the weak Gricular language, it seems easy to imagine both cases in which synonymy holds between "gricular" and "green or circular" and cases in which synonymy does not hold, as well as borderline cases.

The situation seems different for the strong Gricular language. In the latter language, "gricular" must be learned ostensively (or at least not by way of a standard definition), and must be learned of course without first learning "green" and "circular." Evidently, "gricular" would not be synonymous with any complex expression in the strong Gricular language. Moreover, there seems in general to be a presumption against supposing that a word in a language which is not synonymous with any complex expression in that language is nevertheless synonymous with a complex expression in another language. Hence, there would be a presumption against the claim that "gricular" in the strong Gricular language means the same as the English expression "green or circular." If a case for the synonymy claim can be made, it would apparently have to depend on the answer to the following counterfactual question: If speakers of the strong Gricular language were to learn English, would it seem immediately obvious to them that "gricular" can apply to something if and only if "green or circular" applies to it (but not equally obvious that "green" can apply to something if and only if "gricular and grincular" applies to it)? Even if there were evidence for an affirmative answer to this question, it seems far from obvious that the synonymy claim would be warranted. Certainly if there were no such evidence, the claim would appear not to be warranted.

Essentially the same points apply to examples of individuative strangeness, though with a slight complication. The complication is that, on the disbeliever's position, whereas the Contacti word "ctable" ostensibly denotes ctables, no ordinary English expression denotes or even ostensibly denotes ctables. Should we say, on this position, that no English expression is equivalent to "ctable"? Or perhaps that "ctable" is equivalent to a necessarily inapplicable English expression, such as "square and circular"? I am inclined to say the former and to allow the notion

---

[21]These remarks about synonymy are intended to be very rough; I do not suppose that any of the three conditions is strictly necessary for synonymy, or that their conjunction is strictly sufficient.

of "(a priori necessary) equivalence" to be sensitive to differences in ostensible denotation. In any case, it seems quite clear that, on the disbeliever's position, the question could not arise whether there is an English expression *synonymous* with "ctable"; there can be no such expression.

Nevertheless, there are English sentences equivalent to Contacti sentences containing "ctable," and the question can arise whether these sentences are not just equivalent but synonymous. Certainly, it can happen that, while a word has no outright synonym, any sentence containing it is synonymous with a more complex sentence containing several different words in place of it. (For instance, though the word "average" in "the average plumber" is evidently not synonymous with any complex expression, it is plausible to hold that any meaningful sentence of the form "The average *F* is *G*" is synonymous with a more complex sentence containing several words in place of "average.") When I speak of words having synonyms, I should henceforth be understood to include the contextual case. It may, then, be relatively easy to imagine that the word "ctable" in weak Contacti is synonymous (in context) with an ordinary expression; it seems harder to imagine this instance of synonymy with respect to strong Contacti.

In general, when I refer to strong versions of strange languages, I am trying to imagine a case in which the strange words are not synonymous with any ordinary expressions. This seems like the most provocative kind of case. In a later chapter, I will in fact attempt to develop an argument against the coherence of any conception of a strange language in which words or sentences are not synonymous with ordinary words or sentences.[22] Until that argument is addressed, however, we should try to conceive of the strange languages, especially in their strong versions, in the provocative way.

d. Strange Propositions

I anticipate that some readers will immediately want to raise a question about what "propositions" are expressed in the strange languages. Let me make a few preliminary remarks about this.

Many philosophers find it plausible to say that if two sentences (as uttered in certain contexts) are necessarily equivalent, they express (in those contexts) the same condition or state of the world, the same way the world is. Likewise, if two terms (as uttered in certain contexts) are necessarily equivalent, they express (in those contexts) the same condition or state of a thing, the same way a thing is. I assume that this view is acceptable, and I will call the two kinds of "conditions" or "ways," those expressed respectively by sentences and terms, *world-conditions* and

---

[22]See principle IC3 in section 6.4.a.

thing-conditions. Some philosophers identify a world-condition with the set of possible worlds in which the condition obtains, and a thing-condition with a function from possible worlds to sets (or *n*-tuples) of things satisfying the condition in those worlds.[23] I leave it open for now whether this identification is correct, though it will certainly be useful at times to note the correspondence between the conditions and the sets and functions.

Besides the conditions, many philosophers posit more fine-grained items, items that are not invariant under necessary equivalence.[24] I will call these items *fine-grained propositions* and *fine-grained properties*, the first being expressed by sentences and the second by terms. The fine-grained items are often said to have a unique set of constituents structured in a unique way. The same world-condition or the same thing-condition may correspond to any number of different fine-grained propositions and properties. For example, the sentences "Something is green" and "Something is both green or circular and green or non-circular" express the same world-condition but different fine-grained propositions, only the latter containing as a constituent the property of being circular. Analogously, the terms "green" and "both green or circular and green or non-circular" express the same thing-condition but different fine-grained properties.

A proponent of fine-grained propositions may perceive some special difficulties with strong versions of the strange languages. In those versions, as I have recently elaborated them, there are strange words that are not synonymous with any ordinary expressions. It may seem to follow that the sentences containing the strange words cannot express ordinary fine-grained propositions, that is, propositions expressible in ordinary language. How then can we make intelligible to ourselves what fine-grained propositions are expressed in the strange languages?[25]

The force of this question is not immediately clear, however. If it is granted that, because the strange words are not synonymous with ordinary expressions, the sentences containing those words cannot express ordinary fine-grained propositions, all that seems to follow is that these sentences express *strange* fine-grained propositions, ones that are not expressible in ordinary language. It would seem that these strange propositions have in effect been specified by describing the strong versions of the strange languages in the way that I have, that is, as containing words that are not synonymous with any ordinary words.

It is therefore not obvious how the fine-grained propositions affect the division problem. Our apparent situation might be envisioned as

[23]See especially Lewis 1986, pp. 27ff., pp. 50ff.

[24]On the distinction between the coarse-grained and fine-grained items, see especially Bealer 1982.

[25]A parallel question might perhaps be raised about what fine-grained properties are expressed by the strange words.

follows: When we consider two sentences that are equivalent, one ordinary and the other strange, it is not initially clear to us how one can be said to be better than the other, although our strong intuition may be that the ordinary one somehow is better. Now someone comes along and tells us that the two sentences, and their identical truth-conditions, are not the only relevant items to consider, that there are also the different fine-grained propositions expressed by the sentences. How will this information help us? If the structural differences between the two sentences do not explain why the ordinary one is better than the strange one, how will the structural differences between the fine-grained propositions do the trick?

I think that it will in fact emerge that a theory of the fine-grained propositions has a deep bearing on the division problem. (See chapter 6.) What I am saying at present—still in the spirit of introducing the problem—is that it is far from obvious what that bearing is.

e. Strange Primitives

A strange language may strike us as especially disturbing if strangeness affects the primitives of the language. Strange primitives seem in a sense stranger than strange non-primitives. There are a number of notions of a primitive implicit in the literature, but the following seems most pertinent to the present discussion: A *semantic* primitive is a word that is not synonymous (to a relatively high degree) with any complex expression of any language. (Semantic primitiveness, on this account, is a matter of degree or, at least, is indeterminate with respect to many cases.)

If we assume that, at least in strong versions of the strange languages, strange words are not synonymous with any ordinary expressions, then it is plausible to suppose that they are not synonymous with any complex expressions in any language. The strange words would then be semantic primitives.

One should not conflate the notion of a semantic primitive with that of an *unanalyzable* word. If synonymy depends substantially on obviousness of equivalence, it follows that philosophical (conceptual) analysis, which is notoriously non-obvious, does not preserve synonymy. If so, even a semantic primitive may be analyzable. In analyzing a semantic primitive "W," we seek an expression "E" such that, first, "E" is equivalent to "W," and, second, the (non-logical) constituent words of "E" are in some sense "prior to," "more basic than," "W."[26] Such words as "table" and "dog" may possibly be regarded as analyzable semantic primitives, whereas "body" and "green" are perhaps more readily regarded as unanalyzable. I have suggested that, to take

---

[26]I will say something more about the relevant sense of priority in section 6.2.c and in appendix 3.2.

the strange languages in the most provocative way, we should try to regard the strange words as being semantic primitives. It is an additional question whether the strange words can be viewed as unanalyzable.[27]

There is a special class of words that I want to single out in connection with the notion of primitiveness. These are words built up out of other words, such as "uninteresting" or "workable." I take these to be semantic non-primitives. The division problem may relate only marginally to such words. (This is especially true for a language such as German in which the distinction between complex words and complex expressions is nebulous.) It may be indeed that the intuitions that generate the division problem are strictly not about words but about *morphemes* (i.e., the smallest semantic building blocks of a language): It intuitively seems to us that the morphemes that figure in the strange languages are an unreasonable set of building blocks.[28] Although I will continue to talk about words for ease of exposition, this qualification should be noted.

4. Further Examples of Strangeness

My topic in this book is significantly circumscribed by the fact that I am concerned only with the contrast between intuitively ordinary and strange ways of dividing up reality, but not with various other contrasts that might be drawn between ordinary and strange uses of language.[29] I want to take it as given, therefore, that all of the languages under consideration are essentially ordinary in their formal and syntactic aspects, and that they contain words that can be said to (behave as if they) classify and individuate things. The only examples of strangeness that concern me are classificatory and individuative examples. In this section, I want to provide a general characterization of such examples.

a. Classificatory Examples

A famous example of classificatory strangeness is the Grue language. The reason why that example would not have served well to introduce the division problem is that it is too closely associated in the literature with the problem of projectibility, a problem which, as we will see in the next chapter, may be only marginally related to the division problem. Furthermore, the "grue" example involves some very special difficulties

---

[27]On the account of analysis sketched in appendix 3.2, it will turn out that the strange words must be analyzable.

[28]It must therefore be understood that "cular" is not a morpheme in the Gricular language. I use words like "gricular" and "grincular" only as a mnemonic device; we should imagine that these words in the Gricular language have no relevant phonetic relations.

[29]Perhaps this is, then, only one part of what ought to be a larger study.

related to the (ostensible) temporal components in "grue" and "bleen."[30] These special difficulties too tend to divert attention away from the general division problem. It is best, therefore, in much of what follows not to have the "grue" example foremost in mind.

The general scheme for constructing a strange classificatory language is to form some complex English expressions and then imagine a language containing words that are equivalent to the expressions. A further constraint that I have imposed on these languages is that they should have the same descriptive content as English. This constraint limits examples of strong classificatory strangeness.

The simplest construction would be a language in which every (or some) English word "*W*" is replaced by a word that is equivalent to the complement of "*W.*" One might be momentarily tempted to dismiss this as only a trivial stylistic difference, but I think that a little reflection will convince most people that this is actually a serious example. Our intuition—the problem-generating intuition—seems to say that some properties are "positive" and that our words ought to express these properties rather than their complements.

In the Gricular language, the words "grincular" and "ngricular" derive from English expressions involving not only disjunction but also negation. One can also construct purely disjunctive examples. Imagine that the three words "car," "apple," and "ocean" are replaced by the two words "carple" and "apcean," which apply, respectively, to things that are either cars or apples and things that are either apples or oceans. Then "car," "apple," and "ocean" are equivalent, respectively, to "carple and not apcean," "carple and apcean," and "apcean and not carple." In general, any three mutually incompatible words can be reduced to two words in this manner.

Strange languages constructed on the model of the last example I will call "incompatibility languages."[31] Such languages have a number of properties that are worth noting. First, whereas in the examples of the Grue and Gricular languages, a given number of English words are replaced by an equal or greater number of strange words, in the incompatibility languages a given number of English words are replaced by

---

[30]Indeed, Shoemaker 1975 has argued that typical characterizations of the Grue language are not even coherent. It is obvious that there is no argument (along Shoemaker's lines at least) against the coherence of my characterization of the Gricular language. (In fact, I will point out later in section 4.3.d that Shoemaker's argument does not even work against the Grue language as this language relates to the division problem.)

[31]The incompatibilities that figure in constructing the incompatibility languages must be both a priori and necessary if these languages are to have the same descriptive content as English. My assumption is that there are examples of incompatibilities in terms of which such languages can be constructed. The particular examples that I give may indeed be open to question.

fewer—in some cases far fewer—words. This will have some relevance when we discuss pragmatic arguments for rejecting these languages.

There is a certain respect in which the Gricular language differs from both the Grue language and the incompatibility languages. The words of the Gricular language stand to each other in somewhat peculiar logical relations. For example, the complements of "gricular," "grincular," and "ngricular" are mutually incompatible. There probably is no trio of English words whose complements are mutually incompatible.[32] By contrast, the strange words (and their complements) in both the Grue language and the incompatibility languages seem to be logically interrelated in quite ordinary ways. (In the case of the Grue language, this point follows from the well-known symmetry of logical relationship between the pair "grue" and "bleen" and the pair "green" and "blue.") Of course, if there is anything *good* about this, it remains to be shown.

Can we derive strange examples by *conjoining* English words? We can, but I think the effect here is generally not as striking. For example, we have in English words for young dogs and young cats but not (as far as I know) words for old dogs and old cats. If we imagine a language containing such words, this probably does not strike us as very odd at all. What about a language containing a word for anything that is green *and* circular? This seems odder than the last case but, I think, not nearly so odd as "gricular." Of course we can pile up conjunctions in ways that will seem very weird, especially if we allow ourselves to utilize relational properties, for example, if we imagine having a word that denotes anything that is green and circular and touching a brown dog. A completely satisfactory account would have to deal with our diverse intuitions about these various cases.[33]

b. Individuative Examples

In the individuative case, a general recipe for constructing many examples is to imagine a language containing words that denote sums, or parts, or stages, or sums of parts or stages, of ordinary things. To make sure that we satisfy even the believer who thinks that many ordinary words denote such items, we should try to imagine that in the strange languages these items are denoted by individuative words.

One of the simplest constructions along these lines would be to imagine a language in which words denote sums of things that do not stand

---

[32]At least if we do not count "non-*F*" as a word. See Hirsch 1989, pp. 222–29.

[33]A very extreme example of classificatory strangeness is found in Quine 1954. In Quine's imagined language, all ordinary words are replaced by a single relational word whose domain contains highly abstract items on the level of numbers. Since this example seems perplexing in certain rather special ways, I will not employ it in what follows. A more complete treatment of the topic, however, should certainly take it into account.

in any special relationship to each other, for example, a language containing a word "trable" that denotes the sum of any tree and table. Conditions of transtemporal and transworld identity for a trable would still have to be fixed, and that could be done in a number of ways.

To achieve the strongest sense of individuative strangeness, I think we need examples like Contacti in which strange things are concocted by combining the temporal stages of different ordinary things. Another example of this sort has been discussed in several places by Shoemaker. He imagines a language containing the word "klable" such that "if you have both a kitchen table and a living room table, the midnight till noon stages of the one and the noon till midnight stages of the other are together the stages of a klable, a table-like object which shifts back and forth twice a day between your kitchen and your living room."[34] Shoemaker's example is in one respect stranger than Contacti. It seems that an ordinary human being could learn how to make identity judgments about Contacti-things like ctables and cdogs with unaided perception, but in order to make identity judgments about Shoemaker's klables one would need a watch (or some other device to indicate the time). Consequently, whereas an ordinary human being could perform an action that one might naturally call "(perceptually) tracking a ctable," it seems less clear that he could do anything that could be called "tracking a klable."[35]

In both Contacti and Shoemaker's example, stages of different ordinary things are jumbled together discontinuously; that is, both ctables and klables undergo radically discontinuous changes at certain points in their careers. One can, however, also construct striking examples of strange things that suffer no discontinuities. An example of this sort is provided by the Incar-Outcar language.[36] In this language, when a car leaves a garage, an incar is said to gradually shrink and vanish, as it is replaced by an outcar that gradually grows. Incars and outcars are extremely strange things, although their careers are perfectly continuous.

There is another important kind of example of individuative strangeness that has a very high degree of intuitive impact. An ordinary thing can be viewed as a sum of "slices" of the thing in different worlds. We can construct intuitively strange things by combining the slice of one thing in one world with the slice of another thing in another world, where each thing-slice is quite ordinary in its respective world. One such strange thing might combine, for instance, an ordinary dog-slice in one world

---

[34]Shoemaker 1988, p. 201. See also Shoemaker 1984, pp. 258–59 (reprinted from Shoemaker 1979).

[35]See Shoemaker 1988, p. 206.

[36]This is introduced in Hirsch 1982, p. 32.

with an ordinary car-slice in another world. A language is likely to strike us as extremely absurd if it contains words that denote such modally strange things.[37]

In what follows, I will most often use Contacti as the example of individuative strangeness. This language is fairly easy to grasp while, at the same time, its intuitive strangeness is striking. The other kinds of examples should, however, be kept in mind.

5. The Weight of the Intuitions

A "strange language" is one that intuitively strikes us, at least at first, as being absurd. This is, of course, a matter of degree. There will be a spectrum of cases going from the mildly odd to the overwhelmingly strange. The near end of the spectrum merges with familiar and relatively unchallenging examples of actual differences in human languages, such as the variety of words Eskimos are said to have for different kinds of snow. The far end of the spectrum contains some of the examples of strange languages that I have mentioned. I have already indicated several different dimensions along which this spectrum seems to vary. In general, examples of strong strange languages seem to have a greater intuitive impact than weak ones. This appears to be related to the fact that strangeness with respect to thinking or with respect to semantic primitives seems especially serious. Within the categories of classificatory and individuative strangeness, the particular constructions seem to make a difference, for example, disjunctive constructions seeming in general more absurd than conjunctive ones. Perhaps there is a general difference too in how we react to the two categories themselves, for I gather that many people will at first react more strongly to the individuative cases.

I take all of this to constitute a certain kind of philosophical data. I will not here belabor points of philosophical methodology which I think are widely accepted. Briefly put, in philosophy we are often seeking a kind of reflective equilibrium that typically requires the balancing of conflicting intuitions and arguments.[38] Philosophical intuitions, especially if they are strong, must be taken seriously. However, an intuition, perhaps even the strongest one, may eventually be abandoned after reflection. The most painless case of this is where reflection convinces us that we misunderstood the content of the intuition. In this case we really do not abandon the intuition so much as correct an initially mistaken interpretation of it. In more difficult cases, we are led to take up a posi-

---

[37]Note that Contacti-things are not modally strange in the relevant sense; given their strange conditions of transtemporal identity, their conditions of transworld identity are supposed to be as ordinary as possible.

[38]See Rawls 1971, p. 20.

tion that runs against the intuition even though the intuition remains naggingly alive. We do this only if there are compelling countervailing intuitions and arguments.

I take it as obvious that at least at the far end of the strangeness spectrum our intuitions are extremely strong. For the most part, in this book I concentrate on cases at this far end of the spectrum. Reflecting on such cases should make it as easy as possible to uncover, in a relatively clear and pure form, principles that normatively constrain our division practices. Given such principles, we could then undertake the more delicate task of determining to what extent they apply to less extreme cases.

When considering our intuitions about the extreme cases, it is essential not to whitewash what these intuitions seem to say: they seem to say that the strange languages in question would be (at least for creatures in our general life situation) in some way *wrong*, or *bad*, or *unreasonable*. These intuitions may allow for a variety of interpretations (as the parenthetical insertion in the last sentence already intimates). But on any interpretation they conflict with the following *extreme relativist position*: "It is simply an empirical fact of human psychology, or human culture, that we speak and think in ordinary ways rather than the imagined strange ways, but other creatures (even if their life situation were essentially like ours) might very well use the strange languages and there need be nothing at all wrong with this." The extreme relativist is clearly denying the intuitions, something which one may indeed be led to do after reflection, but which must not be one's starting point.

One way to elicit someone's intuitions about extreme relativism is by asking certain questions about how we would react to various kinds of extraterrestrial creatures. Scientists often speculate that there are an indefinite number of intelligent life forms out in the galaxies, which probably differ from us in various striking ways. There might be highly intelligent creatures whose physiology differs somewhat from ours, so that they find it natural to hop around, sleep standing up, eat while submerged in water, and so on. We can imagine this sort of thing without too much trouble.

Now let us try to imagine the following. There are creatures in some faraway galaxy who are in many ways remarkably like us. They look and behave essentially like us. Their sensory apparatus is, at least on the face of it, just like ours: they see with their eyes, hear with their ears, and so on. Their biological needs are much like ours too: they need to eat, breathe, sleep, avoid illness, and so on. And even their emotional or psychological needs are like ours: they need affection, status, security, excitement, and so on. But there is one striking difference between them and us: they speak the strong Gricular language or strong Contacti (or a strong version of one of the other strange languages).

The question we may now ask is how this fantasy compares to the previous ones, about the intelligent creatures who hop around, sleep standing up, and so on. I think anyone should agree that our intuitive reaction to these fantasies is quite different. The crucial point is that we have virtually no inclination, at least after a moment's reflection, to *criticize* the denizens of the former fantasies or to criticize their imagined forms of life. No one wants to say: "What! They hop around like kangaroos and also do mathematics? How foolish!" But that is precisely the sort of thing we do want to say with respect to the creatures in the latter fantasy. Intuitively, it seems that if we met up with such creatures we should be able to make a speech beginning like this: "Can't you see how foolish it is for you to be operating with a language in which . . . ?" The problem of finding the continuation of that speech or, better, of determining whether the speech really has a continuation, is the division problem.

Let me say that some creatures are "in essentially our life situation" if (1) they employ a language that has the same descriptive content as ours, (2) their physical environment and their physical capacities are the same as ours, (3) their sensory apparatus is the same as ours, and (4) their beliefs and motives are equivalent to ours (unless these are related to the use of language). Condition (4) implies that in any circumstances in which they would be disposed to believe or to desire that a certain world-condition obtains, and would express their belief or desire using a certain sentence, we, in those circumstances, would be disposed to believe or desire that the same world-condition obtains, and would express our belief or desire using a sentence that is equivalent to theirs. The parenthetical qualification in (4) allows that, since they speak a different language from ours, their beliefs and motives about their language (e.g., their desire to use the word "gricular") are not equivalent to our beliefs and motives.

Conditions (1)–(4) seem to capture all that is essential in the fantasy about the extraterrestrials who speak a strange language. (The stipulation that they look like us does not seem significant.) Our division intuitions, even on the most minimal interpretation, imply that creatures in essentially our life situation, in the sense just defined, ought not to be using the (strong) Gricular language. The extreme relativist winds up denying the intuitions even in this minimal sense.[39]

Certainly the intuitions may be interpreted in a stronger sense, for one may be prepared to dispense with some of the conditions (2)–(4). One may intuitively feel that no language with the same descriptive content as ours ought to be a strange language, even if it is employed by creatures whose physical environment, or physical capacities, or sensory apparatus, or beliefs and motives are not like ours.[40]

---

[39]The notion of a life situation, and its bearing on the relativist position, will be discussed further in section 5.1.

[40]The theory eventually developed in chapter 6 will imply that, in any imaginable context, (strong) strange languages are inadmissible as primary languages.

Throughout this book I am going to formulate a series of "division principles." These are principles designed to defend our intuitions about the strange languages. An example, roughly put, might be: "The words of a language should denote things that are similar to each other." A division principle may be viewed as presumptive rather than absolute. Even so, a language may be seen as absurd if it violates the principle to a much higher degree than ordinary languages do, and for apparently no good reason. A division principle should be assessed in two ways: first, by asking whether it seems plausible on reflection and, second, by asking to what extent it would sustain our intuitions about the strange languages. The most positive outcome from an intuitive standpoint would be to find plausible division principles that sustain the intuitions even when broadly interpreted. At the other extreme is the possibility that we cannot find plausible principles that can even sustain the intuitions minimally interpreted. Such a negative outcome might lead one to accept extreme relativism. Of course, there are many intermediary possibilities.

6. The Distinctness of the Division Problem

Has the division problem already been adequately addressed in the general literature? I think that, though the problem may sound familiar, it has typically been either brushed aside with a few perfunctory remarks or conflated with various other problems. One of my main aims in this book is, indeed, to isolate the division problem as a separate problem requiring extended and focused discussion. I am almost tempted to claim that the division problem is a "new problem" in order to emphasize the importance of keeping it distinct from other problems that have been more widely discussed. Some problems with which the division problem might be confused include: the problem of projectibility, the problem of universals, the problem of the existence of mereological sums and temporal parts, and the problem of the inscrutability of reference. Those problems are surely related to the division problem, perhaps deeply so, but the division problem is *another* problem. Even if all of those problems were solved, *it* would remain. That, at any rate, is a contention that I will attempt to back up in subsequent chapters.

2

Projectibility and Strange Languages

1. Goodman's Problem and the Division Problem

Goodman's problem of projectibility is to explain why it is rational to project ordinary terms such as "green" and "circular" rather than strange terms such as "grue" and "gricular."[1] Let us imagine that we have a solution to Goodman's problem (his own proposed solution is based on the relative degrees of "entrenchment" of ordinary terms and strange terms). We still do not have an obvious solution to the division problem. If it is rational to project "green" but not "green or circular," then it seems to follow that it is rational to project "gricular and grincular," which is equivalent to "green," but not "gricular," which is equivalent to "green or circular." I am appealing here to the widely accepted *evidential equivalence principle*, which says that if p is equivalent to p' and q is equivalent to q', then if p is good evidence for q, p' is good evidence for q'. This principle seems unassailable in general, and any exceptions to it do not seem likely to be related to the sort of examples I am considering.[2] So speakers of the Gricular language ought (everything else being equal) to project "gricular and grincular" rather than "gricular." How would this make their language irrational? It appears that their projections can be equivalent to ours, despite their strange way of dividing up reality. If their way of dividing up reality is irrational (as our intuition seems to say), this cannot be shown, at least in any obvious way, by appealing to the issue of projectibility.

[1]See Goodman 1973.
[2]For purported exceptions to the principle, see Achinstein 1983, pp. 363–64. It should be understood that the evidential equivalence principle relates to the ordinary intuitive notion of one statement being evidence for another. There may, of course, be useful technical notions in confirmation theory that do not satisfy any equivalence condition; see Goodman 1972, p. 361.

This suffices, I think, to establish that the division problem must be kept distinct from the projectibility problem.[3] The essential point to notice is the difference in orientation (or one might say *dis*orientation) that is appropriate to the two problems. When we are considering the projectibility problem, we typically try to imagine people who speak a strange language and who project hypotheses incompatible with those we project. In this sort of fantasy we may also try to imagine that their "sense of similarity" is in some sense different from ours. Our question, then, is why our projections, and perhaps our "sense of similarity," are superior to theirs. When we are considering the division problem, however, we should be trying to imagine primarily people who speak a strange language *despite* the fact that their projections and their "sense of similarity" are equivalent to ours. It strikes us as intuitively absurd that, *given* the ordinary projections and the ordinary "sense of similarity," they would divide up reality as they do. The problem here is to explain why this would be absurd.

2. *The Projectibility Principle*

Given that the division problem is distinct from the projectibility problem, I now want to consider whether there is any important connection between the division problem and the notion of projectibility. One might be tempted to formulate the following division principle:

The Projectibility Principle. A general word ought to be projectible.

The hope would be to explain why the strange languages seem intuitively absurd by appealing to this principle. In this section and the next, I will consider several arguments in behalf of the principle, with the aim of showing that these arguments do not succeed. The general focus in these sections will be on examples of classificatory strangeness; in the final section 2.4 of this chapter, I will extend the discussion to individuative issues.

a. *Projectible Terms*

The Projectibility Principle evidently presupposes the notion of a projectible term. This notion is in fact widely used in the literature, but there are serious difficulties in properly explicating it. I am not, of course, referring to the projectibility problem, which is the problem of explaining (or perhaps justifying) our criteria for assessing the projectibility of hypotheses. Rather, I am referring to the difficulty of clearly explaining what it means to say that a *term* is projectible, given that we have already decided on which *hypotheses* are projectible. I attempt to give a detailed answer to this question in appendix 1. For the immediate pur-

---

[3]Goodman indicates an awareness of the distinction in Goodman 1978, pp. 128–29.

poses, however, I think we can accept the following rough explanation of what a projectible term is.

The intuitive idea is that for a term to be projectible it must not apply to two classes of objects having no special evidential relationship to each other. The term "green or circular" seems to be non-projectible because it applies to two classes, the green things and the circular things, such that if one were given that, say, all green things are radioactive, this would not constitute evidence for the hypothesis that all circular things are radioactive. Perhaps this point needs to be hedged slightly. If our only relevant evidence were that all green things are radioactive, this might be said to support the conclusion that everything is radioactive, in which case we would be saying that all circular things are radioactive. The point is that, once we are given that some things are not radioactive, we do not take the information about the green things to reflect in any special way on the circular things.

Contrast "green or circular" with a term such as "dog." Any term is of course equivalent to many disjunctive terms. The term "dog" is equivalent to the disjunction of the two terms "fat dog" and "non-fat dog." But what we find out about one class of dogs is evidence with respect to the other class. The truth of "All fat dogs have spotted tongues" is evidence for the truth of "All non-fat dogs have spotted tongues," even after we are given that some things (or some animals) do not have spotted tongues. We take the fact about the fat dogs to provide special evidence about the other dogs, evidence that would not bear on some arbitrarily chosen class of objects.

It seems clear that many strange words are not projectible (if we assume, as I am, our ordinary judgments of projectibility). In general, strange words that are formed by disjoining or negating ordinary words are not projectible.[4] Hence, at least many of the strange languages do not satisfy the Projectibility Principle. Does English satisfy it? That is, are ordinary words projectible? I noted in the last chapter that the division problem seems primarily to apply only to words that are not constructed from other words. Perhaps we can assume—not just for the present division principle but for all the subsequent ones too—that the words in question are not constructed from other words. If so, we need not worry about words with negative prefixes. Indeed, we may be inclined to stipulate that the words in question are semantic primitives (to a high degree), for we may care most about finding division principles that at least exclude strange primitives. If the Projectibility Principle is limited to semantic primitives, it is arguably satisfied by English to a very high extent, perhaps even completely.

Let us assume that the Projectibility Principle is in fact satisfied by English but not by (strong versions of) some of the strange languages. The fundamental question to raise is why the principle is plausible. The

[4]For a defense of this claim, see appendix 1.2.

principle implies that there is some *virtue* in having only projectible words in a language. Why is that? One needs some explanation of why it would be worse to have a language whose words are not projectible but many of whose complex expressions are.

The temptation to accept the Projectibility Principle has several possible sources. First, there may be some considerations of "efficiency" or "practical convenience" which seem to support the principle. I want to put such considerations aside until chapter 5, which will be devoted to various pragmatic arguments against the strange languages. Another argument, which I will address in the next section, derives from an alleged connection between projection and ostensive learning. Let us temporarily ignore questions about whether the strange words can be ostensively learned. What I want to consider now is a different kind of defense of the Projectibility Principle.

b. The Epistemological Claim

We are tempted, I think, to say that there is a purely *epistemological* reason why the Projectibility Principle is valid. It may seem to us that people who speak (and think in) a language in which the principle was violated could not rationally make the right projections. That is, they could not rationally make the projections in their language that are equivalent to the ones we make in ours. Let me call this the *epistemological claim*.

A short rebuttal of the epistemological claim has in effect been given in the last section, where it was pointed out that the evidential equivalence principle seems to imply that speaking a strange language is compatible with rationally making projections equivalent to the ordinary ones. I want now to examine this point more closely and to consider what arguments might be advanced in support of the epistemological claim.

The most trivial argument for the epistemological claim is little more than a fallacy of equivocation with respect to the expression "sense of similarity." The use of that expression in the literature is typically ambiguous in a way that is critical to the present discussion. Three criteria commonly used to determine people's "sense of similarity" are, first, the projections they tend to make (where equivalent projections determine the same "sense of similarity"); second, the explicit judgments they tend to make about what is more similar to what (where equivalent judgments of similarity determine the same "sense of similarity"); and third, their tendencies for grouping certain things but not others under a single word. When I suggested in the previous section that, in the context of the division problem, speakers of a strange language should be imagined as having our ordinary sense of similarity, I meant to apply only the first two criteria. As regards the third, it may be trivially correct to say that they do not have our ordinary tendencies for grouping things under a single word.

Suppose we distinguish between sense-of-similarity$_p$, which is defined in terms of projective tendencies; sense-of-similarity$_j$, which is defined in terms of tendencies to make certain explicit similarity judgments; and sense-of-similarity$_w$, which is defined in terms of tendencies to group things under single words. One may be tempted to argue that since speakers of the strange languages do not have our ordinary sense-of-similarity$_w$, they cannot have our ordinary sense-of-similarity$_p$, hence their rational (or even irrational) projections cannot be equivalent to ours. This argument obviously has no force unless one has some independent argument to show why there has to be a connection between their sense-of-similarity$_p$ and their sense-of-similarity$_w$. That connection is, of course, precisely what needs to be questioned.

It may be suggested that the connection can be established via their sense-of-similarity$_j$. The argument might go as follows:

> *Premise 1.* People who do not have an ordinary sense-of-similarity$_w$ cannot, insofar as they are rational, have an ordinary sense-of-similarity$_j$.
>
> *Premise 2.* People who do not have an ordinary sense-of-similarity$_j$ cannot, insofar as they are rational, have an ordinary sense-of-similarity$_p$.
>
> *Conclusion.* Therefore, people who do not have an ordinary sense-of-similarity$_w$ cannot, insofar as they are rational, have an ordinary sense-of-similarity$_p$.

The conclusion of this argument amounts to the epistemological claim, that is, the claim that if people speak a strange language whose words are non-projectible, they cannot rationally make projections equivalent to the ones we ordinarily make.

There is a serious consideration in behalf of Premise 2. There are two influential views in the literature as to what makes a term projectible. Goodman's view is that this depends on the term's degree of entrenchment. It seems that this view does not offer any clear support for Premise 2. But Quine holds that a term is projectible if and only if it denotes a "natural kind," where a necessary (though perhaps insufficient) condition for a class to constitute a natural kind is that its members stand in some suitable similarity relations to each other.[5] Precisely what these relations are will be considered in section 3.3 (and at greater length in appendix 2) but, for the present, it will suffice to say roughly that, on Quine's view, a term is projectible only if it denotes a class whose members are more similar to each other than to other things. Such a class I will simply call at present a "similarity class" and postpone discussion of "natural kinds (or properties)" until the next chapter. That notion is metaphysically charged and may, on some interpretations, invoke contentious issues (relating perhaps to Platonism or to causality) that go well beyond the relatively innocuous notion of similarity. The latter notion will be accepted, in one form or another, by almost anyone. In the present

---

[5]See Quine 1969a, p. 116, and Quine and Ullian 1970, p. 57.

chapter, therefore, I want to appeal only to that notion. Many people will accept at least the part of Quine's view which says that a necessary condition for a term to be projectible is that the term be related in some intimate way to similarity judgments. From this, Premise 2 may seem to follow: People who make strange judgments of similarity cannot rationally make ordinary projections.

But what about Premise 1? The question remains why we should suppose that people who group things under words in strange ways cannot rationally make our ordinary similarity judgments. This question can be understood in two ways. We are asking, first, why there could not be people who rationally apply the word "similar" in a perfectly ordinary way though many (or perhaps all) of their *other* (non-logical) words are strange in the manner of "gricular." Second, we are asking why there could not be people, *all* of whose (non-logical) words are strange but who rationally make judgments equivalent to ordinary similarity judgments. (Suppose that their language contains, instead of the word "similar," the two words "simose" and "simnose," which apply, respectively, to any pair of things that are either similar or close and to any pair of things that are either similar or not close. Then "a is similar to b" is equivalent to "a is simose to b and a is simnose to b.") Given the principle of evidential equivalence, Premise 2 must be understood as meaning that people who do not make judgments equivalent to our ordinary similarity judgments cannot rationally make projections equivalent to our ordinary projections. If Premise 1 is to be combined with Premise 2 to yield the desired conclusion, Premise 1 must be understood in the same spirit, as meaning that people who group things under words in strange ways cannot rationally make judgments equivalent to our ordinary similarity judgments. It is not obvious why this holds true even for people who have no ordinary (non-logical) words, let alone for people who may have the ordinary word "similar."

The presented argument, therefore, does not succeed in defending the epistemological claim.

c. The Similarity Principle

In Premise 1 of the argument, a certain connection is expressed between the similarity relation and people's use of words. It may be tempting to put forth a somewhat different connection in the form of the following division principle:

> *The Similarity Principle.* A general word ought to denote only things that form a similarity class.[6]

---

[6]I will limit my present consideration of this principle to monadic words, though it might be extended to n-adic words if one can talk of n-tuples being similarly related. (See section 3.6.a.)

If we accept Quine's criterion of projectibility, the Projectibility Principle may have much the same effect as the Similarity Principle. It is essential not to allow these two principles tacitly to feed off each other in a tiny vicious circle. We cannot say that words ought to be projectible because that will ensure that they denote similarity classes and they ought to denote similarity classes because that is necessary for them to be projectible.

The Similarity Principle can be interpreted in two ways, depending on whether one thinks of similarity judgments as expressing objective conditions of the world or as merely expressing a special kind of subjective reaction to the world.[7] If one holds the first view, then the principle can be interpreted most straightforwardly as requiring words to denote objective similarity classes. On the second view, the principle should be interpreted as requiring words to denote things that, in terms of the speakers' subjective similarity space, qualify as a similarity class. Even the first view would permit a subjective interpretation of the principle as requiring words to denote things that the speakers would judge, perhaps mistakenly, to be a similarity class. On any interpretation, the principle must be questioned. The most general form of the question is this: Why should there be *any* kind of special connection between the use of words and the similarity relation?

I am not unaware of the extreme oddity of this question. One might be tempted to reply that here is a place where explanations or justifications come to an end. Obviously, if we can have any hope of defending our intuitions about the strange languages, we must be prepared to arrive at some division principles on which we rest our case. The Similarity Principle, it may be felt, is such a principle. Here we have reached the bottom line.

But have we? Suppose one asked a group of philosophers, outside the context of the present discussion, to give a list of cognitive or intellectual virtues. Leading the list would surely be knowledge, true beliefs, and rational beliefs. Various other subsidiary virtues include intelligence, clarity, originality, and so forth. What is presently being suggested, apparently, is that there is another irreducibly new entry on the list: having words (in thought) that denote similarity classes. This seems astonishing. Why should *that* be a cognitive virtue? If we can imagine that the speakers of the strange languages compare favorably with us in knowledge, rational beliefs, and so on, how could it possibly be a *criticism* of them that their words do not denote similarity classes?

If the Similarity Principle is where our case rests, if this is the bottom line, then we have made a major discovery of an irreducibly new kind of cognitive virtue. Put in this light, it may seem doubtful that the Similarity Principle is where our case rests.

[7]This controversy will be discussed in section 3.5.c.

The epistemological claim would attempt to derive both the Projectibility Principle and (assuming Quine's criterion of projectibility) the Similarity Principle from the standard cognitive virtues, for the claim is that people who use a language whose words are not projectible could not possibly have the kind of knowledge or rational beliefs that we have. But so far we have not seen any justification for this claim.

d. Another Argument for the Epistemological Claim

One might try to argue for the claim as follows: "People who use a language whose words are not projectible could have no rational basis for projecting some terms rather than others. The way *we* know what to project is by implicitly appealing to some such system of rules as the following:[8]

The System S

1. Words (without negative prefixes) are typically projectible.
2. The complement of a projectible term is typically not projectible.
3. If two terms are projectible, and neither entails the other, then their disjunction is typically not projectible (where "F" entails "G" if "Anything that is F is G" is a priori necessary).
4. If two compatible terms are projectible, then their conjunction is typically projectible.
5. If one term is projectible and another term is not projectible, and the first does not entail the second, then their conjunction is typically not projectible.
6. If "F" and "G" are both projectible, and our evidence includes instances of "F" that are instances of "G" but no instances of "F" that are instances of "non-G," then, other things being equal, "All F are G" is more credible than any conflicting universal sentence.

This whole system of rules depends on rule 1, for we could have no way of applying rules 2 through 6 unless we had the starting point provided by rule 1. In a language that does not satisfy the Projectibility Principle, since rule 1 could not apply, the speakers could not know what terms to project. The System S, or some variation of it, constitutes our rules of inductive logic. To try to imagine people who cannot avail themselves of such rules is to imagine people who do not operate with our logic, and who are therefore illogical at least by our lights."

One might of course question the final move from their "not operating with our logic" to their being "illogical by our lights." But I think the argument is misguided in a more fundamental way. The System S, precisely because it depends on rule 1, *cannot* constitute our rules of inductive logic. For rules of logic must not depend on the contingencies of a language's lexicon, as rule 1 does. Any rules of logic (whether formal or informal) must depend entirely on the meanings or denotations

---

[8]I think that many of these rules will seem immediately plausible. Rules 2–6 are suggested by the analysis of term-projectibility given in appendix 1.

or other semantic values of the expressions that enter into the arguments to which the rules apply. If we in fact relied on rule 1, so that our inductive reasoning would be altered by a mere change of lexicon, then it would be *we* who are "illogical." But there is no reason to think that we do rely on rule 1. What we do apparently rely on, in deciding whether to project a term, is either the term's entrenchment (as in Goodman) or the term's denoting a natural kind (as in Quine). Speakers of the strange languages can apparently rely on those same criteria to decide to project complex expressions that are equivalent to our words.[9]

Of course, it might still be suggested that the System S functions as a kind of efficient heuristic device, helping us to pass on to future generations our communal assumptions about which terms are projectible. As I said, I will discuss various issues of practical efficiency in chapter 5, but let me comment briefly on this particular point. Apart from serious questions that can be raised about the accuracy of the System S as it stands, obviously it is inadequate as a general prescription for what projections to accept. It is, at best, the beginning of a characterization in terms of our ordinary lexicon of the conditions for what Goodman calls "presumptive projectibility."[10] In order to decide on the actual degree of credibility of some sentences, we typically need an enormous amount of information about what "overhypotheses" bear on these sentences and other competing sentences. That is to say, an enormous amount of information critical to inductive reasoning must anyway be passed on from generation to generation. Seen in this larger context, the heuristic provided by the System S may seem of marginal significance.[11]

e. *Transcendental Arguments and the Epistemological Claim*

Kantian "transcendental" arguments are generally construed as purporting to show that we could have no knowledge (or "experience") unless we employed certain basic categories of thought, such as causality and persistence.[12] How do such arguments relate to the division problem and, specifically, to the epistemological claim?

It would take me too far afield to attempt to examine such arguments in any detail, but I think it is quite clear that they have little bearing on the division problem. For it seems that what such arguments purport to show is that certain *conditions* of things or the world must be represented in thought in order for us to have knowledge. The arguments have no tendency to show that these conditions need to be represented in one form of words rather than another equivalent form. Even if there

---

[9]I leave open whether rules 2–6 can figure in a genuine system of inductive logic. The crucial point is that rule 1 cannot so figure.

[10]Goodman 1973, p. 108ff.

[11]I will have something more to say on this point in section 5.4.f.

[12]See, especially, Strawson 1966.

were a transcendental argument to show that, in order for us to have knowledge, we must represent the world as containing such conditions as colors and shapes, this would do nothing to show that a color is better represented as "green" than as "gricular and grincular," or that a shape is better represented as "circular" than as "gricular and ngricular."

Perhaps this point needs special emphasis with respect to a language like Contacti, which might be said in a sense to affect the concept of persistence, or even the concept of self-identity. The crucial point is that speakers of Contacti could represent the same conditions of the world that are ordinarily represented, including conditions involving persistence and self-identity. Suppose that Contacti contains such "cpersonal pro-nouns" as "I" and "you" (or, if one prefers, "Ci" and "cyou"), which function in the intuitively obvious way (i.e., a cperson uses "I" to refer to that cperson, and uses "you" to refer to the cperson being addressed). Then a speaker of Contacti will sometimes say such things as "I do not remember my own past" or even "I did not begin this (act of) thought." Such remarks, if made in English, might violate what Kant meant by "the unity of apperception," which is claimed to be a fundamental necessity of knowledge. But the remarks made in Contacti are perfectly innocent, implying, for instance, that someone came into physical con-tact with someone else while in the middle of a thought. And the ordi-nary condition of the unity of a person can be expressed in Contacti, albeit in more complicated sentences. So there seems, surely, to be no transcendental argument against Contacti, and one cannot look to such arguments for a defense of the epistemological claim as a response to the division problem.[13]

3. Projectibility and Ostensive Learning

I suspect that some readers have been waiting impatiently for me to get to what may seem like an obvious argument for the Projectibility Principle. This is an argument to the effect that, unless the words of a language are projectible, the language cannot be learned. According to a familiar empiricist picture, general words divide into two classes: the first class consists of words that are learned ostensively; the second class consists of words that are learned by way of definitions in terms of words of the first class.[14] Even if this distinction is somewhat problematical,

---

[13]I am assuming that transcendental arguments purport to show that certain coarse-grained conditions must be represented in thought; the arguments do not purport to show anything about which fine-grained propositions must be represented. In chapter 6, I will examine at length an argument to the effect that the strange languages are ruled out because of their failure to represent fine-grained propositions in the required way, but I consider that argument to be "metaphysical" rather than "transcendental" (it makes no special appeal to the requirements of knowledge or self-consciousness).

[14]How to fit logical words into the empiricist picture is a well-known difficulty. Since the Projectibility Principle deals only with general words, perhaps this difficulty can be put aside.

it may be sufficiently clear to support the idea that, if people spoke a strong version of the Gricular language (a language in which they could not define the word "gricular"), they would have to be able to learn "gricular" ostensively. But, it may be continued, to learn a word ostensively is to project observed instances of its application to new instances. Hence, the word must be projectible—or, at least, the language learner must be treating the word as projectible. (A closely related conclusion would be that instances of the word must be viewed by the language learner as forming a similarity class.)

Although this argument evidently cannot speak against weak versions of strange languages in which some derivative words are not projectible, it may seem to speak decisively against strong versions of the strange languages. With respect to these versions, the argument may be viewed as defending the epistemological claim. It implies that speakers of the strong Gricular language, for example, would have to treat "gricular" and other strange words as projectible and would therefore be led to making incorrect projections.

The argument depends on the following two premises:

(1) Any general word in a language must either be ostensively learned or be definable on the basis of words that are ostensively learned.

(2) In order for people to ostensively learn a general word, they must treat the word as projectible.

I shall maintain that this argument for the Projectibility Principle (and for the epistemological claim) is highly problematical, indeed in four separate ways. The first two problems pertain to (1) and the other two to (2).

Let us assume as a point of terminology that what is called "ostensive learning" cannot be a blind causal process but must involve something on the order of rational inference from observed instances of a word's use. Certainly the argument under consideration presupposes such a notion of ostensive learning. The substantive claim made by (1) is that the undefinable general words of a language must be ostensively learnable in this inferential sense. But that claim can be challenged.

We recall that many of the views on the relationship between language and thinking imply that people sometimes think in a language other than their public language. If there is a non-public language of thinking, certainly there appears to be no reason to suppose that (1) holds for this language. It is not even clear that it makes sense to talk about ostensively learning a word of the non-public language. The typical view would be that having certain sense experiences somehow "triggers" or "activates" certain mental words without inference or reasoning entering into the process.[15]

---

[15]This is essentially all that Jerry Fodor seems to mean when he says that many of our concepts are "innate." See Fodor 1975, pp. 65ff. and 96, and Fodor 1981, especially pp. 272–73.

If (1) applies only to the public language and (some of) our thinking takes place in another language, then the relevance of (1) to the division problem is limited. One of our strongest intuitions is that the strange languages should not figure in thinking. Apparently (1) does nothing to support that intuition.

But I think that (1) can really do little to support our intuition even about the public language. The rationale for (1) is that people have to acquire their public language by learning it, and the only way they could learn it is if the undefinable words are ostensively learned in the inferential sense. It seems, however, that we can imagine people who acquire their public language non-inferentially (perhaps words of the public language are "triggered" or "activated" by experience) and (1) would not apply to them. These imaginary people might even be in essentially our life situation, in the sense given to that notion in section 1.5. As I said then, our minimal intuition seems to be that people in our life situation should not be using a strange language. The argument from (1), however, would allow that it is perfectly all right for people in our life situation to use a strange language so long as they do not acquire it inferentially.

One should not react to this point by suggesting that the relevant notion of "people in our life situation" has to be strengthened to include the stipulation that they learn their language as we do. I think it is clear, really, that our intuitions about the strange languages are quite independent of how people acquire the language. The intuitive wrongness of the Gricular or Grue language does not seem to derive essentially from an *acquisition problem*. To suggest that it does sounds a bit like saying that some exotic disease is bad because it is hard to get. The (strong) strange languages strike us as being somehow bad to *have* (as the only or primary language), at least for people in our life situation in the previously defined sense. When we reflect on this, I think we see that the argument from (1) is really off the track as a defense of our intuitions.

The two problems I have stated for (1) are, first, that it does not apply to the non-public language of thinking (if there is such a language) and, second, that it does not apply to every imaginable public language. The two problems I am going to state for (2) are, first, that it presupposes a dubious model of ostensive learning and, second, that, even given that model, it seems to be false.

The underlying assumption in (2) is that to ostensively learn a word is simply to make a projection about the word's application. On this model, if one were to ostensively learn "gricular," one would have to project the two hypotheses:

H_1: Anything that is gricular is called "gricular."

H_2: Anything that is called "gricular" is gricular.

One's evidence would consist of positive instances of the hypotheses in which gricular things are called "gricular", and the absence of negative instances. (I will ignore the question of what it means to observe that something is called by a particular word.) Premise (2) asserts that one could project these hypotheses in this way only if one treated "gricular" as projectible.

A question that must be raised is how the learner of "gricular" is supposed to be entertaining the hypotheses H_1 and H_2 prior to knowing the meaning of the word "gricular." One possibility is that these hypotheses are entertained in a non-public language of thinking. Suppose that this language is in fact a version of the Gricular language (that is, it contains a word corresponding to every word of the Gricular language). If this is so, it seems clear that the projection of these hypotheses cannot be viewed on the model of ordinary cases of projection. For the learner is in effect inferring the following hypothesis (where "M" represents the mental word that translates "gricular"):

H: "Gricular" means the same as "M."

Someone who infers H_1 and H_2 *together* with H is not simply in the position of someone making projections of the form "Anything that is gricular is F" and "Anything that is F is gricular." On the surface, H does not even involve projecting "gricular" ("gricular" is mentioned but not used in H). One can easily imagine (indeed it is difficult not to imagine) that the learner is predisposed to assume that words in the public language can be translated into words in the non-public one. If such an assumption can be deemed rational, the inference of H, and therefore of H_1 and H_2, seems entirely unproblematical, whether or not "gricular" is being treated as projectible. Hence, contrary to (2), the ostensive learnability of "gricular" does not presuppose that "gricular" be treated as projectible.

The model of ostensive learning presupposed by (2) might be sustainable if one supposed that the learner starts out by thinking without a language. In this case, projecting H_1 and H_2 might indeed be like projecting any other hypothesis involving "gricular."

However, this brings me to the second problem with (2). Even if H_1 and H_2 require straightforward projections, there is no reason to suppose that someone who makes these projections must treat "gricular" as projectible. We treat "gricular" as non-projectible if we regard the class of green things as not being evidentially related in any special way to the class of circular things. This implies that we will project a hypothesis about gricular things only on the basis of evidence drawn from the two evidentially unrelated subclasses of "gricular." Hence, if we observed both green things that are called "gricular" and circular things that are called "gricular," and a variety of other things that are not called "gricular," then we could rationally infer that all and only gricular things are called "gricular." Therefore, contrary to (2), even when "gricular" is treated as non-projectible, there need be no problem in ostensively learning "gricular."[16]

---

[16]There is empirical literature about learning words like "gricular" ostensively. See Fodor 1975, pp. 34–42.

Indeed, practically speaking, it need not be significantly harder in general to find evidence for a hypothesis about gricular things than, say, a hypothesis about dogs, though "gricular" is non-projectible and "dog" is projectible. Roughly speaking, one needs to be a bit more cautious in the former case to make sure that one's positive instances include the evidentially unrelated subclasses of green things and circular things. In the latter case, since "dog" is projectible, positive instances drawn from any class of dogs provide evidence with respect to any other class of dogs. In practice, however, this difference may be of negligible significance, since even in the latter case one's positive instances ought to include a wide variety of dogs, at least if one wants one's hypothesis about dogs to have a relatively high degree of credibility. Hence, if ostensive learning is indeed a matter of making projections, it may be as easy to learn "gricular" ostensively as to learn "dog" ostensively. In any case, I am, as usual, not yet worrying about considerations of "practical efficiency" which might be thought to favor words that are more easy to learn ostensively. My claim at present is that (2) is false in that many non-projectible words *can* be learned ostensively, even when they are treated as non-projectible. Hence the Projectibility Principle cannot be based simply on (2).

My point about the ostensive learnability of "gricular" carries over, perhaps with a few minor complications, to other strange words like "grincular" and "ngricular." It should be noted, however, that the case of "grue" is quite special in the present connection. In order to project "Anything that is grue is called 'grue'" on the model of ostensive learning being assumed, one *would* have to treat "grue" as projectible. For one would have to project (sentences equivalent to) both "Anything that is green and examined before t is called 'grue'" and "Anything that is blue and not examined before t is called 'grue.'" Prior to t, one's evidence for the second sentence could only consist of green things examined before t, which would amount to treating "grue" as projectible. Perhaps we do have in this an argument against strange languages modeled on the Grue language. The argument does not, however, generalize to any of the other examples of strangeness. Moreover, even for the case of the Grue language, the argument is vulnerable to the other three points that I have made in this section: It does not apply to the Grue language as a non-public language of thinking, it does not apply to every imaginable public Grue language, and it presupposes a questionable model of ostensive learning.

4. Projectibility, Similarity, and Individuation

Although the discussion thus far does not appear to support the Projectibility and Similarity Principles, these principles, perhaps in some modified form, may yet turn out to be correct. It is therefore of interest to clarify their scope of application. One reason why it is important to distinguish between classificatory and individuative strangeness is that division principles applicable to one case may not be applicable to the other. The question I want to consider in the present section is whether cases of individuative strangeness violate the Projectibility and Similarity Principles. I will argue (perhaps surprisingly) that they do not.

a. Strange Similarity Classes

Let me first concentrate on the Similarity Principle. Do words like "ctable" and "klable" denote similarity classes? When I first introduced the distinction between classificatory and individuative strangeness, I suggested that in the latter case we have intuitively ordinary classifications (of intuitively strange things).[17] This seems to imply that individuative strangeness involves classifications in terms of similarity classes. I think that this is correct, but the issue is complicated in several ways.

A similarity class is such that its members are more similar to each other than to other things (where the precise meaning of this remains to be elucidated in the next chapter). Red things presumably constitute such a class. Since a thing's color varies from time to time, I assume that when we assess the similarity between red things we ignore times at which they are not red. But there is another question to ask: If x is red at the instant t_1 and y is red at the instant t_2, are we to compare x as it is at t_1 with y as it is at t_2, or are we to compare x's whole period of being red with y's whole period of being red? It seems clear that this question will make no difference in assessing the similarity between red things, but it may make a difference in assessing the similarity between ctables. Since any instantaneous stage of a ctable is indistinguishable from the instantaneous stage of some table, it trivially follows that if we compare things at a given instant the class of ctables is a similarity class if and only if the class of tables is. To make the question interesting, let us assume that we compare ctables by comparing their whole periods of being ctables.

Even looked at this way, it seems that the class of ctables is a similarity class. Ctables are entities that are otherwise like tables except for the bizarre transformations when they come into contact. Certainly, such entities seem to form a strikingly similar class. Perhaps we need immediately to insert the following qualification. There may of course be some tables that throughout their entire histories never come into contact with other tables. If we regard even these tables as corresponding to ctables in Contacti, then these would be ctables that never undergo the strange exchange of characteristics. Can we say that there is a similarity class that includes both these things and the ctables that do undergo the exchanges? I think we can answer this question in the affirmative. Given the most obvious conditions of transworld identity for ctables, any ctable has the

---

[17]See section 1.2.d.

possibility of undergoing the exchanges; that is, any ctable has the dispositional property of being such that it would undergo the exchanges in a possible situation in which it comes into exclusive contact with another ctable. It seems that if we take such dispositional properties into account, we can include in one similarity class both ctables that do and ctables that do not actually undergo the exchanges. But if someone disagrees with this, all that would follow is that in order for Contacti to satisfy the Similarity Principle, it would have to have separate words for things that do and things that do not undergo the strange exchanges. If this is so, let it indeed be stipulated that such words as "ctable" and "cdog" denote only things that do undergo the strange exchanges.

b. Intrinsic Similarity Classes

There are still questions to be raised about whether the class of ctables is a similarity class. One sort of doubt derives from the following consideration. Let S be a succession combining the stages of one table up to time t followed by the stages of another table after t. Then S constitutes a single ctable only if the two tables are exclusively in contact with each other at t, that is, only if the stage of S at t stands in a suitable unique contact relation to the stage of another ctable. S constitutes a single ctable, therefore, only if it has certain *extrinsic* properties, that is, only if it stands in a certain required relation to something outside itself.[18] Hence, certain non-ctables—namely, those comprised of successions combining stages of different tables where the required unique contact relation does not hold—may be as intrinsically similar to ctables as ctables are to each other. (This is especially clear, perhaps, for non-ctables that combine stages of different tables that do enter into contact with each other, but not unique contact.) If, then, we interpret the Similarity Principle as requiring words to denote "intrinsic similarity classes"— that is, classes of things that are similar to each other with respect to intrinsic properties—it may seem that this condition will not be met by such words as "ctable."

The trouble is that the condition will not be met even by ordinary words like "table." I am not making the seemingly obvious (though possibly controversial) point that a thing could not qualify as a table unless it were actually used in certain ways by entities outside it. I want to make a point that will apply to *every* count noun, such as "dog" or "pebble." No ordinary count noun can apply to a thing in virtue of its purely intrinsic properties. Consider "dog." Evidently a four-legged dog cannot be said to contain a three-legged dog as a proper part, though if the dog actually lost a leg, what was previously a certain three-legged part of a dog would come to constitute a three-legged dog. If x is a bit of matter that constitutes every part of a dog except for one leg, then x

[18]See Lewis 1983a, 197–200; also section 3.6.a here.

by itself fails to constitute a dog because x is suitably connected to the leg. Hence certain non-dogs—namely, large three-legged parts of dogs—may have the highest degree of intrinsic similarity to three-legged dogs. These non-dogs fail to qualify as dogs because of their extrinsic properties. This point applies to any count noun.

Nevertheless, it may seem intuitively correct to say that the extrinsic properties of things often do not count in our ordinary judgments of similarity. Might it be that some count and some do not? Perhaps the extrinsic property of being spatially connected in a certain kind of way to a certain kind of thing strikes us as "almost intrinsic," since this property inheres, as it were, at a thing's surface. If spatial connectedness but no (or few) other extrinsic properties count in similarity judgments, then both dogs and cdogs might constitute similarity classes while strange things modeled on Shoemaker's klables might not. (I will have something more to say about intrinsic and extrinsic similarity in the next chapter.)

c. Similarity and Salience

There is an influential approach to similarity that might be thought to have a bearing on the foregoing questions. Amos Tversky, in a widely cited paper, states that "the contribution of any particular (common or distinctive) feature to the similarity between objects" is measured in part by "the salience or prominence" of the feature, where salience is determined by a wide variety of factors, some of which are highly contextual.[19] Along these lines, one might question my claim that ctables or cdogs constitute similarity classes. Such items (or their distinctive features) are not salient for us, it might be said, and hence these items are not sufficiently similar to each other.

I would like to resist the mixture of similarity and salience, however. Imagine that a and b are two qualitatively identical cats that are both brightly colored and conspicuously in motion, and that c and d are two qualitatively identical cats that are dully colored and inconspicuously at rest. Tversky would presumably say that a is more similar to b than c is to d. Surely, this seems intuitively questionable. One would have thought that any pair of qualitatively identical things must be similar to the same degree, to the highest degree. Salience seems to have nothing to do with the matter. The point seems to hold even if we imagine the pairs as not being qualitatively identical. If a is slightly bigger and rounder than b, and c is to the same degree slightly bigger and rounder than d, then a ought to be no more similar to b than c is to d.

On the face of it, Tversky is simply confusing "a is similar to b" with "It is easy to notice that a is similar to b." Why should there not be this distinction? Obviously there *must* be this distinction if similarity is to be

---

[19]Tversky 1977, p. 332. See also Quine 1973, p. 25.

an objective relationship. But I think the distinction should be made even if we regard similarity judgments as subjective reactions. Being disgusting, I take it, is a subjective matter, but can we not distinguish between "*a* is more disgusting than *b*" and "It is easy to notice that *a* is more disgusting than *b*"? If we hide away some disgusting object or conceal its disgusting features, do we make it less disgusting? Well, perhaps in a sense, yes, but there is surely a sense in which it remains as disgusting as ever, though one would have to bring it into the light to notice this.

I am not necessarily attempting to challenge the significance of Tversky's psychological insights. From a philosophical standpoint, however, I think that clarity is served by prizing apart similarity and salience as much as possible. The similarity judgments that ought to concern us most philosophically are those that might be called *reflective*. Similarity judgments are reflective if, first, they are made after the objects in question and their relevant properties have been noticed and, second, they can withstand some reflection. The relevance of the first condition was illustrated in the earlier example, in which it was assumed that a similarity judgment about the non-salient pair of cats should take into account the relevant properties of these cats. The following may bring out the relevance of the second condition: Tversky offers evidence that people are sometimes more willing to accept a sentence of the form "*a* is (very) similar to *b*" than "*b* is (very) similar to *a*," particularly if *b* is more salient than *a* (e.g., people more readily accept "North Korea is similar to Red China" than "Red China is similar to North Korea"). From such examples Tversky draws the paradoxical conclusion that similarity is not symmetrical.[20] But surely the similarity judgments cited by Tversky are not likely to be reflective judgments. It seems that virtually everyone would dismiss as ill considered and silly a set of similarity judgments they made once it is pointed out that these judgments imply an absence of symmetry. So we should, at least for our philosophical purposes, discount such judgments.

In attempting to prize apart similarity and salience, I do not mean to suggest that salience has no important role to play in the division problem. Indeed, in section 5.2 I will formulate a "salience principle" that requires, roughly, that words should represent things and properties that are salient. But I think it best not to mix this principle together with the Similarity Principle.

d. Predictable Things

Fine details aside, I expect that many will find it intuitively satisfactory to say that the class of cdogs is a similarity class. If this is so then, at least on Quine's view of projectibility, it may also seem plausible to hold that "cdog" is projectible. There is, however, another important angle

[20]Tversky 1977, pp. 333–34.

on this question, one that may suggest a new division principle. Let Cfido be some particular cdog, and suppose we are given an extensive description of Cfido's intrinsic properties up to some time t. This will not enable us to make any detailed predictions as to what Cfido's intrinsic properties will be after t if there is any likelihood that Cfido may alter its (exclusive) contact relations with other cdogs after t. In this, Cfido seems to contrast with the dog Fido, for many of the details of Fido's intrinsic future properties seem to be predictable on the basis of its intrinsic past properties. This contrast between Cfido and Fido evidently has something to do with the fact that it is reasonable to project certain hypotheses about dogs but not reasonable to project the corresponding hypotheses about cdogs. Examples of such hypotheses are:

Hd: Any dog is such that if it eats poison it will later be ill.

Hc: Any cdog is such that if it eats poison it will later be ill.

One may be tempted to conclude that "dog" is projectible but "cdog" is not. But, as I shall now explain, this is misguided; assuming that "dog" is projectible, so is "cdog."

We said earlier that "dog" is projectible because any division of dogs into two subclasses (e.g., the fat dogs and the non-fat dogs) is such that information with respect to one subclass is evidence with respect to the other subclass. Can one make a comparable remark about "cdog"? The example of Hc may superficially suggest that one cannot. For suppose we divide cdogs into those that do and those that do not alter their contact relations with other cdogs after t. Consider the property of being such that if it eats poison at t it will later be ill. Evidently, if we are given the information that this property is possessed by the subclass of cdogs that do not alter their contact relations after t, this will not be evidence that the property is possessed by the subclass of cdogs that do alter their contact relations after t. It is a mistake, however, to suppose that this implies that "cdog" is not projectible. A term is projectible if any division of its instances into two subclasses is such that information that one subclass has a certain property is evidence that the other subclass has the property, for *some* properties. This condition cannot possibly hold for all properties. Even in the case of "dog," it holds only for some properties. Take the property of being a fat dog with a spotted tongue. Obviously, the information that fat dogs have this property would not be evidence that non-fat dogs do. If this point is borne in mind, we realize that "cdog" is projectible, just as "dog" is. With respect to many properties not involving change after t (or, more simply, not involving change at all), the information that this property is possessed by the subclass of cdogs that do not alter their contact relations after t will be evidence that it is possessed by the other subclass.

This is not to deny, of course, that there is an important difference between "cdog" and "dog" that is relevant to the hypotheses Hc and Hd. The nature of cdog-identity (together with the general fact that cdogs tend to differ intrinsically from each other) entails that a cdog's intrinsic properties are liable to change drastically when it enters into contact with another cdog. No corresponding entailment is derivable from the nature of dog-identity. This is why we would project Hd but not Hc.

If we want to express a division principle that brings out the relevant difference between "dog" and "cdog," the most obvious formulation would be the following:

> *The Predictable Things Principle*. A general word ought to denote things whose future intrinsic properties are predictable, to a significant degree, on the basis of their past intrinsic properties.[21]

We should note certain immediate limitations of the principle. It will evidently not exclude strange things constructed simply by summing things, such as trables (sums of tables and trees). Trables are intuitively strange, though we could evidently associate conditions of transtemporal identity for them which would make them roughly as predictable as tables or trees. (A thing is "predictable" in the relevant sense to the extent that its future intrinsic properties are predictable on the basis of its past intrinsic properties.) The principle would not even exclude such strange things as incars (things that shrink when cars leave garages), which seem to be predictable to a high degree. When an incar is shrinking, it will predictably continue to shrink until it vanishes, and when it is not shrinking only one of its ends is prone to change unpredictably, at which time it will be shrinking and predictable. Ice cubes that shrink and vanish when removed from the freezer are not more predictable than incars; nor perhaps are many other ordinary objects that are subject to externally caused change or destruction. The Predictable Things Principle may, however, seem at least to effectively exclude Contacti-things.

My argument has been, in effect, that this principle is entailed by neither the Projectibility Principle nor the Similarity Principle. It may nevertheless have a great deal of independent appeal. My impression is indeed that many who philosophize about identity through time implicitly assume that some such principle is beyond question. Of course, I am going to urge that it must be questioned. If one is tempted to say that this principle is the bottom line, that here is where justifications come to an end, I would press the same sorts of questions as those I raised

---

[21]The principle should be taken to imply that n-adic relational words ought to denote n-tuples of things whose future intrinsic properties. . . . Note that if "ought to denote things whose future . . ." is understood to mean "ought to denote *some* things whose future . . . ," rather than "ought to denote *only* things whose future . . . ," the principle can satisfy the believer discussed in the last chapter who held that even ordinary (non-individuative) words denote strange things as well as ordinary things. The restriction is against words denoting only strange things. The believer could also be satisfied by restricting the principle to individuative words. These qualifications in behalf of the believer should be assumed in what follows.

earlier. If we can imagine people who compare favorably with us in true beliefs, rational beliefs, intelligence, and so on, how could it possibly be a criticism of them that their words denote unpredictable things?

The crucial point to grasp here is that (at least as far as we have hitherto been able to show) people whose language violated the principle need not thereby make fewer accurate predictions than we do. They may, in fact, make predictions equivalent to the ones we make. The difference between their predictions and ours has to do only with different structures of language and thinking. We still seem far from understanding how that difference can matter.

It is at least roughly correct to say that a word "F" will satisfy the Predictable Things Principle only if instances of "F" have histories with a high degree of causal interconnectedness. ("F"-instances would have to be "causal lines" in Russell's sense.[22]) There is a possible fallacy here that seems completely trivial but may be worth mentioning. The sentence

(3) Causal connectedness is an important condition of identity

may mean either

(3a) Causal connectedness is a (or the) leading condition of identity for things denoted by the words of ordinary language

or

(3b) It is important for any language to contain only words that denote things with causally interconnected histories.

I am not at present questioning (3a).[23] But it is clear that what is required to support the Predictable Things Principle is (3b) and that (3a) does not entail (3b). If one confusedly runs together the two senses of (3), one will fail to see how difficult it is to find any support for the principle.

---

[22]Russell 1948, pp. 458–60.

[23]In fact, I believe that (3a) may be an exaggeration; see Hirsch 1982, pp. 218–23.

3

Reality's Joints I: Properties

1. Reality's Joints and the Division Problem

The idea that there are in some sense "natural joints" in the world goes back to Plato.[1] What this idea seems to suggest is aptly expressed by David Lewis as follows:

> Among all the countless things and classes that there are, most are miscellaneous, gerrymandered, ill-demarcated. Only an elite minority are carved at the joints, so that their boundaries are established by objective sameness and difference in nature.[2]

I think it has often been tacitly assumed in the literature since Plato that the division problem is immediately solved (or at least substantially diminished) for someone who believes in the objectivity of reality's joints, for this belief may seem to imply the division principle that language should divide reality at the joints (or come sufficiently close to that ideal). I should hope that by now it would be clear that such an assumption is misguided. A belief in reality's joints does not, at least obviously and of itself, entail a belief in any division principle. The latter makes a normative claim about language, which cannot follow, at least obviously, from a metaphysical claim about objective sameness and difference in nature. Even if one believes in reality's joints, a separate argument is needed to support the division principle.

The crucial difference to note is that between "carving at the joints" and "saying where the joints are." If we believe in the objectivity of reality's joints, it perhaps follows immediately that we ought to have the wherewithal to say where they are. This would require that we have certain words in our language, perhaps indeed the word "(reality's) joints." But to carve at the joints, in the sense relevant to this discus-

[1]See Plato, *Phaedrus* 265.
[2]Lewis 1984, p. 227.

52

sion, is to arrange for there to be a special kind of structural fit between one's language and reality's joints. An argument is needed to show why that kind of fit is required.

In seeking an argument for the division principle that language should carve at the joints, we should begin by distinguishing between the principle as it applies to classification and as it applies to individuation. I will discuss the former in this chapter and the latter in the next chapter.

2. Natural Properties

As the quote from Lewis indicates, the issue of reality's joints is closely related to questions about sameness and difference. These questions must certainly impinge on some of the issues about similarity already discussed in the last chapter. The general connection between these chapters might be put by saying that I am moving from an epistemologically centered discussion to a metaphysically centered one. In the last chapter I was primarily seeking arguments to show that speaking the strange languages would adversely affect people's ability to make correct projections about the world (or about their language). Now I am primarily seeking arguments to show that the strange languages are somehow ruled out by metaphysical or ontological considerations.

One version of a Classificatory Joints Principle would indeed be the Similarity Principle of the last chapter. In the present context one would require the proviso, which was inessential to the previous discussion, that similarity is being viewed as an objective relationship (since reality's joints are certainly supposed to be objective). It will be more instructive, however, to now formulate a somewhat different version of a Classificatory Joints Principle and afterward to inquire how that version relates to the Similarity Principle.

The Classificatory Joints Principle. A general word ought to express a natural property.

The initial plausibility of this division principle may be enhanced if we recall two earlier points: First, any division principle may be viewed as applying primarily to the semantic primitives of a language; second, any division principle may be viewed as presumptive rather than absolute. In any case, what the Classificatory Joints Principle is evidently driving at is that such words as "grue" and "gricular" do not express natural properties, whereas such words as "green" and "circular" do. Most of this chapter is devoted to examining the notion of a natural property, which is presupposed by the principle. In the final section 3.7, I will turn to arguments for the principle.

I have generally been using the word "property" to cover both thing-conditions and fine-grained properties (where, we recall, this distinction depends on whether necessary equivalence entails identity). To keep the present discussion within manageable limits, however, I am going to stipulate that the properties under consideration in this chapter are coarse-grained thing-conditions. Much of what I say could be carried over easily to the fine-grained domain.[3] I have been assuming—and will continue to assume—that all philosophers will accept thing-conditions at least in the sense of functions from possible worlds to extensions or, for short, sets of actual and possible things. Clearly, such words as "grue" and "gricular" do express thing-conditions, and hence properties, in this broad sense. The "natural properties" are supposed to correspond to only a restricted group of thing-conditions.

Since the purported distinction between natural and unnatural properties is somewhat technical, it needs to be introduced in a preliminary way before we embark on an attempt to analyze it; otherwise, we are at risk of putting forth analyses without having any real idea of what we are aiming at. Let me indicate the general route by which a preliminary sense of the distinction may be imparted. First of all, we start out with examples that purport to exemplify the distinction. On one list we have properties like Green, Circular, and Apple; on the other, properties like Grue, Gricular, and Carple. These examples tend to elicit in us intuitions of two closely related sorts. First, there are intuitions about the properties themselves. Those on the first list strike us as being "genuine properties," the sharing of which constitutes things really having something in common and being similar to each other. (I intend to use "natural property" and "genuine property" interchangeably, but the latter expression seems more apt to capture the intuition I am now attempting to invoke.) Those on the second list do not seem to make things that share them really have something in common or be similar; these properties strike us as being "merely disjunctive" or "merely arbitrary (or artificial) constructions."

Second, the examples elicit intuitions about what constitutes a sensible practice of linguistic classification. These are, of course, the intuitions that generate the division problem. I have been assuming all along that languages containing words for such properties as Grue and Gricular strike us as intuitively strange. This gives an immediate sense in which such properties can be said to be "psychologically unnatural" (for us). It must be clearly noted that this is not the sense of naturalness currently in question. The Classificatory Joints Principle seeks, rather, to normatively ground our use of words for some properties and not for others in an objective distinction between natural and unnatural properties, a distinction that holds independently of our language or thought or interests.

To sum up the last two paragraphs, let the following stand as the "official" preliminary introduction of the distinction:

---

[3]I will discuss fine-grained properties in appendix 3.4, where I will attempt to fill any lacunae left in the present discussion.

We believe in a distinction between natural and unnatural properties if we
believe that there is an objective distinction that corresponds at least roughly
to our intuitions about "genuine properties" versus "merely arbitrary constructions" and to our intuitions about ordinary versus strange classifications.[4]

Of course, there may turn out to be more than one objective distinction relevant to the intuitions in question, and the intuitions themselves
may need to be sorted out in various ways. (For instance, we have
already seen that intuitions about strangeness are a matter of degree,
which may suggest that property-naturalness is itself a matter of degree;
I will turn to that refinement in a later section of this chapter.) Nevertheless, I think the official introduction gives a sufficiently clear sense of
the prima facie distinction that we would like to explain.

Explanations of what property-naturalness consists in divide up into
two sorts, depending on whether they essentially turn upon an ontological
claim. The ontological claim would be that, whereas both ordinary and
strange words answer to sets of actual and possible things, only ordinary
words answer to *another* kind of item, a universal that things share. The
natural properties, on this view, are Platonic universals, whereas unnatural
properties are merely set-theoretical items.

The ontological position should be contrasted with the *elitist* position. The elitist does not say that there is an additional abstract item
attaching to "green" which does not attach to "gricular." The number
of attaching items is the same but those attaching to "green" have
the elite status of being objectively "genuine" or "natural." The elitist
may be a Nominalist who accepts properties only in the sense of set-
theoretical items. Or the elitist may be a kind of Platonist who believes
that even such words as "gricular" express universals, albeit unnatural
ones. The distinction this philosopher wants to draw is neutral as
between these ontological positions.

If someone rejects both the ontological and elitist positions, let us
call that position *egalitarian*. The egalitarian, too, may be a Platonist
or a Nominalist. In either case this philosopher holds that the number
of abstract items attaching to the strange words is the same as those
attaching to ordinary words and, moreover, the latter items have no
objectively special status lacking in the former.[5]

---

[4]Perhaps it needs to be added that the objective distinction in question must not be of
a normative nature. It cannot simply be the distinction between properties that may reasonably
be expressed by single words and those that ought not to be expressed by single words.
Nor can it be the distinction between properties on which projections ought to based and
those on which projections ought not to be based. What we are seeking is an objective non-
normative distinction that may serve to explain such normative distinctions.

[5]The ontological position is close to that of Armstrong 1978. (Various questions about
the nature of universals—for example, whether they are "immanent" or "transcendent"—
will be left open.) The elitist position is advanced in Lewis 1983b, pp. 347ff., and in Lewis
1986, pp. 59–63; however, Lewis assumes that the elitist is a Nominalist whereas I leave

We have, then, ontological inegalitarianism, elitist inegalitarianism, and egalitarianism. I will begin by looking at the elitist position. One version of this position, suggested by Lewis, is that naturalness might be accepted as an unanalyzable primitive.[6] This view is, I think, quite plausible in that it is hard to think of any notion more fundamental than that of a "genuine property." Nevertheless, that notion seems to be intimately tied to two others, similarity and causality, and this has encouraged some elitists to attempt either a similarity analysis or a causal analysis of property-naturalness. I will consider these analyses in the next two sections.

It should be noted that each of these analyses can be divided into two claims. The first claim is that property-naturalness is equivalent to some condition involving similarity or causality.[7] The second claim is that this equivalence constitutes an analysis. Even inegalitarians who reject the second claim—because they regard property-naturalness as properly analyzable in ontological terms or because they regard it as primitive—may accept the equivalence. The analyses are therefore of potential interest to all inegalitarians.

3. The Similarity Analysis

The point of departure of the similarity analysis is the seemingly obvious idea that a property P is natural if and only if P-bearers constitute in some sense a class of things more similar to each other than to other things (this is what was called a "similarity class" in the previous chapter). It would seem quite surprising if this idea could not be explicated in some reasonable fashion.[8] Yet there are formidable difficulties in the way of accomplishing this.

a. The Problem of Imperfect Community

The first point to appreciate is that we cannot accept the simple principle that a property is natural if and only if any two of its bearers are

---

that open. (Strictly, Lewis does not reject Armstrong's view, but he claims that the alternative elitist view is equally plausible.) A somewhat different ontological position (involving "tropes" rather than universals) is also formulated in Lewis 1986, pp. 64–69; I will, however, stick to the more standard ontological position. The terminology of "elitism" and "egalitarianism" is derived from Lewis. The ontological, elitist, and egalitarian positions are closely related to the three positions discussed in Shoemaker 1988.

[6]Lewis 1986, p. 63. Throughout this discussion, I assume that the relevant notion of a primitive is that of an unanalyzable semantic primitive in roughly the sense indicated in section 1.3.e.

[7]That is, a sentence of the form "P is natural" is (a priori necessarily) equivalent to a sentence of the form "P satisfies such-and-such condition of similarity (or causality)."

[8]Note that the similarity analyst's suggestion here is not that every natural property can be analyzed in terms of similarity (which seems immediately implausible), but that one particular property, the property of being natural, can be so analyzed.

more similar to each other than either is to any non-bearer. Presumably, there are pairs of natural properties P and Q which are compatible and such that some possible things have one but not the other. The principle in question must fail for at least one of these properties. For suppose that x has both properties, y has P but not Q, and z has Q but not P. If x is more similar to y than to z, then the principle fails for Q, and if x is not more similar to y than to z, the principle fails for P. It follows that the principle cannot be correct.[9]

Quine considers, and ultimately rejects, a somewhat more complicated principle. This says that a set constitutes a natural kind if and only if "all its members are more similar to one another than they all are to any one thing outside the set. In other words, each non-member differs more from some member than that member differs from any member."[10] Recasting this in terms of properties, the condition on the naturalness of a property P being considered by Quine seems to be this:

For any x that lacks P, there is a y that has P such that, for any z that has P, the degree of dissimilarity between x and y is greater than that between y and z.[11]

Quine argues that this condition cannot be a sufficient condition of naturalness because it succumbs to a version of Goodman's "problem of imperfect community."[12] Suppose that I is the property of having at least two of the three properties Green, Circular, and Wooden. The intuitive judgment would appear to be that I is not a natural property, but, argues Quine, I does satisfy the condition. For if x lacks I, we can always choose an I-bearer y that shares none of the three properties with x; since y may also be chosen to differ from x in every other relevant respect, y may be as far away from x as one wishes. Any z that has I, by contrast, must share at least one of the three properties with y. Hence, the degree of dissimilarity between x and y is greater than that between y and z.

---

[9]The principle that is shown to be incorrect says that if P is a natural property, and x and y have P while z lacks P, then the degree of similarity between x and y must be *both* greater than that between x and z *and* greater than that between y and z. A slightly more complicated argument of the same general sort would refute a principle that required that the degree of similarity between x and y must be *either* greater than that between x and z *or* greater than that between y and z. (Let P, Q, and R be natural properties such that x has P and Q but not R, y has P and R but not Q, and z has Q and R but not P. Then there is no possible way of assigning similarity distances between x, y, and z which will satisfy the stated requirement for all three properties.)

[10]Quine 1969a, p. 120.

[11]A slightly different interpretation of Quine's condition will be discussed in appendix 2.1. Let it be noted that I assume throughout this discussion that every property under consideration is such that some (possible) things have it and some do not.

[12]See Quine 1969a, pp. 120–21, and Goodman 1977, p. 119. In what follows, I am summarizing Quine's characterization of the problem of imperfect community; I will try to show in appendix 2.3 that this characterization of the problem is inaccurate in a certain respect.

Let us note that similarity conditions such as the one mentioned by Quine can be understood in two senses, depending on whether one takes the variables to range only over actual things or also over possible things.[13] On the first interpretation, it will be a contingent matter whether a property satisfies the condition. If we want it to be a matter of necessity whether a property satisfies the condition, we need to adopt the second interpretation. That is the interpretation that I will generally have in mind.

The problem of imperfect community, explained by Quine, is that the specified condition will be satisfied by properties of the form "having at least m of the following (mutually compatible) n natural properties," where m is more than half of n. Properties of this form have often been associated with Wittgenstein's notion of a "family resemblance."[14] So the problem is that the specified condition provides us with a notion no stronger than that of a family resemblance, whereas we seem to have a stronger intuitive notion of a natural property.

Let me suggest how one might formulate a stronger condition that appears to solve the problem of imperfect community. The basic idea in this formulation is that a natural property is *similarity-making*. Intuitively, this is a property the sharing of which necessarily increases the similarity between things. We might start out by saying that P is similarity-making if and only if, for any x and y, if x has P and y lacks P then, for any z, if z is just like y except for having P, z will be more similar to x than y is. As an explication of "z is just like y except for having P" we might be tempted to give "Nothing that has P is more similar to y than z is." This will not do, however, if there are an infinite number of P-bearers and, for any one of them, there is another one more similar to y. To circumvent this problem, our definition should say, roughly, that a property P is natural if and only if:

> For any x and y, if x has P and y lacks P, then, for any P-bearer z, if z is sufficiently similar to y, z is more similar to x than y is.

To put this a bit more precisely, we should treat z as marking a degree of similarity to y beyond which any P-bearer must be more similar to x than y is. Our definition might then be that P is natural if and only if:

> (N) For any x and y, if x has P and y lacks P, there is a z such that z has P and, for any w, if w has P and w is at least as similar to y as z is, then w is more similar to x than y is.

Note how this definition gets around the problem of imperfect community. Where I is the property of having at least two of the three properties Green, Circular, and Wooden, there will be an x that has I in

---

[13]For expository convenience, I here treat "possible things" as if they were Lewisian objects, each existing in only one world. This can be reformulated in terms of world-slices of things or ordered pairs of worlds and things.

[14]See, e.g., Bambrough 1966, p. 189.

virtue of having Circular and Wooden but not Green and a *y* that lacks *I* in virtue of having only Wooden. Then there may be *I*-bearers as close as one can get to *y* having Green and Wooden but not Circular, and these need be no more similar to *x* than *y* is. (Whereas *y* may have the same substance and color as *x*, *I*-bearers close to *y* may only have the same substance as *x*.) Hence the imperfect community property *P* fails to satisfy (N). Evidently, this argument will generalize to any imperfect community property.

b. Dimensions of Comparison

Similarity conditions such as (N) or the one specified by Quine are couched in terms of a notion of overall similarity. (I always use "similarity" *simpliciter* to mean overall similarity.) It has often been noted, however, that the task of defining naturalness in terms of similarity is made easier if one presupposes various general dimensions of comparison, such as color and shape.[15] One might then try to say that *P* is natural if, for some accepted dimension of comparison *D*, the maximal dissimilarity with respect to *D* between any non-*P*-bearer and some *P*-bearer is less than that between any *P*-bearers. The obvious problem is that the accepted dimensions of comparison are themselves being accepted as natural second-order properties, so at most one is defining what a natural first-order property is in terms of natural second-order properties. To this I would add the further observation that not all natural second-order properties appear to function as dimensions of comparison. Although Animal Species is presumably a natural second-order property, we do not typically compare particular animals as being more or less similar with respect to Animal Species.[16] Hence, it is not clear how the dimension-relativized definition could apply to such a natural property as Dog.

Let us note, further, that Quine's condition and condition (N) are designed to explain first-order naturalness. Suppose that the properties Grue, Bleen, and other gruified colors are called "schmolors."[17] If we tried to apply these conditions to the second-order property Schmolor, we might very well get the result that this is a natural property. (All the gruified colors seem to be more similar to each other than to other properties, including non-gruified colors.) It might be said, perhaps, that Schmolor is not natural because a necessary condition for a second-

---

[15]See, e.g., Quine 1969a, pp. 119–20 and 136.

[16]We can indeed say "Fido and Lassie are similar with respect to (what) species (they are)," which is like saying "Fido and Lassie are similar with respect to being dogs." What we cannot apparently say is "Fido is more similar to Lassie than to Benji with respect to (what) species (they are)," in the way we can say of three red things that the first is more similar to the second than to the third with respect to (what) color (they are).

[17]See Ullian 1961.

order property to be natural is that its instances are natural. (This does not seem to be a sufficient condition, since the property of being either the property Red or the property Round is presumably unnatural, even if its instances are natural.) But if second-order naturalness needs to be explained by reference to first-order naturalness, this is another reason not to welcome the account suggested in the last paragraph, in which first-order naturalness is defined in terms of natural second-order properties.

c. The Property P*

Although (N) appears to solve the problem of imperfect community, it faces another problem (which applies as well to Quine's condition). Suppose that Red_{60} is some arbitrarily designated shade of Red and that $Orange_{40}$ is some arbitrarily designated shade of Orange. If P* is the property of having a color between Red_{60} and $Orange_{40}$, it would seem that P* will be similarity-making in the sense of condition (N).[18] Properties like P* can evidently be constructed for shapes and other qualities. But some elitists will wish to deny that all such properties are natural.

The status of such properties is, I think, a pivotal question in our understanding of naturalness. It may seem obvious that these properties are in some sense "psychologically unnatural" (for humans), but that is not the issue.[19] As regards the relevant notion of (objective) naturalness, it seems extremely tempting on reflection to say that this must somehow boil down to facts about (objective) similarity, that a natural property just is a property that makes for similarities. If we hold to this idea, then it seems we must accept such natural properties as P*.

A point that I especially want to emphasize is that it appears that any form of similarity analysis must have this consequence. Consider the dimension-relativized analysis of a few paragraphs back. That analysis implies that a property P is a natural color if and only if the maximal (objective) dissimilarity with respect to color between any non-P-bearer and some P-bearer is less than that between any P-bearers. I think it is clear on reflection that P* must then be a natural color (if any ordinary color is).

Lewis mentions another kind of similarity analysis of naturalness, one that requires us to accept as primitive an artificial similarity relation that is tailor-made to provide a definition of naturalness.[20] Lewis remarks that

---

[18]I am assuming that color is a "natural phenomenon" (see Kripke 1980, p. 134), and I take this to imply that a property such as Red is natural and satisfies condition (N). It then follows that P* also satisfies (N). If colors are not viewed as natural properties then my examples would have to be altered, but the problem remains the same.

[19]On the psychological unnaturalness of properties such as P*, see Rosch 1977a, pp. 3–15.

[20]The relation would have to be "both contrastive and variably polyadic. Something like $x_1, x_2, \ldots$ resembles one another and do not likewise resemble any of $y_1, y_2, \ldots$ (where the strings of variables may be infinite, even uncountable) must be taken as understood without further analysis" (Lewis 1983b, pp. 347–48). A similar idea is found in Quine 1973, p. 18.

there seems to be no clear difference between this view and simply taking naturalness as primitive. I would suggest, however, that there may be the following difference: So long as we analyze naturalness in terms of a similarity relation, even an artificial similarity relation, we can conclude that, if Red is natural, then so are such properties as P*. For it seems that there can be no relevant difference between the latter property and Red as regards the general structure of their similarity relations. Lewis was apparently motivated to consider the artificial similarity analysis because the problem of imperfect community seemed to stand in the way of any other similarity analysis. If an analysis in terms of (N) solves this problem (and gives rise to no other problems), it would appear that this analysis should be favored. As regards the problem of P*, a similarity analyst of any stripe should be prepared to bite the bullet on this.

d. Other Consequences of (N)

If we accept condition (N) as definitive of naturalness, certain conclusions seem to follow with respect to disjunctions, conjunctions, and complements of properties. It seems immediately obvious that arbitrary disjunctions of properties satisfying (N) will not satisfy (N). This is, of course, the result that we want for naturalness. I think the following is also quite clear: If two (compatible) properties satisfy (N), then so does their conjunction.[21] I would regard this as intuitively satisfactory—at least not intuitively disturbing—with respect to naturalness. (If P-bearers "really have something in common," and so do Q-bearers, it surely seems to follow that so do bearers of P and Q.)

The case of complements is far more complicated, and I am postponing discussion of it until appendix 2.4. There are a number of other intricate issues related to the similarity analysis which I will take up in appendix 2. However, my conclusion there is that, although (N) may require some refinements, it seems plausible to suppose that some such condition is equivalent to property-naturalness.

4. The Causal Analysis

There is another possible analysis of property-naturalness to consider. Many inegalitarians, whether adopting the ontological or elitist position, have claimed that there is an important connection between causality and property-naturalness. It might be suggested, then, that naturalness can be analyzed in terms of causality.

---

[21] I do not see how to demonstrate this conjunctive principle. I suppose it could be demonstrated given certain assumptions about the structure of similarity space. But the principle itself is likely to be as intuitive as any such assumption. (Armstrong 1978, chapters 14 and 15, also arrives at the view that conjunctions but not disjunctions of natural properties are natural.)

a. The Standard Causal Analysis

The most obvious idea along these lines would be to analyze a natural property as a property that has causal powers.[22] But I think this idea has little promise.

In order for the analysis to hold, it must at least be true that:

(1) Necessarily, only natural properties have causal powers.

An example might be this. We say that the presence of oxygen is a cause of combustion, and that the presence of radium is a cause of death. Let "oxium" apply to anything that is either oxygen or radium and let "combeth" apply to anything that is either combustion or death. Can we say, then, that the presence of oxium is a cause of combeth? A believer in (1) would hold that we cannot say this because the properties being related are not natural.

If we want to define a natural property as a property that has causal powers, we need not only (1), but also:

(2) Necessarily, all natural properties have causal powers.

However, (2) seems untenable in the light of another highly plausible principle put forth by Lewis:

(3) If a property is natural, it is necessarily natural.[23]

I take it for granted that

(4) Any law of nature is contingent.[24]

Obviously (4) implies that if *P* has certain causal powers, it might not have had those particular powers. But I think that (4) should also be understood as implying that if *P* has certain causal powers, it might not have had any causal powers at all, for there might not have been any laws of the required sort involving *P*. (But note that (4) does not imply that events might have had no causes.) On this reading, (2), (3), and (4) are incompatible. I conclude, therefore, that (2) cannot be accepted.

I should make explicit a certain assumption in this argument. I take it that a property defined dispositionally in terms of certain causal powers cannot itself be said to have those causal powers. Consider the prop-

---

[22]This may be implied by Shoemaker's position in Shoemaker 1979, 1980, 1988. (I should add that Shoemaker's overall position includes an intricate general theory of the nature of properties, which I do not attempt to do any justice to in the argument that follows.) A similar view is Fodor's suggestion that a natural property is one such that some natural law applies to events in virtue of their instantiating it; see Fodor 1975, p. 14.

[23]Lewis 1986, pp. 60–61, note 44.

[24]As is usual in the literature, by "necessity" and "contingency" unqualified is meant metaphysical necessity and contingency. On the basic intuition behind (4), see Lewis 1986, pp. 87–91. Perhaps (4) needs to be restricted to "laws that constrain what can coexist in different positions" (Lewis 1986, p. 91).

erty Q of being able to melt things. I assume that Q has no causal powers, or at least not the causal power to melt things. Something has Q in virtue of having another property P that does have the power to melt things. P may be a certain molecular structure. It is a necessary fact that anything that has Q is able to melt things but a contingent fact that anything that has P is able to melt things. My argument assumes that the causal analyst would regard P as a natural property.

A proponent of the causal analysis might object that this argument is merely question begging. Assuming that (4) is sacrosanct, then (3) must be rejected. If naturalness depends on causality, which is contingent, then naturalness is contingent.

However, (3) is not plausibly rejected. To see the force of (3), consider that a standard way of expressing a belief in naturalness is to contrast natural properties with those that are "merely disjunctive" (or perhaps "merely a construction" of some other sort). But it surely seems wrong to say that some merely disjunctive property is such that in some other situation that very property would not have been merely disjunctive. Note that (3) seems immediately obvious for the ontological inegalitarian who regards a property as natural if it answers to a Platonic universal, for it seems clear that it is a necessary fact whether a given property answers to a universal.[25]

b. A Modified Causal Analysis

The causal analyses generally implied in the literature seem to embrace (2). But one can imagine a modified causal analysis that identifies naturalness not with the actual having of causal powers but with the possible having of causal powers. On this analysis, (3) comes out true (assuming that, at least in this sort of case, what is possible is necessarily possible), and (2) can be denied. I think, however, that even the modified causal analysis is unacceptable.

Consider again the property of being oxium, and compare this to the property of being oxygen. We have the following truths:

> It is physically (nomically) necessary that the presence of oxygen (together with the presence of heat, etc.) is followed by combustion.

> It is physically necessary that the presence of oxium (together with the presence of heat and the presence of life, etc.) is followed by combeth.

That much seems undeniable. Now the causal analyst wants us to say:

> The presence of oxygen is a cause of combustion.

> It is not the case that the presence of oxium is a cause of combeth.

---

[25]Hence, the ontological inegalitarian Armstrong, while apparently accepting (1), rejects (2), presumably in virtue of (3) and (4); see Armstrong 1978, Volume 2, pp. 44–45.

But, then, it seems that we must make some invidious judgment about oxium (or perhaps about combeth) in virtue of which oxium cannot be said to have causal powers, despite its figuring in various physical necessities. The invidious judgment seems to be precisely that the property of being oxium (or the property of being combeth) is unnatural or nongenuine. Since the judgment that oxygen and oxium differ with respect to their possible causal powers depends on the prior judgment that they (or some other properties) differ with respect to naturalness, we cannot analyze the latter judgment in terms of the former. It seems plain that to say, "The reason why being oxium is not a genuine property is because the presence of oxium could not possibly cause anything" is to put things intuitively backward.

One might have immediately objected to the causal analysis on the grounds that our understanding of physical necessity or natural lawfulness already presupposes the notion of a natural property.[26] I am allowing that the former notions might be accepted as independently intelligible. What cannot be independently intelligible, however, is the distinction between "physical necessity that counts as causality" and "physical necessity that does not count as causality." That distinction, if one makes it, seems clearly to depend on a prior notion of property-naturalness. One has implicitly defined "property that has causal powers" roughly in terms of "natural property that figures in physical necessities."[27] It is therefore circular to turn around and pretend to define "natural property" in terms of "property that has causal powers."

I suspect that some proponents of the causal analysis may tacitly suppose that circularity can be avoided as follows. Let a "pure" judgment of physical necessity be one that does not invoke the notion of causality. (Physics, chemistry, and biology seem to be replete with such pure judgments of physical necessity.) It might be thought that a natural property can be defined as one that (possibly) figures in some distinctive way in pure judgments of physical necessity. The analysis need not, therefore, invoke causality in any question begging sense. But this is, I think, a serious misconception. No set of pure judgments of physical necessity entails a distinction between the naturalness of such properties as being oxygen and the unnaturalness of such properties as being oxium.

I do not mean to suggest that a charge of circularity might not also be leveled in other directions. Both the ontological inegalitarian who analyzes naturalness in terms of universals and the sort of elitist who treats naturalness as primitive may possibly accept the similarity analyst's claim that, necessarily, a property is natural if and only if it satisfies condition (N), but may condemn the analysis on the grounds that our understand-

----

[26] This is Lewis's position in Lewis 1983b, pp. 366–68.

[27] This is only a rough partial definition, since the distinction between physical necessity and causality may also relate to temporal order, overdetermination, and other issues.

ing of similarity depends on a prior understanding of what a natural property is. I will not attempt to settle this issue (though I will make a further remark about it in the next section). What we regard as a "circular analysis (definition)" is very likely quite nebulous in many cases, as are our assessments about which concepts depend on other concepts. (The nature of this dependence will, in fact, eventually emerge in chapter 6 as itself a crucial factor in the division problem.) But I would judge the causal analysis to pass over a line beyond which an analysis is so obviously circular as to be no longer illuminating.

c. Metaphysical versus Nomic Naturalness

One might try to view the matter in a somewhat more conciliatory manner. It is not unlikely that there is more than one notion of a "natural property" being expressed in the literature. One might distinguish between "metaphysical naturalness" and "nomic naturalness." Metaphysical naturalness satisfies (3): if a property is metaphysically natural, it is necessarily so. Metaphysical naturalness seems clearly to be the notion that the ontological inegalitarian was trying to formulate, and I took the elitist to be dealing with the same notion. Other people in the literature, however, may be dealing with a different notion, that of nomic naturalness. Nomic naturalness satisfies (1) and (2): a property is nomically natural if and only if it has causal powers. The application of this notion to a property is a contingent matter, for it depends on the contingent causal structure of the world. Hence nomic naturalness does not satisfy (3). One claim I have made is that nomic naturalness presupposes metaphysical naturalness. The only way to begin to explain the former notion is to say, roughly, that a property is nomically natural if it is metaphysically natural and figures in physical necessities. Consider again Lewis's remark, quoted earlier, that "only an elite minority [of properties and things] are carved at the joints, so that their boundaries are established by objective sameness and difference in nature."[28] If we substitute "causality" for "sameness and difference," we get the notion of nomic naturalness. The world has, one might say, similarity joints and causal joints. But the latter presuppose the former.

5. Against Egalitarianism

a. The Counterintuitiveness of Egalitarianism

Even the egalitarian, I assume, would agree that some of our initial intuitions are inegalitarian. Prior to much reflection, anyone will be tempted to say such things as the following about the property Grue:

[28]Lewis 1984, p. 227.

- It's not a genuine property.
- It's merely a disjunction of different properties.
- It's not a property that is intrinsic to a thing (because it involves a reference to time).
- It's a property that doesn't make things similar to each other.

It is true that these initial intuitions turn out not to be equivalent—disjunctiveness and extrinsicness often do not go together (as in Gricular) and some non-genuine properties (e.g., certain negative ones) may be neither extrinsic nor (in any clear sense) disjunctive. Moreover, the remark about similarity needs a good deal of explication, as we have seen. So these intuitions certainly require some fine-tuning, but their force cannot be questioned.

The egalitarian rejects these intuitions. Or, perhaps it would be better to say, the egalitarian accepts them only in a subjectified and relativized form: Grue is different from Green, but only relative to our language, or interests, or innate sense of similarity or saliency. Certainly, this is not what the intuitive idea purports to be. As Quine observes:

> A man's judgments of similarity do and should depend on his theory, on his beliefs; but similarity itself, what the man's judgments purport to be judgments of, purports to be an objective relation in the world. . . . Such would be the acceptable and reputable sort of similarity concept, if it could be defined.[29]

Quine, himself perhaps an egalitarian, seems to conclude that the reputable sort of similarity judgment cannot be defined. But he is surely right in saying that similarity judgments purport to be objective. The same holds for the other intuitive judgments I mentioned.

What impels the egalitarian to reject these intuitive judgments? I want to focus on the issue of metaphysical naturalness, which I have maintained is fundamental. The temptation, surely, is to take the intuitive judgments to express metaphysical necessities. If egalitarians have good reason to reject metaphysical naturalness, they will automatically have reason to reject the derivative notion of nomic naturalness.

One difficulty in clarifying the egalitarian's stance is the pervasive tendency to conflate it with a rejection of the Classificatory Joints Principle (or some related division principle). In the following quotation from the egalitarian Putnam, the words "cat*" and "mat*" express properties that are intuitively highly extrinsic and unnatural.

> The upshot is that viewed from the perspective of a language which takes "cat*," "mat*," etc., as primitive properties, it is "cat" and "mat" that refer to "extrinsic" properties . . . ; while relative to "normal" language, . . . it is "cat*" and "mat*" that refer to "extrinsic" properties. . . . no property is intrinsic or extrinsic in itself.[30]

---

[29]Quine 1969a, p. 135.
[30]Putnam 1981a, p. 38. As I argued in section 2.4.b, such properties as Cat and Mat are not fully intrinsic, but let us waive that point in trying to understand Putnam's remark.

Putnam's reference to "perspectives of language" and the "primitives" of a language makes it difficult not to confuse the following two questions:

> Is there some metaphysical distinction between the properties Cat and Cat* which is expressed by saying that the first is intrinsic and the second extrinsic?

> Is there some metaphysical distinction between the properties Cat and Cat* which gives us good reason to have a (primitive) word in our language for the first property rather than the second?

What makes Putnam an egalitarian is that he answers no to the first question. It is essential to be quite clear that an inegalitarian, who answers the first question in the affirmative, may give a negative or skeptical response to the second question.[31]

We should also be clear—to reinforce a point made earlier—that the issue posed by Putnam's egalitarianism is not the old issue of Platonism versus Nominalism. First of all, Putnam is probably not a Nominalist (he might have nothing against assigning universals both to "cat" and "cat*"). And, quite definitely, traditional Nominalists such as Locke and Berkeley would have found Putnam's remarks astonishing. Those philosophers were inegalitarians who assumed that there are objective similarity relations, and who no doubt would have claimed that these relations suffice to determine whether a property is objectively intrinsic.

b. The Empirical Argument

Let me suggest that arguments for egalitarianism fall into two broad categories, empirical and a priori. The empirical argument might run as follows. Science—or at least the advanced sciences—makes no use of the distinction between natural and unnatural properties. Indeed, it is a "mark of the maturity of a branch of science that it no longer needs an irreducible notion of similarity and kind."[32] We do have our naturalness-intuitions, but the simplest and best explanation of these intuitions is in terms of psychological and cultural mechanisms, not in terms of objective naturalness.[33]

One might be tempted to react to the last sentence of this argument by saying that it really provides the basis for a defense of a form of

---

[31]I criticize Putnam for not being clearer about the possibility of accepting inegalitarianism while rejecting the Classificatory Joints Principle, but I think he is surely right to discern a deep connection between the two. However, Hartry Field, in his review of Putnam 1981a, seems to refuse to see even a prima facie connection between the doctrine of inegalitarianism and any claim about an ideal structure of language; see Field 1982, pp. 553–54.

[32]Quine 1969a, p. 138.

[33]See Goldman 1987, p. 544. Goldman is defending egalitarianism for things, but his argument could be applied as well to properties.

*in*egalitarianism. If we do have uniform naturalness-intuitions, then we can rigidly fix the reference of "naturalness" by the description "(higher-order property of belonging to) the set of properties that normally elicit positive naturalness-intuitions." This description can be used to rigidly fix the reference of "naturalness" to an objective property, that is, a property that might have been instantiated even if no people existed, let alone had naturalness-intuitions. Compare this with Kripke's account of how "heat" can rigidly refer to an objective phenomenon in virtue of having its reference fixed by a description of the form "the phenomenon that normally produces such-and-such sensation."[34]

Egalitarians risk incoherence if they respond to this point by saying that the difference between heat and naturalness is that the latter is merely constituted by a disjunction of different properties that happen to elicit in people the same naturalness-intuitions. Egalitarians cannot say this because they deny any real distinction between disjunctive and non-disjunctive properties.

Nevertheless, I do not think that inegalitarianism in the relevant sense can properly be sustained by treating "naturalness" as having its reference fixed by a description that mentions our naturalness-intuitions. Someone is not an inegalitarian in the sense at issue merely in virtue of believing that some properties happen to elicit a certain reaction in us. Let us say that an *objective description* is, roughly, a description *D* such that it is not knowable a priori that satisfiers of *D* normally (or in certain specified circumstances) produce (or stand in other specified relations to) certain specified experiences or judgments in people. If the reference of "naturalness" were fixed by the description "the set of properties that normally elicit positive naturalness-intuitions," then to say that a property is natural would not be an objective description (even though "naturalness" would rigidly refer to a property that could be instantiated independently of people's experiences or judgments). Let us assume that an inegalitarian must hold that to call a property natural is to describe it objectively.

The egalitarian's empirical argument against this is that science has no need for any such descriptions. One might debate whether science really does have such a need.[35] But I think that the deeper rejoinder to this argument is that a priori issues cannot be settled empirically. As an inegalitarian, I claim to know a priori that some properties are natural and some unnatural. If empirical science should have no particular use for this a priori truth, this need have no more significance than the fact that science has no use for various a priori truths of mathematics and logic.

I say that it is a priori evident that some properties are and some are not natural. But this does not imply that it is knowable a priori whether

[34]Kripke 1980, pp. 131–34.
[35]See Lewis 1983b, pp. 364–65.

a certain specific property (e.g., Red) is natural. That may be a posteriori.

On one view, indeed, there are no cases in which we know a priori of a given property that it is natural.[36] But I do not agree with that. There are actually three possibilities to consider: First, it may be a priori that there is the property *P* and that it is natural; second, it may be a priori that if there is the property *P* then it is natural but not a priori that there is the property *P*; third, it may not even be a priori that if there is the property *P* then it is natural.

Kripke says that we might discover that there are two kinds of tigers that have absolutely nothing to do with each other.[37] This would then be an example of the third sort; we cannot even know a priori that if there is the property Tiger, it is not merely disjunctive. Perhaps other examples treated by Kripke would fall under the second category. If the reference of "heat" is fixed by a description of the form "the natural property that produces such-and-such sensation," then we can know a priori that if there is such a property as Heat, it is natural. But we cannot know a priori that there is such a property as Heat, for it may be that no natural property produces the sensation.

As an example of the first sort, I think we know a priori that there is such a property as Spherical and that this property is natural.[38] The difference between this example and the ones mentioned in the last paragraph is that the reference of the term "spherical" does not seem to depend on any contingent facts about spherical things. Rather, in understanding the word "spherical" we pick out a certain property "essentially," in virtue of grasping the property's essential nature.[39] We can therefore know a priori both that there is such a property and that it is natural.

(The notion of picking out a property essentially may augment my previous remarks about the objective description of naturalness. The inegalitarian will almost certainly believe that in calling a property natural we are picking out the property of naturalness essentially. However, I will not impose this as a condition on inegalitarianism.)

In cases such as Tiger and Heat, we do rely on empirical science to judge that there is a certain natural property. There seems to be no special problem about this, once the distinction between natural and un-

---

[36]This appears to be Armstrong's view; see his "a posteriori Realism" throughout Armstrong 1978.

[37]Kripke 1980, p. 121.

[38]I am assuming the familiar distinction between the conditions for understanding a proposition and the conditions for knowing that the proposition is true. Experience may be required to understand what it means to say that there is the natural property Spherical, but once one understands the proposition, no experience is required to know that it is true.

[39]On "picking something out essentially," see Kripke 1971, p. 162, and Kripke 1980, p. 152. I discuss this notion more fully in Hirsch 1986, pp. 249ff.

natural properties is taken as a priori established. Other things being equal, the simplest theory is one that posits laws of nature involving the fewest number of natural properties (this seeming indeed to be one basic criterion of simplicity).[40]

But to repeat the main point: Since it is an a priori truth that some properties are natural and some unnatural, no empirical argument can undermine this distinction.

c. The A Priori Argument

I turn now to the a priori argument against inegalitarianism. It might be set forth as follows:

> *Premise 1.* We can objectively describe properties as being natural or unnatural only if we can objectively describe one thing as being more similar overall to a second thing than to a third thing.
>
> *Premise 2.* But we have no coherent objective notion of overall similarity.
>
> *Conclusion.* Therefore, we cannot objectively describe properties as being natural or unnatural.

I suspect that this is really the underlying argument that has converted many people to egalitarianism. It is, I think, a serious argument, presenting a serious challenge to inegalitarianism. But I think the challenge can be met.

Let us first consider Premise 1. I am inclined to accept this premise. Obviously the premise would have to be accepted by an elitist inegalitarian who attempts to analyze naturalness in terms of conditions on similarity such as (N). But I think that even the ontological inegalitarian, who gives a different analysis of naturalness, or the sort of elitist who takes naturalness as primitive may feel impelled to accept the premise. For it seems that our intuitive grip on the notion of naturalness does depend on our grasp of the similarity relation. These notions are wed throughout the literature, apparently in all camps. Lewis, who does not analyze naturalness in terms of similarity, nevertheless remarks that, whereas "sharing of [unnatural properties] has nothing to do with similarity," "sharing [natural properties] makes for qualitative similarity."[41] And Putnam attacks the notion of naturalness by saying that "'of the same kind' makes no sense apart from a categorical system which says

---

[40]Compare with Lewis 1983b, pp. 367–68. Armstrong's view seems to be that our "quality space" determines which properties we initially judge to be natural and that we alter these judgments in the light of empirical knowledge so as to achieve the simplest system of natural properties (Armstrong 1978, Volume 2, pp. 49–52). On my view, there is the additional constraint imposed by our a priori knowledge of the existence of certain natural and unnatural properties.

[41]Lewis 1983b, pp. 59–60.

what properties do and what properties do not count as similarities."[42] Finally, consider this from Quine:

> The relation between similarity and kind, then, is less clear and neat than could be wished. Definition of similarity in terms of kind is halting, and definition of kind in terms of similarity is unknown. Still the two notions are in an important sense correlative. They vary together. If we reassess something *a* as less similar to *b* than to *c*, where it had counted as more similar to *b* than to *c*, surely we will correspondingly permute *a*, *b*, and *c* in respect of their assignment to kinds; and conversely.[43]

Premise 1 seems acceptable to me, but I want to challenge Premise 2. Premise 2 has been defended with great force in Goodman's "Seven Strictures on Similarity."[44] I will here reformulate and adapt some of the points that he makes.

Point A. We cannot measure overall similarity by counting the properties that things have in common, for there is no clear way to count these. So similarity judgments must be relativized to properties that are contextually relevant. Strictly speaking, we never do make judgments of "overall similarity."

Point B. Even given a list of contextually relevant properties, we cannot simply count them up, for we assign different weights to different properties when we make similarity judgments. These weights are highly variable and subjective, depending largely on which properties we happen to regard at a given time as being important.

Point C. Judgments of similarity must also take into account degrees of similarity with respect to qualitative dimensions such as color and shape. However, there is no uniquely correct way of ordering qualities. Similarity judgments must therefore also be relativized to some particular choice of a quality ordering.

These are powerful points, and I think they have succeeded in persuading a large segment of the philosophical community that similarity judgments must always be highly contextual and subjective. But I believe that such conclusions are misguided.

The main mistake being made by points A through C, I think, is a failure to acknowledge, or to fully appreciate, the phenomenon of vagueness. This leads to what might be called the fallacy of generalizing from borderline cases. I think that the subjectivism and relativism in points A through C do indeed hold for borderline cases of similarity but not for clear-cut cases.[45]

I want to give some examples of clear-cut cases of overall similarity. Let *a*, *b*, and *c* be a trio of things that are purported to be such that the first is more similar overall to the second than to the third. The first

---

[42]Putnam 1981a, p. 51.
[43]Quine 1969a, p. 121.
[44]In Goodman 1972.
[45]Compare with Lewis 1973, pp. 91–95.

clear-cut case is where $a = b$ but not $a = c$. Obviously Reagan is more similar overall to Reagan than to Bush. This is not vacuous because had Bush been an exact duplicate of Reagan it would have been false. As things are, however, it is an incontrovertible truth.

The second clear-cut case is one in which a and b are exact duplicates of each other but not of c. In such a case, a is more similar overall to b than to c. A committed egalitarian may deny that we have any objective notion of "exact duplication," but that only shows how far-fetched this view is, since it seems clear that we do have such a notion.

The third clear-cut case is where a is more similar to b in certain respects and a is not more similar to c in any respects. Suppose that a, b, and c are all homogeneous spherical objects that do not differ in any respect except color. Suppose that a and b are both red, but of different shades, and c is green. Then a is more similar overall to b than to c. One should not be tempted to reply that what we are really saying here is that a is more similar with respect to color to b than to c. For let d, e, and f be another trio of homogeneous spheres that differ only with respect to size, with the size of d being closer to e than to f. Then d is more similar overall to e than to f. It seems plain that what we are saying is that there is a certain relation exemplified by the trio a, b, and c and also by the trio d, e, and f. That relation is overall similarity.

Point C, taken to the extreme, would imply that there is never a clear-cut fact as to degrees of similarity in a given qualitative dimension. If that were so, the third kind of case would fail to be clear-cut. But this version of Point C seems wildly implausible (and I doubt that Goodman intended it). If y is twice as big as x and z is ten times as big as x, it is surely a clear-cut fact that x is more similar in size to y than to z. We need only appeal to such examples to sustain the third kind of case. Of course, a committed egalitarian may protest that my description of the third kind of case presupposes that only certain respects of comparison are legitimate and that this begs the question. However, I think the question is settled rather than begged. The clear-cutness of the third kind of case speaks for itself.

The fourth kind of clear-cut case will be more controversial. Let me begin by giving a few examples. I take it to be clear that any pair of typical wire coat hangers are more similar overall to each other than to any typical apple, that any pair of typical apples are more similar overall to each other than to any typical cat, that any pair of typical cats are more similar overall to each other than to any typical snowflake, and so on for untold many such examples. It seems absurd to suggest that these statements must really be relativized to some properties that are contextually important. No matter what may be contextually important, anyone who is sane and knows how to speak English must accept these statements.

I think that part of the temptation to deny this stems from a tendency to conflate, for example, "That cat is more similar in color to the snowflake than to the other cat" with "From the standpoint of (an interest in) color, that cat is more similar to the snowflake than to the other cat." The second statement may indeed function as a harmless periphrasis of the first. But confusion sets in when we go on to take "similar" *simpliciter* in the second statement to be tantamount to "similar overall." We then wind up concluding that there is a standpoint from which one could deny that the cats are more similar overall to each other than to the snowflake. It seems clear that there is no such "standpoint."

Can the fourth kind of case be defined in some general way? It may be tempting to suggest that this is a case in which *a* and *b* share many natural properties, whereas *a* and *c* share only a few natural properties. Of course, "many" and "few" are vague, but that is for the good, since the fourth kind of case might then be seen as gradually merging into borderline cases of overall similarity. A major problem, however, is whether it makes sense to count the number of natural properties that things may be said to share. (If two things are alike in color, or in shape, or in internal structure, how many colors, or shapes, or internal structures can they be said to be alike in?) I do not know whether this problem can be solved. If it cannot, the conclusion ought to be that the notion of overall similarity is not exhaustively analyzable; the conclusion is not that the notion is incoherent or subjective. If overall similarity cannot be analyzed, even given property-naturalness, this makes it more tempting to regard overall similarity as primitive and to try to analyze property-naturalness in terms of similarity. (It remains a plausible option, however, to regard both overall similarity and property-naturalness as closely related primitives.)

I think that Goodman's discussion goes wrong in ignoring these clear-cut cases of overall similarity. In such cases, there is no relativization, no variability, no subjectivity. Those characterizations apply only to borderline cases of overall similarity, for if we want to make a similarity judgment in such cases, we naturally slide off in a rather variable and subjective fashion into a judgment relativized to some contextually relevant set of properties. Of course, there are an indefinite number of such cases, for the notion of overall similarity is exceedingly vague. But one must not be blinded by these cases to the indefinite number of clear-cut cases.

Vagueness is sometimes viewed as a kind of multiple ambiguity, the different possible precisifications of a vague term constituting its multiple senses. Looked at in this way, we have multiple senses of "overall similarity," each one answering to a different similarity relation.[46] One thing that is (almost) invariant throughout these relations is naturalness,

---

[46]The psychological and taxonomic literature contains various attempts to formulate quantitative measures of overall similarity. See, for example, Garner 1947 and Tversky 1977. These quantitative measures should be seen as attempts to precisify our ordinary notion, and are subject to the constraint that they be compatible with the clear-cut facts about similarity.

for (almost) the same set of natural properties will emerge as enhancing similarity, regardless of which precise similarity relation one chooses. That just those properties enhance similarity is essential to a relation's being a *similarity* relation. Contrary to what one might be tempted to think, therefore, naturalness does not inherit the vagueness of similarity. Naturalness may have its own areas of vagueness, but they are of a different order. Even if we attempt to analyze naturalness in terms of similarity (e.g., in terms of condition (N)), the vagueness of similarity seems to have virtually no effect on which properties we regard as natural.[47]

Naturalness might be compared in this respect to another notion: *continuity of change*. The logic of the egalitarian's position seems to imply that there is no objective distinction between continuous and discontinuous change. For, if there is no objective distinction between gruified and non-gruified properties, then it is difficult to see how an instantaneous change in an object from middle blue to middle green or from spherical to cubical can be said to be objectively discontinuous. This only shows again how very farfetched this view is. However, I want to appeal to the notion of continuity to show something else. There is a familiar way of analyzing continuity in terms of similarity. Roughly put, the idea is that a succession of states is continuous if, for any state s in the succession, and for any small degree of dissimilarity d, there is a time interval I around s such that the degree of dissimilarity between s and any state within I is less than d. The point to note is that, although continuity is here being analyzed in terms of similarity, it does not inherit the extreme vagueness of similarity. In much the same way, property-naturalness does not inherit the vagueness of similarity.

I conclude that we have an objective idea of similarity, as well as of property-naturalness.

6. Degrees of Naturalness

In the last chapter I was rather vague about the extent to which ordinary language seems to satisfy the Projectibility and Similarity Principles. My assumption was that these principles might be thought to be substantially satisfied at least by the semantic primitives of ordinary language. A corresponding assumption can, I think, seem fairly plausible with respect to the current Classificatory Joints Principle. But first the principle needs to be clarified in a certain way.

---

[47] I am inclined to think that the vagueness of similarity affects the application of (N) only in very difficult sorts of cases, such as those discussed in appendix 2.5 (cases of "conjunctive entailment"). I could not see how the vagueness of similarity might affect, for instance, someone's reaction to my earlier argument that imperfect community properties do not satisfy (N).

Both the ontological inegalitarian Armstrong and the elitist Lewis hold that properties can be said to be natural *to varying degrees.*[48] Certainly many, perhaps most, ordinary words would not be regarded as expressing fully natural properties. Words for artifacts, such as "car" and "table," would not be so regarded; nor would words for functional stuffs, such as "food," "medicine," and "clothing"; nor would words for various institutional items, such as "war," "government," and "law." One might conceivably attempt to relegate all such words to the surface level of semantic non-primitives, but this has no immediate plausibility. It seems, therefore, that if the Classificatory Joints Principle can plausibly be regarded as substantially satisfied by ordinary language, the principle must be interpreted as requiring, not naturalness of the highest degree, but only a sufficiently high level of naturalness. We might indeed construe the principle in the following spirit:

> There is a presumption against having a general word express an unnatural property, the presumption being stronger to the degree that the property is unnatural.

The principle in this moderated form might still go far toward vindicating our strong negative intuitions about the strange languages, if many words in those languages express properties that are highly unnatural, and if there appears to be nothing to defeat the presumption against this.

Let me sketch a scale of naturalness which combines both metaphysical and nomic considerations. We want a scale that seems intuitively acceptable and that looks hopeful from the point of view of the Classificatory Joints Principle.

a. *Degrees of Metaphysical Naturalness*

First, on the metaphysical dimension, I will assume that some properties are perfectly or fully natural. Perhaps these are the ones that satisfy (N) or some refinement of (N). Lewis and Armstrong differ interestingly in how they scale degrees of naturalness. Armstrong takes family resemblance properties—which I assume to be the same as imperfect community properties—to be more natural than simple disjunctions. Lewis, however, measures the naturalness of properties by the extent to which "they can be reached by not-too-complicated chains of definability from the perfectly natural properties."[49] A family resemblance property would be in this sense more complex than a simple disjunction. Certainly Armstrong's scale is more promising if we are looking to defend the Classi-

---

[48]Armstrong 1978, Volume 2, pp. 48–49; Lewis 1986, p. 61. For the ontological inegalitarian, lesser degrees of naturalness are "fallings away" from the exemplary case in which a property corresponds to a universal (Armstrong 1978, Volume 2, p. 49).

[49]Lewis 1986, p. 61.

ficatory Joints Principle. Many ordinary words are standardly regarded as expressing family resemblances, but there seems to be a strong intuitive presumption against having a word (such as "gricular") that expresses a simple disjunction.

The following may qualify as an explanation of why family resemblance properties are more natural than simple disjunctions. Consider all properties of the form "having at least m of such-and-such n perfectly natural properties." At the extremes, if m is zero, the property is vacuous, and if m is n, the property is itself perfectly natural (assuming that, on the metaphysical dimension, conjunctions of perfectly natural properties are perfectly natural).[50] In the intermediary cases, therefore, the closer m is to n, the closer the property might be said to being perfectly natural. The difference between a family resemblance property and a simple disjunctive property is that in the former, m is more than half of n. In this sense, at least, family resemblance properties are more natural than simple disjunctions.

Family resemblance properties may relate in another way to metaphysical naturalness, if the latter is equated with satisfaction of the similarity condition (N). I previously construed the variables of this condition as ranging over both actual and possible things, and I was then able to show that family resemblance properties do not satisfy the condition. Some family resemblance properties may, however, satisfy (or admit of relatively few counterexamples with respect to the satisfaction of) a *restricted* version of (N), where the variables are taken to range only over actual things, or over things in some extended spatiotemporal region. It may well be that only such family resemblance properties strike us as intuitively natural. Although this would be a contingent kind of naturalness, it is closely related to metaphysical naturalness (if the latter is equated with satisfaction of the unrestricted version of (N)).[51]

Let us note that the distinction between natural and unnatural properties must be understood as applying not only to monadic properties but also to relations. Gruified or disjunctive relational constructions evidently strike us as unnatural. Moreover, the intrinsic-extrinsic distinction applies to relations; for example, the relation of having the same owner can be said to be extrinsic in that it relates two things in terms of a third thing external to them.[52] If similarity conditions such as (N) can be applied to relations, we must be able to assess the relative similarities of pairs (or higher n-tuples) of things.

---

[50]It may be tempting to try to distinguish between natural properties that are simple and complex, treating only the former as metaphysically natural to the highest degree (cf. appendix 3.2.) If so, the assumption mentioned in the text would have to be qualified.

[51]One might have thought to suggest that the reason why family resemblance properties have a significant degree of naturalness is that they at least satisfy Quine's similarity condition, if not (N). However, it will emerge in appendix 2.3 that (contrary to what Quine implies) typical family resemblance properties do not in fact satisfy Quine's condition.

[52]For further clarification of this point, see Lewis 1986, p. 62.

Suppose that we accept Lewis's judgment that "all perfectly natural properties are intrinsic."[53] It would follow that no property expressed by an individuative term, such as "dog" or "tree," is perfectly natural, since no such properties are entirely intrinsic (for the reasons explained in section 2.4.b). Nevertheless, such properties often seem highly natural and are evidently apt to be expressed by ordinary words. It seems easiest to explain this in terms of the notion of similarity, for it is obvious that sharing an extrinsic property may, in some cases, be said to enhance the extrinsic similarity between things. In order for a property to be perfectly natural, sharing it must enhance intrinsic similarity, but a property may acquire a degree of naturalness in virtue of enhancing similarity of any sort, intrinsic or extrinsic. To this may be added the point made in section 2.4.b, that some extrinsic similarities weigh more than others, because they are in a sense close to being intrinsic. In particular, extrinsic similarities that depend only on an object's natural relations to things with which it has contact may have great weight, so that individuative properties may wind up with a high degree of metaphysical naturalness.

b. Degrees of Nomic Naturalness

Let us turn very briefly to nomic naturalness. If we are not egalitarians, we try to view degrees of nomic naturalness as reflecting the objective causal structure of the world, rather than purely psychological or pragmatic features of scientific inquiry. It is not obvious how such a view might be precisely formulated, but a rough idea might be along the following lines. Let us first say that a "strict law of nature" is expressible by a sentence of the form "It is physically necessary that all *A* are *B*," where both "*A*" and "*B*" express perfectly natural properties in the metaphysical sense. These properties will be said to "figure" in the law. A law may be not strict because it is statistical rather than universal, or because it presupposes various "boundary conditions," or because the properties that figure in it are not perfectly natural in the metaphysical sense. In terms of these factors, strictness of laws can itself be treated as a matter of degree, and the properties figuring in laws will have correlative degrees of nomic naturalness.

c. The Overall Scale

Our overall scale of naturalness may combine metaphysical and nomic considerations. Let me roughly indicate a few ways in which this may be done. In some cases, a property may have a high degree of metaphysical naturalness but a low degree of nomic naturalness, so that on the overall scale it is not very natural. Moreover, objects may be intrin-

---

[53]Lewis 1986, p. 61.

sically similar in virtue of the similar causal processes within them, and they may be extrinsically similar in virtue of their similar causal interactions with other things. Properties that apply in virtue of any similarities were said earlier to be metaphysically natural to some degree, and the overall naturalness of a property might be ranked much higher if the relevant similarities involve nomic factors. This consideration may provide a further reason why typical individuative properties have a high degree of naturalness despite not being entirely intrinsic. The consideration may also suffice to justify according a relatively high degree of naturalness to many artifactual properties, such as being a car, and to many functional kinds of stuff, such as food. Perhaps this kind of consideration could even be extended to some institutional properties, such as being a government.

It may be that our overall scale of naturalness ought to include certain factual considerations that are related only obliquely to nomic or metaphysical factors. Let us say that a property P is *locally bounded* if and only if there is a spatiotemporal region R such that (a) R is relatively large, (b) there are relatively many instances of P within R, and (c) no instances of P within R are highly similar to any instances of Non-P within R. For example, if the relatively large region R contains many dogs and contains no non-dogs that are very similar to the dogs, then the property Dog will be locally bounded with respect to R. It seems that if we are examining objects within R, a property that is locally bounded with respect to R has a better chance of appearing in a sense to "stand out." Local boundedness is evidently a matter of degree, depending on how large R is, on how many instances of P it contains, and on the degree of similarity between instances of P and instances of Non-P in R.[54] Our overall scale of naturalness may reflect the degree to which a property is locally bounded. Note that since I seek a notion of degrees of naturalness that is arguably objective, I do not count a property as more bounded in virtue of its being bounded in a region R that contains us. It does seem plausible to suppose, however, that, other things being equal, we are more disposed to have a word for a property if it is bounded in a region containing us.

Local boundedness may enhance the naturalness of any property, but this consideration has a special bearing on family resemblance properties, given my earlier suggestion that such properties may be intuitively natural to a high degree only if they satisfy (or come close to satisfying) a restricted version of (N). It seems clear that this is most likely to happen only if the family resemblance property has a high degree of local boundedness.[55]

---

[54]I will maintain in Appendix 2.2 that typical natural properties are not bounded to the highest degree. For example, there are (or were, or could have been) non-dogs very similar to dogs.

[55]The supposition that only bounded family resemblance properties are significantly natural is, I think, implicit in some recent psychological literature. See Rosch 1977a and Tversky 1977.

What I have indicated here is, of course, merely the most rudimentary sketch of a scale of naturalness. But this may suffice to suggest how a scale could be defined in terms of which English, or at least the semantic primitives of English, substantially satisfy the Classificatory Joints Principle. And it seems clear that the scale might allow us to say that the strange languages being considered substantially violate the principle.[56] All we need now is a defense of the principle.

7. Explanation and Classification

Many of the points discussed in the previous chapter, with respect to the Projectibility and Similarity Principles, carry over directly to the present principle and need not be rehearsed at length. Three crucial points, adapted from the last chapter, might be worth emphasizing. First, in trying to imagine a language that violates the Classificatory Joints Principle, we are not primarily trying to imagine people who disagree with us about which properties are natural but rather people who use words for properties that they themselves may regard as unnatural. Second, the temptation to regard the principle as expressing an ultimate intellectual virtue seems hard to sustain, for it does not seem correct on reflection to criticize people simply because their words express unnatural properties, if their knowledge and rational beliefs are equivalent to ours. Third, we cannot defend the principle by appealing to the claim that only terms for natural properties are projectible unless we have some independent defense of the Projectibility Principle; we must not lapse into defending each principle by appealing to the other one.

The principle may initially seem obvious if "genuine or natural properties" are taken to contrast with what can be called "spurious properties." It may then seem that it must be, at the very least, *misleading* to have words for unnatural properties, for speakers would tend to assume that properties expressed by words are natural.[57] But a moment's thought should convince us that this simple line of reasoning only begs the question. We are trying to imagine a language in which words standardly

---

[56]Peter Unger has raised another kind of question about the application of the Classificatory Joints Principle. According to some philosophers, many ordinary ethical and esthetic words (e.g., "good" and "beautiful") do not express properties of any sort, natural or unnatural. Rather, they function within sentences to evoke emotions or direct behavior. But, surely, even within ethical-esthetic discourse there is an intuitive distinction between ordinary and strange words. Does this show that the distinction really has little to do with natural properties and "reality's joints"?

I think it does not show this. Even according to these philosophers, there is some very close semantic connection between ethical-esthetic words and properties of emotions or behavior. The Classificatory Joints Principle might be reformulated so as to require that these properties be (relatively) natural. (Unger's question may show, however, that my account is sketchy in more ways than one.)

[57]Compare with Gilbert Ryle's notion of a "systematically misleading experession" in Ryle 1931.

express unnatural properties. This might indeed mislead unwary speakers of the language if they had some reason to expect words not to express unnatural properties. And they might have such a reason if they were aware of a normative presumption against words expressing unnatural properties. But it is precisely that presumption that is presently under question. If there is no such presumption then there is no reason for the speakers to be misled.

a. The Explanation Claim

Apart from the arguments already canvassed in the last chapter, and postponing as usual pragmatic considerations for a later chapter, I suspect that there may be only one seriously tempting defense of the Classificatory Joints Principle. I will call this the *explanation claim*. It says that, if the words of a language expressed (highly) unnatural properties, this would prevent, or at least significantly obstruct, the formulation of correct explanations. Having a language that divides reality at the joints serves our explanatory aims.

This claim will, I think, seem initially plausible to many people.[58] But it seems difficult on reflection to see what it amounts to. The claim is immediately threatened by the following *explanatory equivalence principle*: If S and T are (a priori necessarily) equivalent, respectively, to S' and T', and S is the explanans in a correct explanation in which T is the explanandum, then S' is the explanans in a correct explanation in which T' is the explanandum.[59] If this principle is correct then, since we have been assuming that any ordinary sentence has an equivalent in any of the strange languages, the explanation claim would seem to fail.

Let me use an example of a strange language of chemistry to bring out the issue. (This will be an "incompatibility language" of the sort discussed in section 1.4.a) Imagine that such words as "oxygen," "radium," and "carbon" are replaced by such words as "oxium" and "rabon," which are equivalent, respectively, to "oxygen or radium" and "radium or carbon." Then, assuming that "oxygen," "radium," and "carbon" are mutually incompatible, these words are equivalent, respectively, to "oxium and not rabon," "oxium and rabon," and "rabon and not oxium." Let us imagine such replacements to occur in a large-scale fashion throughout the language of chemistry. We want to try to imagine that speakers of this strange language will agree with us about every

---

[58]The claim is, I think, implicit in many discussions but, since the division problem is almost never clearly isolated, it is difficult to find unambiguous citations. The claim is almost clearly stated in Wiggins 1980, pp. 144–45, footnote 18.

[59]This is a cautious formulation of the principle, which suffices for the present discussion. In fact, the principle may seem plausible even if the sentences are just necessarily equivalent, without being a priori equivalent. (It should be remembered that, in this book, "equivalent" unqualified always means "a priori necessarily equivalent.")

condition of the world. They will agree with us also about which terms are projectible and about which terms express natural properties. Would their explanations have to suffer because of their strange language?

Imagine a situation in which it would seem reasonable to explain:

(5) Combustion occurred

by appealing to:

(6) Heat and oxygen were present

and some such law as:

(7) It is physically necessary that whenever heat and oxygen are present, combustion occurs.

Assuming that "combustion" is also a word of the strange chemical language (otherwise the example would have to be complicated slightly), we apparently have as the equivalent explanation of (5) in that language:

(6') Heat and oxium were present, and the oxium was not rabon.

and:

(7') It is physically necessary that whenever heat and oxium are present, combustion occurs, if the oxium is not rabon.

Instead of (6'), I could have put more simply "Heat and oxium that is not rabon were present" (and correspondingly for (7')), but I intend to reinforce the point that a strange word such as "oxium" can occur in many syntactic contexts (not just in the context of the complex terms "oxium that is rabon" and "oxium that is not rabon"), and that this may hold even for strange sentences equivalent to sentences about oxygen. In any case, if some version of (6') and (7') correctly explains (5), it would seem that any ordinary chemical explanation will have a correct equivalent in the strange language.[60]

(According to some views, the law relevant to (5) ought to be expressed, not quite as (7), but rather as a second order relation between properties, perhaps as "The conjunction of heat and oxygen nomically necessitates combustion." But it seems that this would not substantially affect the point at issue, for in the strange language we presumably have

---

[60] I am assuming that "oxygen" is a general term that denotes any bit of stuff that is oxygen, and that "oxium" denotes any bit of stuff that is either oxygen or radium; and the same for the other chemical terms. On this construal, "Oxygen has a valence of minus two" means that any bit of oxygen has a valence of minus two, and the equivalent sentence would be "Oxium that is not rabon has a valence of minus two" or "Oxium has a valence of minus two if it is not rabon." There are other ways to construe the semantics of a mass term such as "oxygen"; these might complicate somewhat the present example but would not, I think, substantially alter its import. (And, of course, examples of the same general sort could be constructed for non-mass terms, such as those that figure in biology or physics.)

"The conjunction of heat and oxium that is not rabon nomically necessitates combustion."[61])

The explanatory equivalence principle seems to be tacitly assumed
in many examples; I will mention three related to physics. First, in clas-
sical mechanics motions of objects are described typically by way of rectangular coordinates and sometimes by way of polar coordinates. Insofar
as these descriptions are assumed to be equivalent, it seems to be taken
for granted that any explanation of physics couched in terms of one
description is correct if the equivalent explanation in terms of the other
description is correct. As a second example, there are equivalent formulations of Newton's laws, some of which are more succinct and perhaps
more elegant than Newton's. But it seems never to be suggested that
one of these formulations may provide a correct explanation of something that is not correctly explained by another formulation. Consider, third,
that discussions of the nature of geometry often center on the question
whether Euclidian descriptions are equivalent to non-Euclidian descriptions, but it is standardly assumed that if the descriptions are equivalent, they yield equivalently correct explanations in physics. These examples seem representative of many others in various branches of science.

b. Putnam's Constraint

A well-known paper by Putnam may be thought to cast doubt on the
equivalence principle.[62] He says that one constraint on an explanation is
the following: "The relevant features of a situation should be brought
out by an explanation and not buried in a mass of irrelevant information."[63] I will refer to this as *Putnam's constraint*. He illustrates it by
imagining that we want to explain why a square peg slightly less than
one inch across will not go through a round hole one inch across but
will go through a square hole one inch across. A correct explanation
would appeal to the rigidity of the objects involved and the fact that
one hole is big enough for the peg and the other is not. The rigidity of
the objects might be in principle deducible from some enormously complicated facts about the attractions and repulsions of elementary particles.
However, those facts cannot enter into an explanation of why the square
peg does not go through the round hole; relative to the requirements
of that explanation, those facts bury the relevant information.

---

[61]See Armstrong 1978, Volume 2, pp. 148–57. I am assuming that, if we accept the
explanatory equivalence principle, we will also accept the following related principle: If the
terms "F" and "G" are equivalent, respectively, to "F'" and "G'" then, if the property of
being F can be said to necessitate the property of being G, the property of being F' can be
said to necessitate the property of being G'. (If the properties under consideration are coarse-
grained, which has been my general assumption in this chapter, then the latter principle is
trivial.)

[62]See Putnam 1981b.

[63]Ibid., p. 206.

Putnam calls his constraint a "pragmatic constraint."[64] The "pragmatics of explanation," as this notion is generally used in the literature, deals with constraints on an explanation which derive contextually from the knowledge and interests of the people seeking the explanation.[65] Presumably, the reason Putnam regards his constraint as "pragmatic" is that the "burial" of information is described by him as follows: "Suppose I subject the statements G and I to logical transformations so as to produce a statement H that is mathematically equivalent to G and I (possibly in a complicated way), but such that the information G is, practically speaking, virtually impossible to recover from H."[66] Then G is "buried" in H, and H may fail to explain something that G explains. Putnam might allow, therefore, that if there are people who—perhaps because of special training or innate capacities—are adept at calculating the implications of enormously complicated facts about elementary particles, relative to that pragmatic context, the particle explanation of the peg's behavior could be correct.

It is doubtful that Putnam's constraint directly conflicts with the explanatory equivalence principle. In all of his examples, if *A* is buried in *B*, then *B* is equivalent not to *A*, but to the conjunction of *A* and some other sentence *C*. The constraint, at least narrowly interpreted, would allow that, if *A* and *B* are equivalent, they must have the same explanatory role. Nevertheless, it seems that Putnam's argument for his constraint would immediately carry over as an argument against the equivalence principle. For suppose that *A* explains *E* and *A* is equivalent to *B*, but it is, practically speaking, virtually impossible to know that *A* is equivalent to *B*. In such a case, one might conclude, *B* may fail to explain *E*.

It seems evident that the explanation in terms of (6') and (7') does not violate Putnam's constraint, even as generalized in the last paragraph. It is not impossible, or even difficult, to see that (6') and (7') are equivalent, respectively, to (6) and (7) (nor, of course, is it difficult to see that (5) follows from (6') and (7')). Nevertheless, a proponent of the explanation claim may want to appeal to Putnam's constraint to show that the explanatory equivalence principle is invalid.

c. Strict Correctness and Pragmatic Adequacy

Let us note that such relations as "known to explain" or "easily known to explain" obviously do not satisfy any equivalence principle. That is, we can obviously have a case in which *A* is equivalent to *B*, it is known

---

[64]Ibid.

[65]See van Fraassen 1980, pp. 97–157.

[66]Ibid., p. 207. If we produce H by performing a logical transformation on G and I, should we not be able to perform the converse transformation to recover G from H? I take Putnam to mean that H is the *sort* of statement that, had we not deliberately produced it, would "bury" G.

(or easy to know) that A explains E, but it is not known (or not easy to know) that B explains E. Anyone who takes the explanatory equivalence principle seriously must assume a distinction between the explanatory relation and such epistemically qualified relations. Putnam's discussion of his constraint suggests that he does not accept such a distinction, for if he did, he should have asked whether the constraint holds for the explanatory relation rather than just for the epistemically qualified relations.

To reject this distinction seems of a piece with van Fraassen's view that there is no notion of explanatory correctness which can be divorced from contextual facts about the interests and knowledge of those seeking the explanation.[67] An alternative view would hold that an explanation may be "strictly correct" without being "pragmatically adequate." For any explanandum, there are any number of explanantia that figure in a strictly correct explanation, but only some of these fit the explanatory needs determined by the context. If we accept a distinction between the strict correctness and the pragmatic adequacy of an explanation, it is obvious that Putnam's constraint holds—and the equivalence principle fails to hold—for pragmatic adequacy, but the question remains whether the principle holds for strict correctness.

There is a further distinction we should draw, between "pragmatic adequacy" and "possible pragmatic adequacy." Even one who rejects the notion of strict correctness should allow that, for any sentences A and B, it makes sense to ask whether there is any possible context relative to which A would constitute a pragmatically adequate explanation of B. It is not obvious that Putnam's constraint holds for possible pragmatic adequacy, or that the equivalence principle fails to hold.

I stated earlier that the equivalence principle threatens the explanation claim (i.e., the claim that the strange languages would defeat our explanatory aims). Can the claim be sustained by the simple observation that pragmatic adequacy (relative to some particular context) does not satisfy the equivalence principle? This seems doubtful. It is trivially true that an explanation of (5) in terms of (6') and (7') would be pragmatically inadequate relative to a context in which we are seeking an explanation couched in ordinary terms. The relevant question, of course, is whether the explanation would have to be pragmatically inadequate for people who speak the strange chemical language. The burden of argument is on someone who wishes to answer this question in the negative. A negative answer would follow if it could be shown that the strangely couched explanations are not even possibly pragmatically adequate. They

[67]See especially van Fraassen 1980, p. 130: "It is sometimes said that an Omniscient Being would have a complete explanation, whereas these contextual factors only bespeak our limitations due to which we can only grasp one part or aspect of the complete explanation at any given time. But this is a mistake. If the Omniscient Being has no specific interests (legal, medical, enconomic; or just an interest in optics or thermodynamics rather than chemistry) . . . then no why-questions ever arise for him in any way at all—and he does not have any explanation in the sense that we have explanations."

may not be if the equivalence principle fails to hold for possible pragmatic adequacy.

The following example suggests that the equivalence principle in fact fails to hold for possible pragmatic adequacy. Suppose that the explanandum is (5) and the explanans is, instead of (6) and (7), (6'') and (7).

(6'') Heat and oxygen were present, and all tables are tables.

I assume that (6'') is equivalent to (6). But it is surely difficult to imagine any possible context relative to which an explanation of (5) couched in terms of (6'') would be pragmatically adequate.

The example of (6'') may cast doubt on the application of the equivalence principle even to the strict correctness of an explanation (if we accept that notion). One may be inclined to say that an explanation of (5) couched in terms of (6'') is not correct in any sense.

Other examples also may challenge the application of the equivalence principle even with respect to an explanation's possible pragmatic adequacy or strict correctness. One general problem area is mathematical explanation. It seems that we sometimes want to say (though perhaps not very often) that one mathematical truth explains another. Since unrelated a priori necessary truths are automatically equivalent, if mathematical truths are a priori necessary, they are all equivalent to each other, but surely could not in general be substituted one for another in a mathematical explanation. Another problem case concerns the phenomenon of "emphasis." If the explanandum is "John *strangled* Mary last night" a suitable explanans might include "John has strong hands" but not "John was alone with Mary last night." The latter explanans but not the former might be suitable for the explanandum "John strangled Mary *last night*." Since "John *strangled* Mary last night" is presumably equivalent to "John strangled Mary *last night*," the equivalence principle appears to have no application in this sort of case.[68]

To sustain the explanation claim, however, it does not suffice to point out examples in which the application of the equivalence principle is problematical even with respect to possible pragmatic adequacy or strict correctness. It seems clear that the principle applies in many standard examples (such as the example of switching from rectangular to polar coordinates) and that there is in general a presumption in favor of its applying. One needs to look at the recalcitrant examples and see whether they generalize to the case at issue, the case of the strange languages.

d. Explanatory Equivalence and the Strange Languages

I think we may assume that neither the example of mathematical explanation nor the example of emphasis has a direct bearing on the case of the strange languages. The sort of example that seems most likely to have

[68]See Achinstein 1983, pp. 193–217, and van Fraassen 1980, pp. 127–30.

a bearing is (6''). The reason why (6'') is pragmatically inadequate as an explanation of (5)—at least relative to any ordinary context—might be put as follows. Ordinarily, when we ask for an explanation (when we express a why-question), we expect and want an explanans that contains no *superfluous words*. A sentence contains superfluous words if we can delete some of its words and use the remainder to form an equivalent sentence. Superfluous words in an explanans would ordinarily strike us as confusing, as pointing in the wrong direction.[69] This consideration may be enough to show that an explanation of (5) in terms of (6'') is not even possibly pragmatically adequate, because it is difficult to imagine any possible context in which seekers of explanations would not object to superfluous words.

This consideration does not, however, generalize to the critical case of (6'); (6') contains no superfluous words. So it now appears that if (6'') is our model of a pragmatically inadequate explanation, then the explanation in terms of (6') turns out to be pragmatically adequate for people who speak the strange chemical language.

It might be answered that (6') still compares with (6'') in being too long, complicated, inelegant, and so on, so that at least these pragmatic considerations apply in both examples. I think, however, that the latter considerations in themselves have little to do with what philosophers such as van Fraassen and Putnam mean by the "pragmatics of explanation." These philosophers deem an explanation pragmatically inadequate if it would frustrate the contextually implied expectations of those who seek the explanation. But surely if we are imagining people who speak the strange chemical language (as their only chemical language), and who ask for an explanation of (5), we must suppose that the sort of explanation they expect is precisely something on the order of (6'). So that explanation would not be pragmatically inadequate in the relevant sense. Of course, one may want to raise a more general question about the efficiency of a language that requires the utterance of such sentences as (6'). But that is the kind of general pragmatic issue that I have all along been postponing until a later chapter.

I think we can conclude that an explanation in terms of (6') is not pragmatically inadequate relative to the context being imagined, at least if (6'') is our model of pragmatic inadequacy. The only hope for the explanation claim seems to be to hold that (6') provides an explanation that is strictly incorrect. The claim must imply, then, that there is a distinction between pragmatic adequacy and strict correctness, and that the equivalence principle does not hold even for strict correctness. If the example of (6'') is to help elucidate this claim, we must ask whether an explanation of (5) in terms of (6'') is strictly correct. The difficulty of this question may indeed serve as an inducement to join van Fraassen in repudiating any notion of explanatory correctness divorced from prag-

---

[69]Perhaps we should restrict superfluous words to terms; superfluous syncategorematic words may not matter so much. Note that "Heat and oxygen were present, and heat and oxygen were present" can also be said to contain superfluous words (i.e., word-tokens).

matic adequacy. If we hold to the notion, we may try to bite the bullet about (6″) and claim that the explanation is strictly correct. The view might be that the correctness of an explanation depends entirely on the relationship between the conditions of the world expressed by the explanans and the explanandum. Since the condition expressed by (6″) is the same as that expressed by the good explanans (6), the former qualifies as a correct explanation. Of course this view would also imply that (6′) so qualifies.

Supposing it is held instead that an explanation in terms of (6″) does not qualify as strictly correct, if the purported reason for this is that (6″) contains superfluous words, then (6′), which contains no superfluous words, again remains unscathed.

The only alternative line that I can think of, favorable to the explanation claim, would have to be in the following vein. The *fine-grained proposition* expressed by (6″) is distinct from that expressed by (6), and only the latter stands in the right kind of explanatory relation to the fine-grained proposition expressed by (5). What may disqualify the former proposition is that it contains *superfluous constituents*, in rather the same sense that the sentence (6″) contains superfluous words. To work this idea out would require, at the very least, a theory of the structure of propositions. If we want to generalize from the case of (6″) to the critical case of (6′), we need to be able to say that the proposition expressed by (6′) also contains superfluous constituents. Perhaps one can say this, but it would require considerable clarification. For all that now seems obvious, the proposition expressed by (6′) contains a constituent, answering to "oxium," that is not contained in the proposition expressed by (6), just as the latter proposition contains a constituent, answering to "oxygen," that is not contained in the former. If that were so, the proposition expressed by (6′) would not contain any superfluous constituent. So the explanation in terms of (6′) may be correct even if the one in terms of (6″) is not.

I will return to some of these points in chapter 6 when I discuss the structure of fine-grained propositions.[70] The conclusion I would draw at present is that the explanation claim is obscure; the burden is on proponents of the claim to clarify it. The claim seems to involve at least the following problematical assumptions:

(a) There is a distinction between the pragmatic adequacy and the strict correctness of an explanation.

(b) The explanatory equivalence principle does not hold even for strict correctness.

(c) The fine-grained propositions expressed in the strange languages somehow render those languages unsuitable for providing strictly correct explanations.

[70]See especially section 6.5.a.

4

Reality's Joints II: Things

1. Natural Things

In the previous chapter I considered the classificatory implications of the claim that language ought to divide reality at the joints. Although no satisfactory defense of the claim was presented, it may yet seem plausible. In the present chapter, I want to consider the implications of the claim for the individuative case.

My argument in section 2.4 implies that "cdog" and other strange individuative words may satisfy such conditions on similarity as (N) to much the same extent as ordinary individuative words do. Similarity conditions would seem, therefore, not to render the property of being a cdog significantly less metaphysically natural than the property of being a dog. It might still be suggested that, as a contingent matter of fact, the former property is significantly less nomically natural than the latter. It is true that dogs but not cdogs are predictable things and this constitutes a nomic difference between the two properties. Nevertheless, there are many truths of the form "All (or most) cdogs are F," where "F" does not involve change. Moreover, the sense in which cdogs are not predictable things is that the future intrinsic properties of a cdog cannot be predicted on the basis of its past intrinsic properties. If we take into account extrinsic properties, particularly the contact relations between cdogs, we can evidently formulate a law involving cdogs equivalent to any law involving dogs.

It is unclear, therefore, why "cdog" should fail to qualify under the Classificatory Joints Principle. It might be suggested that being a cdog is not a natural property because cdogs are not natural things and natural properties must be exemplified by natural things.[1] On this view, we may still need to explain what a "natural thing" is, but, given that

---

[1]Lewis 1983b, pp. 372–73, implies that a property that does not belong to any natural things is thereby rendered unnatural.

notion, individuative strangeness will turn out to be disqualified by the Classificatory Joints Principle. Such a view may seem quite plausible if we are ontological inegalitarians, but not, I think, if we are elitists. If unnatural things lack a certain elite status, that need not imply that properties exemplified only by unnatural things must lack an elite status. This will not be implied, certainly, if our elitism with respect to properties is based on a similarity analysis. As elitists, we may regard the property Cdog as natural and the things having the property as unnatural. We then need another division principle to deal with individuative strangeness:

> *The Individuative Joints Principle.* A general word ought to denote natural things.[2]

Corresponding to the earlier case of natural properties, let the following be my "official" preliminary introduction of the purported distinction between natural and unnatural things:

> We believe in a distinction between natural and unnatural things if we believe that there is an objective distinction that corresponds at least roughly to our intuitions about "genuine things" versus "mere logical constructions" and to our intuitions about ordinary versus strange individuative words.

As for the earlier case, we seek an account based on objective considerations, rather than pragmatic or psychological ones. And, as for that case, we anticipate that naturalness of things may be a matter of degree, the principle imposing an increasingly strong presumption against increasingly unnatural things.

a. Egalitarian and Inegalitarian Views

Let us try to formulate three views about natural things corresponding to the three views considered for natural properties: the ontological inegalitarian, elitist inegalitarian, and egalitarian views. The ontological view with respect to natural things would be the disbeliever's position of chapter 1. It would reject the existence of any such strange things as Contacti-objects.[3] Both the elitist and the egalitarian accept the existence of such things. The elitist holds that there is an objective distinction

---

[2]Again (as for the case of the Predictable Things Principle of section 2.4.d), the present principle should be taken to imply that n-adic relational words ought to denote n-tuples of natural things. And, to satisfy those who believe that ordinary (non-individuative) words denote both natural and unnatural things, we should either restrict the principle to individuative words or read "ought to denote natural things" as "ought to denote some natural things," i.e., "ought not to denote only unnatural things." These points will be taken to qualify all subsequent individuative principles.

[3]That is, the ontological inegalitarian would reject English sentences of the form "There are such-and-such things that exchange their characteristics when they touch." As I explained in section 1.2.c, I expect it to be understood that when addressing alternative ontological positions, I am expressing those positions in (what purports to be) plain and strict English, rather than in the ontologically casual hybrid meta-language that I sometimes employ.

between things that can be called natural and things that can be called unnatural. The egalitarian rejects any such distinction.

I am going to assume in this discussion that the inegalitarian takes ordinary bodies, such as trees and cars, as paradigmatic of (highly) genuine things (hence, artifacts are in the relevant sense "natural things"). There may be philosophical views that repudiate the genuineness of many ordinary things, but they can be ignored in the present discussion, for they will surely not sustain the Individuative Joints Principle. If the principle is intended to defend an invidious contrast between ordinary languages and the strange languages, it must be assumed that typical commonsense objects qualify as natural things.[4]

In the case of properties, we supposed that even ontological inegalitarians would allow that there are unnatural properties in the sense of sets of actual and possible things. Let us adopt an analogous assumption for the case of unnatural things.[5] We assume that any party to this discussion will be prepared to associate with any ordinary object such as a dog a set of actual and possible space-time points (or a function from any possible world to a set of space-time points in that world). Space-time points may be viewed as set-theoretical constructions out of places and times, which might themselves be viewed as set-theoretical constructions of some sort. But the assumption here will be that everyone agrees that *some* sense can be given to the notion of a set of actual and possible space-time points associated with an object. Now ontological inegalitarians deny that there are any physical objects that occupy the same places as dogs but that exchange their properties when in contact. They will agree, however, that there are sets of space-time points that correspond to the strange Contacti descriptions of "cdogs." Such sets are all the reality unnatural things have. The difference between natural and unnatural things, for them, is that only in the former case do we have genuine objects in addition to the sets of space-time points.

Elitists do not distinguish in this way between natural and unnatural things. Perhaps they believe that even natural things are nothing but sets of space-time points, or that even unnatural things involve more than such sets. In either case, the distinction for them is not an ontological one.

Elitists might take the distinction as primitive. This would correspond to the option suggested by Lewis for properties. Let us consider what other options are available to us if we are elitists.

---

[4]It may seem that philosophers like Butler, Reid, and Chisholm repudiate the genuineness of many ordinary things. (See Butler 1736; Reid 1785; Chisholm 1976.) Or is it, rather, that they would count ordinary things (in contrast to the strange things) as "genuine" things, but wish to distinguish further among the genuine things a super-elite class of things with "strict" or "perfect" identities? From the standpoint of the present discussion, the critical question is whether these philosophers express a view that might possibly sustain the Individuative Joints Principle.

[5]Here I follow Shoemaker 1988, pp. 216–17.

b. Analyses of Thing-Naturalness

We might simply define a natural thing as a predictable thing (i.e., a thing whose future intrinsic properties are predictable on the basis of its past intrinsic properties), thus collapsing the present division principle into the Predictable Things Principle of section 2.4.d. But we may want to get something more out of the present principle. As noted in section 2.4.d, there are intuitively strange things, such as trables (sums of trees and tables) or incars (things that shrink when cars leave garages), which are predictable to a high degree.

We may attempt to disqualify such things by giving an account of why they are "unnatural." One influential view about the nature of physical objects would seem to imply that the difference between, on the one hand, tables and ice cubes and, on the other, trables and incars must be explained by reference to the fact that our language contains "sortals" that supply identity criteria for the former things but not the latter.[6] If the explanation requires us to refer literally to the fact that we speak a language containing certain sortals, then this kind of sortal-relativized account obviously cannot help us in the present context, for we cannot define an objective notion of naturalness by appealing to facts about our language. We may attempt to eliminate explicit reference to our language by drawing up an exhaustive list of all the sortals in our language, say: $S_1, S_2, \ldots S_n$. We could then make a correlative list of the properties expressed by the sortals: $SP_1, SP_2, \ldots SP_n$. The objectivity of naturalness might be sustained if we define a natural thing as any thing that has either SP_1, or $SP_2, \ldots$ or SP_n. But, if an elitist did offer such a definition, the notion of naturalness thereby defined could offer no immediate intuitive hope for the Individuative Joints Principle, since there is apparently no temptation to suppose that our use of language is normatively constrained by a mere list of alternative properties under which to trace things.

Putting aside the sortal explanation, one might suggest that a trable is unnatural because it consists of parts (i.e., the table and tree) that are spatially and causally disconnected. The example of the incar is harder to deal with. Perhaps it can be said that an incar is unnatural because its career fails to *minimize change*: when we trace the career of an incar, and judge it to shrink upon leaving the garage, we countenance change unnecessarily. To trace the career of a natural thing is to follow a path that is continuous and that minimizes change as far as possible. Cars may seem to qualify in this respect, as perhaps do ice cubes, but not incars.

Lewis implies that a thing is natural to the extent that it is "a locus of causal chains" and "has a boundary well demarcated by differences in

---

[6]This seemed to be Wiggins's view in Wiggins 1967. I elaborate such a view in Hirsch 1982, chapter 2. Wiggins's more recent discussion in Wiggins 1980 is less clear in this respect, for it seems to rely on some version of the explanation claim (criticized in the last chapter).

highly natural properties."[7] The first condition is already implicit in what I have said. The second condition may strike us as intuitively important. And this condition may be enough to deal with the shrinking incars, which do not have highly natural boundaries at their shrinking ends. But there are other examples that cannot be dealt with in this way. At least, there are such examples if a natural thing can be a large part of another natural thing. Consider a trunk x of a tree y containing only one small branch. A succession combining x's early stages with y's later stages will be highly continuous causally (and in every other way). Yet the thing consisting of those stages is about as intuitively unnatural as anything can be. (This thing gains a branch though nothing happens to the branch.) Assuming that both x and y are natural, and hence satisfy the condition of having sufficiently natural boundaries, this condition evidently cannot explain why the trunk-to-tree concoction seems so unnatural.[8] But the condition of minimizing change does explain this.

One possibility, then, is that a thing x is natural to the degree that it satisfies the following conditions:

(P) (a) x always has a boundary demarcated by natural properties, and (b) x always has parts that are spatially and causally connected, and (c) x's career is continuous and change-minimizing.

Continuity in (Pc) may be measured in terms of a combination of spatiotemporal, qualitative, causal, and compositional factors.[9]

Both the sortal analysis and the analysis in terms of (P) admit of a certain general modification. Instead of taking the conditions presented in the analysis as definitive of what constitutes a genuine thing, we can take them as definitive of what constitutes a *stereotypical* case of a genuine thing. A genuine thing can then be defined as anything whose underlying structure is sufficiently similar to most (local) stereotypical cases.[10] I will ignore this complication in what follows, for I do not think that it substantially affects the points I am going to make.

We should try to interpret (P) so that a significant degree of naturalness might be assigned to things other than bodies. A flock of birds, for

---

[7]Lewis 1983b, p. 372.

[8]If we acknowledge such items as trunks (stems, fingers, and so on) as natural things, the following odd question arises: Why are joints in the ordinary sense joints in the metaphysical sense? In what way does a trunk (as opposed to a trunk together with half a branch) have natural boundaries? (See Hirsch 1982, pp. 108–9.) My point in the text might be made with other kinds of examples. Consider the part of a car between the bumpers. This part may be highly articulated and hence qualify as a natural thing on Lewis's definition. A succession combining early stages of this part with later stages of the car may be highly continuous but will certainly not constitute a natural thing.

[9](P) corresponds roughly to the definition of the "basic idea" of an object explained in Hirsch 1982, chapter 3 (see especially p. 111). Compare (Pc) with Robert Nozick's notion of a "closest continuer" in Nozick 1981.

[10]See Hirsch 1982, pp. 227–35.

instance, may qualify under (P) to a significant degree, assuming that the flock's boundary is demarcated by there being a much greater degree of spatial and causal connectedness between members of the flock than between members and non-members. One may even hope that on a suitable interpretation of (P), various natural-seeming events and processes (e.g., noises, storms, and flashes) might qualify to a significant degree.

c. Four Problems for (P)

There are, however, the following four problems for (P), which I present in what I take to be an order of increasing seriousness.[11] *First,* many things clearly satisfying the conditions of (P) do not seem to have the right kind of synchronic unity to qualify as genuine things. Consider, for example, a pair of socks tied together, or the result of attaching a sled to the back of a car.[12] These items seem to show that the synchronic unity conditions (Pa) and (Pb) are insufficient. It might be answered that such items can indeed be plausibly regarded as natural to some degree. But this does not fully answer the problem, at least if we take seriously the intuitive idea that, for example, a car is a more genuine thing than a car-cum-sled. (P) apparently cannot sustain this idea.

Second, (P) will not be satisfied by an undifferentiated portion of matter, such as a drop of water in the sea, which is not demarcated by natural boundaries.[13] Many philosophers would want to regard such portions of matter as genuine things. This problem seems to apply to both synchronic and diachronic unity. Let d be an undifferentiated drop of water in the sea. Obviously d fails to satisfy the condition of synchronic unity (Pa). Moreover, it would appear that d does not even satisfy the condition of diachronic unity (Pc), since it does not seem that d's path minimizes change more than any arbitrary continuous path through the sea of water.

It might be answered that d does in fact satisfy (Pc), since d is composed of atomic (or subatomic) particles. Each such particle is naturally bounded and satisfies (P), and d, as opposed to arbitrary continuous paths through the sea, minimizes change of particle composition. Hence, though d is not perfectly natural because it has no natural boundary, it is natural to a significant degree because it minimizes change. This answer is problematical, however, in that it requires us to regard it as a priori true that, if matter is not composed of articulated particles, then

[11]I have discussed these issues in Hirsch 1982, and the reader is referred for further details to the cited pages in that book.

[12]See Hirsch 1982, p. 110. *Synchronic unity* is lacking where we do not even have stages of genuine things; *diachronic unity* is lacking where we have stages of genuine things that do not, however, combine into the history of a genuine thing.

[13]See Hirsch 1982, chapter 4.

a large undifferentiated portion of matter contains no parts that are genuine things. Many philosophers will find this consequence implausible.

The *third* problem is that (P) does not account for cases in which things are said to go out of existence by continuously turning into other things, such as the case of a tree that goes out of existence by being whittled down to a splinter of wood.[14] This problem actually has two sides. The first is that there is a (P)-satisfying thing that changes from constituting a tree to constituting a splinter of wood, but this thing would not ordinarily qualify as a genuine thing. It might be answered that a "chunk (or lump) of wood" is at least a somewhat genuine thing, and, in the imagined case, a chunk of wood does indeed change from constituting a tree to constituting a splinter of wood. As before, this does not fully meet the problem, if a tree is judged to a be a more genuine thing than a shrinking chunk of wood, for (P) cannot apparently sustain this judgment.

But the second side of the problem is the more serious one. Certainly, our ordinary judgment is that there is a genuine thing, the tree, that goes out of existence when it is reduced to a splinter. But (P) cannot sustain this. In general, (P) cannot sustain the seemingly fundamental distinction we ordinarily make between continuous changes in which things go out of existence by turning into other things and continuous changes in which nothing goes out of existence.

The *fourth* problem is that condition (Pc) gives rise to an indefinite number of cases of *change-minimizing conflict*, that is, cases in which an object's career might be traced in two different ways that have a claim to minimizing change.[15] Compare the case of attaching a missing bumper to a car with the case of attaching a small sled to the back of a car. We would ordinarily judge that in the first case a thing gets larger but not in the second case. In both cases there is a conflict between minimizing change in size and shape and minimizing change in separate movability. Our ordinary judgment can obviously be defended if we appeal to a prior list of sortals; the judgment can then be justified by the fact that our language contains the sortal "car" but no sortal with either the force "portion-of-car-other-than-bumpers" or the force "car-with-or-without-sled." But there seems to be no way to defend the ordinary judgment by reference to (P). Such cases of change-minimizing conflict are pervasive, occurring whenever a small thing is added to or subtracted from a larger thing.

It might be suggested that, in such cases, either conflicting path defines a thing that is significantly natural, for a natural thing need only minimize change in some natural respect. The idea would be to replace (P) by a set of conditions (P') which includes the two synchronic conditions (Pa) and (Pb) but replaces (Pc) with the following condition:

[14]See Hirsch 1982, pp. 25–26.
[15]See Hirsch 1982, pp. 84–90.

(P'c) x's career is continuous and minimizes change with respect to some natural property.[16]

The obvious problem is that (P') does not explain why the car, which gets larger when bumpers are added but not when a sled is added, seems to be a more genuine thing than the portion-of-car-other-than-bumpers, which does not get larger when bumpers are added, or than the car-with-or-without-sled, which gets larger when a sled is added. I think the problem is worse than that, however, for it seems that the latter items really have virtually no degree of intuitive naturalness. Imagine that a missing bumper is added to the car on Monday and that a door handle is removed on Tuesday. It seems flatly wrong to say in this case that some (genuine) thing, consisting of every part of the car except the bumpers, does not alter its size on Monday but does alter its size on Tuesday. But that is the judgment that (P'c) would countenance if we trace the portion-of-car-other-than-bumpers in a way that preserves continuity and minimizes change in size and shape.

It should be noted that neither (P) nor (P') addresses the issue of transworld identity. But an adequate general analysis of what a natural thing is should explain when a set of things-at-a-world constitutes a single modally thick natural thing. This adds an additional layer of complication to the analysis.

d. How Deep Is Thing-Naturalness?

My inclination is to think that it is exceedingly difficult to deal with these various problems except by eventually falling back on something like a list of sortals.[17] But, as I said before, this seems inimical to the hope of defending the Individuative Joints Principle. Let me elaborate a bit on this point. My suggestion is not that the sortal view supports thing-egalitarianism. It is indeed difficult to see what could support that position. What could motivate anyone to deny that we have an objective idea of a distinction in the world answering to our intuitions about "genu-

---

[16]I take (P'c) to be something of an improvement over the suggestion criticized in Hirsch 1982, pp. 91–94. The latter simply allowed a choice of either path in any occurrence of change-minimizing conflict, thus not even ensuring any consistency in how one resolves conflicts that occur at different times in the tracing of x.

[17]I argued in Hirsch 1982, chapter 4, that it is impossible to analyze the identity of (a bit of) matter, even given a list of sortals, which may suggest that the second problem mentioned above cannot be dealt with even by the sortal view. But the present context is somewhat different, for one may propose a disjunctive analysis of what constitutes a genuine thing having the following format:

> Something is a genuine thing if and only if it is either a dog, or a tree, . . . or a car, or a table, . . . or a bit of water, or a bit of wood. . . .

This may be held to qualify as an analysis of what a genuine thing is, even if no analysis can be given of the identity of a bit of water (wood, etc.).

ine" and "non-genuine" things? Perhaps, if a property-egalitarian views continuity as subjective, and if our intuitive notion of a genuine thing is essentially linked to continuity considerations, such a philosopher would have reason to embrace thing-egalitarianism. If we are property-inegalitarians, however, it seems virtually automatic that we will adhere to some form of thing-inegalitarianism as well.[18]

The question is whether we are able to view the distinction between genuine and non-genuine things as metaphysically deep and important. Even the diversity of conditions mentioned in (P)—and this diversity would be more pronounced if we brought in conditions of transworld identity—may somewhat jeopardize the sense of depth in the distinction. Why, one must wonder, should there be a normative constraint on language that requires words to denote things satisfying the apparently diverse conditions mentioned in (P)? But the force of this question is made much stronger if one has to replace (P) with the sortal view. The latter view seems to make the distinction between genuine and non-genuine things metaphysically shallow, as if a metaphysically arbitrary, albeit objective, line is being drawn through logical space. The question might be recast by asking whether we, who are inegalitarians about both properties and things, view the property of being a natural thing as a natural property. The sortal view seems to force us to answer this question in the negative.[19] But, if thing-naturalness is an unnatural property, it seems difficult to appreciate the intuitive force of a division principle which states that our words ought to denote things having this property.

There is in what I have just been saying an implicit contrast between the case of property-naturalness and the case of thing-naturalness. The contrast is sharpest if we concentrate on cases of naturalness to a very high degree. I am now assuming that in both cases we are the sort of elitists who seek an analysis of what naturalness consists in. In the case of properties, we have the principle that a property is natural if and only if its bearers are in some sense more similar to each other than to other things. Perhaps this principle can be analyzed further in terms of (N) or some related condition. The principle, in any case, allows us to capture in a relatively simple and intuitive way what property-naturalness essen-

---

[18]If we reject ontological thing-inegalitarianism but believe that this is the position implicit in the ordinary distinction between "genuine things" and "mere constructions," we would in a sense reject the distinction. Nevertheless, we could still accept the elitist's distinction between "genuine things" and "mere constructions." At least in that sense we could adhere to inegalitarianism.

[19]The negative answer seems to be implied in Wiggins's repeated insistence that there could not be "any usable account of what it is, in general, to make a mistake or avoid a mistake in tracing [an object] *a*. . . . To trace *a* I must know what *a* *is*," where to know "what an object is" in the relevant sense is to be able to apply a sortal to it (Wiggins 1967, p. 35). The negative answer may indeed be taken as definitive of what counts as a sortal analysis, since, if the question could be answered in the affirmative, it is not clear in what sense we need to be appealing to (a list of) sortals.

tially amounts to (at least in the fundamental sense of metaphysical naturalness). If we ask the (somewhat peculiar) question whether property-naturalness is itself natural, it appears possible to answer this question in the affirmative. The case seems quite different for thing-naturalness. The latter notion certainly cannot be captured in any simple or intuitive way if one needs to invoke a list of sortals in its behalf. The notion of property-naturalness appears, therefore, to be a metaphysically deeper and more secure notion than that of thing-naturalness.

This point applies directly only to the form of elitism which analyzes thing-naturalness in terms of a list of sortals. It may not apply to ontological thing-inegalitarianism, or to the form of elitism which regards thing-naturalness as primitive. There is a plausible intermediary position, however, to which it does seem to apply. This position eschews a full-scale analysis of the notion of a genuine thing but embraces various a priori principles of synchronic, diachronic (transtemporal), and transworld identity. A full-scale analysis is eschewed in the sense that the principles may be viewed as in some ways incomplete, or as already presupposing in some ways the notion of (the identity) of a genuine thing. The principles are, nevertheless, deemed necessary to answer the sorts of questions that arose in connection with (P). For example, why is it that only some masses of matter constitute genuine things? Why is it that only certain changes constitute a thing's going out of existence? Why is it that only some cases of attaching two things together constitute a thing's getting bigger? My arguments in connection with (P) seem to show that the principles needed to answer these questions must invoke a prior list of sortals. This may be granted even by someone who holds that the notion of a genuine thing is not (fully) analyzable. But this element of dependence on a list of sortals seems enough to threaten the metaphysical depth of the notion of thing-naturalness.

In the last several paragraphs, I have been advancing some general negative considerations that seem to cast a kind of doubt on the intuitive prospects of the Individuative Joints Principle. Of course, one needs to measure such negative considerations against whatever positive arguments might be put forth in behalf of the principle. To such arguments, I now turn.[20]

2. *The Semantic Argument*

Evidently the explanation claim discussed in the last chapter with respect to the previous Classificatory Joints Principle will apply here again, and will be vulnerable to the same objections. I think that one new kind of argument may first emerge with respect to the present principle. I will call this the *semantic argument*. It is an argument that seems to be avail-

---

[20]But I will return to the general negative considerations, in a slightly different context, in section 7.3.c.

able primarily to the ontological inegalitarian, though I will later mention a version of it that may be available to the elitist.

Let me say that a *truth-conditional semantics* for a language is a finite description of the language which entails, for each sentence of the language, a specification of its truth-conditions. To specify the truth-conditions of a sentence is to specify, for each context in which the sentence can be uttered, what the possible circumstances are with respect to which the sentence holds true.[21] The semantic argument derives from two premises:

> *Premise 1.* Any language must have a truth-conditional semantics.
>
> *Premise 2.* If a language failed to satisfy the Individuative Joints Principle, it could not have a truth-conditional semantics.

From these premises it is concluded that any language must satisfy the principle.

a. Objections to the Argument

Premise 1 is widely accepted in the literature, and is often taken to follow from the simple observation that to understand a language involves being able to determine the truth-conditions for an indefinite number of novel sentences, sentences one has previously never confronted. Harman has argued, I think persuasively, that the simple observation does not really entail Premise 1.[22] But I want to concentrate here on the status of Premise 2.

A truth-conditional semantics is standardly envisioned as made up of two parts that, ignoring irrelevant refinements, might be characterized as follows. The first part is a *reference scheme* that assigns denotations to the non-logical words. The second part consists of a finite set of recursive rules (a "truth definition") that would allow one to calculate the truth-conditions of any sentence on the basis of the reference scheme. As a crude example, consider the English sentence "Some dog is first brown and then white." The reference scheme would assign to "dog," "brown," and "white," respectively, dogs, brown things, and white things. One of the recursive rules for English might be something like this (where I ignore questions about how time is properly to be treated): "Any sentence of the form 'Some F is first A and then B' is true (with respect to a possible world) if and only if there exists something that is denoted by both 'F' and 'A' with respect to one time and by both 'F' and 'B' with respect to a later time." One can then infer that "Some dog is first brown and then white" is true if and only if there exists a dog that is first brown and then white.

---

[21] I assume the general semantic framework of Kaplan 1989, though my argument does not depend on any of the details of this framework.

[22] Harman 1975, pp. 280–88. See also Schiffer 1987, chapter 7.

Suppose we are ontological inegalitarians who believe that there are no such unnatural things as "cdogs"—that is, that there are no things that are like dogs except for exchanging their characteristics when they touch. It may seem that we would then be precluded from formulating any reference scheme for Contacti which, when combined with some recursive rules, yields the stipulated truth-conditions for Contacti sentences. Consider the Contacti sentence "Some cdog is first brown and then white." This sentence is supposed to come out true if a brown dog comes into exclusive contact with a white dog. But there appears to be no assignment of denotations to "cdog," "brown," and "white" which would have this result, assuming that we are precluded from assigning any such things as cdogs to "cdog." Even if we consider a simpler sentence like "Something is first brown and then white," we can apparently formulate no reference scheme to explain the truth-conditions of this sentence, since it is supposed to come out true if a brown dog comes into exclusive contact with a white dog, or a brown table comes into exclusive contact with a white table, etc. Hence Premise 2 seems to follow: there can be no truth-conditional semantics for a language like Contacti.

Now I assume that any reader of this book can determine the truth-conditions of an indefinite number of novel Contacti sentences. This immediately seems to indicate that there is something wrong with the semantic argument. Of course, I never presented a "semantics" for Contacti. In section 1.2.a, I introduced the language by making some remarks about the "identity conditions" that operate in Contacti, by giving a few examples of the truth-conditions of Contacti sentences, and by exhibiting a diagram to portray these truth-conditions. It seems extremely plausible to suppose, however, that with sufficient ingenuity one could formulate a more rigorous description that effectively specified the truth-conditions of all Contacti sentences.

Certainly *within Contacti* there could be no problem in formulating a truth-conditional semantics for Contacti.[23] This semantics would exactly mirror the one for English (with "cdog" replacing "dog," "ctable" replacing "table," and so on). The semantics within Contacti would include:

> (a) "cdog," "brown," and "white" denote, respectively, cdogs, brown things, and white things

and:

> (b) Any sentence of the form "Some *F* is first *A* and then *B*" is true if and only if there exists something that is denoted by both "*F*" and "*A*" with respect to one time and by both "*F*" and "*B*" with respect to a later time,

---

[23]That is, there could be no problem in addition to any (and in fact there appear to be many) that may apply to English. Throughout this discussion I ignore any general problems with the idea of a truth-conditional semantics.

from which it can be inferred that:

> (c) "Some cdog is first brown and then white" is true if and only if there exists a cdog that is first brown and then white.

Of course, (c) is exactly the result we want within Contacti.

It is true that if, standing outside Contacti, we are committed to saying that there do not exist any such strange things as Contacti-objects, then we may also be led to say that (a) is not really a condition involving *denotation*, and (b) is not really a condition involving the *existence of things*. We might say that (a) involves only "ostensible denotation" and that (b) involves only the "virtual existence" of "virtual things."[24] (Indeed, if we are purists, we may even insist that "cdog" in Contacti is only an "ostensible general word.") But it is not clear why this should matter, for if what we mean by a truth-conditional semantics is a finite specification of the truth-conditions of the infinite sentences of the language, then it seems clear that there will be within Contacti such a semantics for Contacti.

But perhaps we mean more than this by a truth-conditional semantics. Let us say that a *standard* truth-conditional semantics is one whose reference scheme involves denotation (as opposed to ostensible denotation) and whose recursive clauses involve the existence of things (as opposed to the virtual existence of virtual things). If we are ontological inegalitarians, we may view Contacti as not having a standard truth-conditional semantics. This would support the semantic argument only if the latter is recast to read:

> *Premise 1'*. Any language must have a standard truth-conditional semantics.
>
> *Premise 2'*. If a language failed to satisfy the Individuative Joints Principle, it could not have a standard truth-conditional semantics.

b. Objections to the Revised Argument

I mentioned that Premise 1 seems to be widely assumed in the literature, but Premise 1' seems far less plausible. The basic intuitive impulse behind Premise 1 is that a finite mind such as ours could not possibly master an infinitely rich language except by way of finite rules. But what reason is there to suppose that these rules should take the form of a standard truth-conditional semantics rather than the non-standard seman-

---

[24]Another way to put this is that (b) does not really involve *objectual quantification*. But one should not be tempted to suggest that (b) involves instead *substitutional quantification*, for there need not be names answering to all of the virtual things ostensibly denoted in Contacti, any more than there need be names answering to all the things denoted in English. Statements of "virtual existence" are statements that have the same formal (syntactic) logic as statements of objectual quantification, although they are not statements of objectual quantification. On ostensible denotation and virtual things, see the reference to Quine in chapter 1, note 16. On objectual and substitutional quantification, see Quine 1973, pp. 98ff.

tics that would be available in Contacti? If there is something wrong with the non-standard semantics, certainly this is not suggested merely by considering the infinite richness of language.

Let us turn to Premise 2'. The ontological inegalitarian may be led to construe the strange words of Contacti as not really denoting but only ostensibly denoting. It is this construal which supports Premise 2'. But there is another way to view Contacti. I have been assuming that even the ontological inegalitarian accepts sets. The words of Contacti may therefore be construed as denoting (as applying to) sets of various sorts.[25] Since I have already supposed that corresponding to any natural or unnatural thing there will be a certain set of actual and possible space-time points, the most obvious idea would be to imagine a version of Contacti in which the words denote such sets. Even ontological inegalitarians accept the existence of such sets corresponding to Contacti-things, though they hold that natural things are entities over and above such sets. If we construe the words of Contacti as denoting sets, we can apply the Individuative Joints Principle to Contacti so long as the principle is understood to imply that a general word ought not to denote sets answering to unnatural things. (We can leave it open how sets answering to natural things may relate to the principle.) It seems, however, that the principle cannot be based on Premise 2'. If we construe the words of Contacti as denoting sets, we can have a standard truth-conditional semantics for Contacti, one that deals with the real denotation of things (i.e., sets) that really exist.

Ontological inegalitarians regard the English sentence "Any dog is identical with a certain set" as necessarily false. If they try to imagine a version of Contacti in which the corresponding sentence "Any cdog is identical with a certain set" is necessarily false, then it does indeed follow that they cannot give a standard semantics for this particular form of sentence. Such sentences would have to be regarded as not genuinely identity sentences and as not deriving their truth-conditions in the standard way. But it is difficult to see how the demand for a standard truth-conditional semantics is seriously breached by our having to make an exception of one rather obscure and exotic form of sentence. In any case, the ontological inegalitarian can shift to a version of Contacti in which the identity sentence is treated as necessarily true—this is surely still a strange language in the relevant sense. It appears that at least for this version of Contacti, even the ontological inegalitarian can easily give a standard semantics.

Might the response be that this is still not a *standard* semantics, for the reference scheme of a standard semantics must not associate words with sets? But the question-begging quality of this response is surely apparent. If our belief is that the world contains just natural things and sets, the response (when conjoined with Premise 1') is merely tantamount

---

[25]As indicated in note 1 of chapter 1, I adopt a usage in which a term denotes whatever it applies to. Hence, "cdog" denotes certain sets if and only if cdogs are sets.

to restating the Individuative Joints Principle (whereas we are seeking an argument for the principle).

If we are allowed to beg the question in this way, even the elitist inegalitarian might join the act by simply insisting that a "standard" semantics must not associate words with unnatural things. Indeed, we might as well defend the Classificatory Joints Principle in the same way, by insisting that a "standard" semantics must not associate words with unnatural properties. I take it as obvious that such defenses of the Joints Principles are empty.

c. Normative and Modal Arguments

There is an important subsidiary point to be derived from the present discussion, one that will eventually alter the structure of the argument in this book. I have been assuming all along that our negative intuitions about the strange languages are of a *normative* nature, to the effect that it would be in some sense irrational or bad to speak such languages. In formulating the semantic argument, however, I deliberately left it ambiguous as between a normative interpretation and a *modal* one. The modal interpretation of Premise 1 (or 1') is that it is *metaphysically necessary* for a language to have a (standard) truth-conditional semantics. The modal point, rather than the normative one, seems to be suggested by considerations having to do with the infinite richness of language. (How could such considerations suggest that it would be bad, although possible, to speak a language like Contacti?) Note that I am not considering here the question whether it is, as a contingent fact of psychology, impossible for humans to speak the strange languages—though I will have a little bit to say on that question in chapter 5, dealing with pragmatic matters. There are only two fundamental philosophical questions to raise about the strange languages: Is it (metaphysically) possible for there to be such languages, and, if so, would such languages be in some sense bad? Until the present section I have considered only the latter question, and I will continue to focus on that question until chapter 6, at which point the modal question will become central.

I do not take this section to have completed a discussion of the claim that language must have a standard truth-conditional semantics in some sense that is inimical to the strange languages. A position related to this claim will indeed be the major topic of chapters 6 and 7. What I do think has been shown in this section is that the claim draws no obvious support from familiar considerations about the infinite richness of language.

3. Inscrutability

In this section, I want to consider certain connections between the problem of the inscrutability of reference and the division problem. The immediate distinction between the two problems is that the former raises a question about why it is rational to reject strange interpretations of ordinary languages, whereas the latter raises a question about why it is rational to reject strange languages. However, the inscrutability problem may seem to threaten the intelligibility of the division problem. I will broach this issue by introducing a new way of viewing Contacti. It will be a puzzling way insofar as it may threaten the assumption that Contacti really involves individuative strangeness.

a. Pseudo-Languages

It will facilitate matters to first introduce a certain abbreviation. Suppose that two dogs are exclusively in contact with each other (i.e., they are in contact with each other but with no other dogs). Then let us say that each is "contact-dog" to the other. Further, if a dog is not exclusively in contact with any dog, let us say that it is contact-dog to itself. In general, "x is contact-F to y at time t" abbreviates "either it is the case that x and y are two F-things that are exclusively in contact with each other at t or it is the case that $x = y$ and x is an F-thing that is not exclusively in contact with any F-thing at t" (where, as usual, "two F-things are exclusively in contact" is taken to mean that neither F-thing is in contact with a third F-thing). In terms of this abbreviation, we can see that a Contacti sentence of the form "There exists a cdog that is A at t_1 and B at t_2" is equivalent to the corresponding (abbreviated) English sentence of the form "There exists a dog that is contact-dog at t_1 to something that is A and that is contact-dog at t_2 to something that is B." Now consider a reference scheme for Contacti which has the following assignments:

"cdog" denotes dogs.

"ctable" denotes tables.

. . .

. . .

. . .

"brown" denotes anything that is either contact-dog or contact-table or contact-. . . to something that is brown.

"white" denotes anything that is either contact-dog or contact-table or contact-. . . to something that is white.

The clauses for "brown" and "white" would have to be completed by attaching a "contact" operator to every word that stands to some word of Contacti in the way that "dog" and "table" stand to "cdog" and "ctable." (To simplify the example, I am tacitly assuming that the strange individuative words of Contacti are mutually incompatible and exhaustive; otherwise the clauses for "brown" and "white" would have to be complicated in certain ways.) This reference scheme (together with the recursive rules indicated earlier) would imply that the Contacti sentence "There exists a cdog that is first brown and then white" is equivalent to the English sentence "There exists a dog that is first contact-dog to something that is brown and then contact-dog to something that is white." In other words, the reference scheme would yield the same truth-conditions for the Contacti sentence as were originally stipulated.

The same would hold for all Contacti sentences if the reference scheme is suitably extended. Demonstrative terms (and proper names) would be treated in essentially the same way as "brown" and "white": "that cdog," uttered while pointing in the direction of a certain dog, would be assigned its contact-dog. The odd consequence is that we have a reference scheme yielding the stipulated truth-conditions for Contacti in which "cdog," "ctable," and all other words denote perfectly ordinary objects.[26]

Let me call the language I originally described "Contacti" and the language I have just described "Pseudo-Contacti." I leave it open at this point whether these are descriptions of two different languages or merely two descriptions of the same language (i.e., whether Contacti is or is not identical to Pseudo-Contacti). All that I take to be established is that these languages have the same sentences with the same truth-conditions. Let us juxtapose the earlier diagram of Contacti with a diagram of Pseudo-Contacti. (See Figures 4.1 and 4.2.) Following the broken arrows in Figure 4.1 and following the unbroken arrows in Figure 4.2 yield the same description of the cdogs. The broken arrows represent the strange identities of the strange things. Figure 4.2 shows only unbroken arrows because no strange things are represented there.

It is obvious that there is a language Pseudo-English that stands to English in the way that Pseudo-Contacti stands to Contacti (Figure 4.3.) In Pseudo-English, we follow the broken arrows. Pseudo-English has the same sentences with the same truth-conditions as English, but it is represented in terms of a reference scheme that assigns words not to ordinary things, but to the strange Contacti-things.

---

[26]Several qualifications are in order. First, throughout this section, when I discuss alternative reference schemes for a language, I exclude from consideration modal sentences of the language. But I do not think that these introduce any additional problems in principle. Second, I exclude from consideration sentences of the language that are either explicitly semantic or that attribute propositional attitudes. I believe that if we have alternative schemes for the language with such sentences excluded, we can extend the schemes to include these sentences. In any case, it would seem in some way question begging to rely on these sentences to settle on the correct reference scheme, since they themselves invoke (at least implicitly) information about the correct reference scheme. Note, third, that this example works only if we are thinking of strong Contacti, which does not contain "dog" as well as "cdog." In weak Contacti, the reference scheme just described would yield the wrong truth-conditions for the sentence "There exists a dog that is first brown and then white." Furthermore, the example works only on the assumption that the Contacti sentence "Any cdog is identical with a certain set" has the same truth-value as the English sentence "Any dog is identical with a certain set."

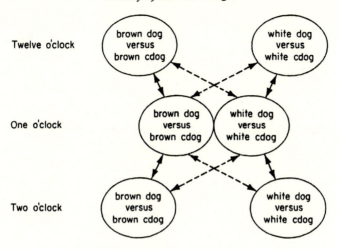

Figure 4.1 English versus Contacti.

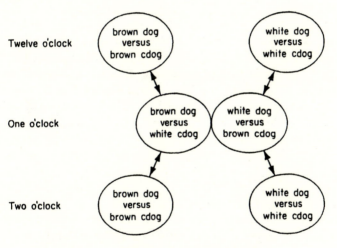

Figure 4.2 English versus Pseudo-Contacti.

The standard way of constructing alternative reference schemes yielding the same truth-conditions is by a permutation that exchanges things in one scheme with things in the other.[27] My examples also operate in this way: one gets from Contacti to Pseudo-Contacti and from English to Pseudo-English by a permutation that exchanges each dog (table, etc.) with the cdog (ctable, etc.) with which it makes exclusive contact (if there is one).[28]

[27]See Wallace 1977, p. 146.
[28]At most one cdog can ever come into exclusive contact with a given dog; this cdog coincides with the dog when not in contact with it.

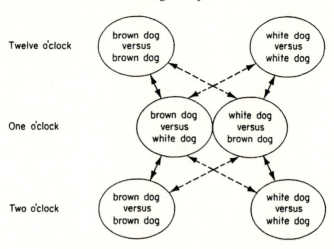

Figure 4.3   English versus Pseudo-English.

If speakers of a language cannot determine whether they are speaking Contacti or Pseudo-Contacti, this may seem to jeopardize the distinction between individuative and classificatory strangeness. Worse, if speakers cannot tell whether their language is English or Pseudo-English, even the distinction between ordinary and strange languages seems to be in jeopardy. My aim in this section is to clarify whether these distinctions can be sustained.

b. Truth-Conditional and Inscrutability Theses

Let us say that two reference schemes are *truth-conditionally equivalent* if (given the same recursive rules) they yield the same truth-conditions for the same sentences. One question to be asked is this: Is it possible for there to be a pair of truth-conditionally equivalent reference schemes that apply selectively to different languages? That is, is it possible for there to be two truth-conditionally equivalent reference schemes R_1 and R_2 such that R_1 is a correct description of one language and R_2 is a correct description of another language, but it is not the case that both R_1 and R_2 are correct descriptions of both languages?[29] To give a "no"

---

[29]The answer to this question will be trivially affirmative if a particular language is identified as an abstract structure associated with a certain reference scheme. However, I am assuming in this discussion that a particular language can be identified as the language employed by certain specified people on certain specified occasions. Without that assumption, our question would be formulated as follows:

Is it possible for there to be two truth-conditionally equivalent reference schemes R_1 and R_2 such that R_1 is a correct description of a language employed by person 1 at answer to this question is to hold what I will call the *truth-conditional thesis*. This thesis implies that in a sense *truth-conditions determine denotation*, but this need not imply that truth-conditions are in any sense "prior" to denotation.

The truth-conditional thesis implies that, if two reference schemes are truth-conditionally equivalent, then either they correctly describe the same languages or one of them is an *impossible* scheme, in the sense that it does not correctly describe *any* possible language. This thesis must be distinguished from the *inscrutability thesis*, where the latter is understood to imply that the correctness of a reference scheme depends on nothing beyond its yielding the right truth-conditions, so that if a scheme is correct, any truth-conditionally equivalent scheme is equally correct.[30] According to the inscrutability thesis, it is impossible for there to be two truth-conditionally equivalent reference schemes R_1 and R_2 such that R_1 but not R_2 is the correct description of some language. One may hold, as against the inscrutability thesis, that there are additional constraints on the correctness of a reference-scheme, constraints that disqualify some schemes yielding the right truth-conditions. If one holds, moreover, that these constraints always pick out a uniquely correct scheme for any language, then one has rejected inscrutability altogether.[31] The truth-conditional thesis, however, need not be rejected if one holds that the relevant constraints render all but one scheme for any language impossible.

When it is often said in the literature that "there is no fact of the matter as to what a term denotes," this is confusingly ambiguous as between the truth-conditional thesis and the inscrutability thesis. Someone who holds the former thesis but denies the latter will agree that, if R_1 and R_2 are truth-conditionally equivalent, it cannot be a straightforward *empirical* fact that R_1 but not R_2 is correct for a given language, because if R_2 is not correct for that language, it is not correct for any possible language. Nevertheless, it may be a "fact," a *necessary* fact (given the truth-conditions in the language), that R_1 but not R_2 is correct.

c. *Constraints on Reference Schemes*

If we accept the truth-conditional thesis, we have to decide whether also to accept the inscrutability thesis. It should be noted that even the latter thesis may not imperil the distinction between ordinary and strange

---

time 1 and R_2 is a correct description of a language employed by person 2 at time 2, but it is not the case that both R_1 and R_2 are correct descriptions of both a language employed by person 1 at time 1 and a language employed by person 2 at time 2?

All of the issues discussed in this section could be reformulated along these lines.

[30]This position seems to be what many people mean by "inscrutability." It is formulated very clearly in Wallace 1977. See also Putnam 1981a, pp. 32–48.

[31]I assume that we can distinguish what we are calling inscrutability from garden variety cases of vagueness or ambiguity, which, of course, everyone acknowledges.

languages. According to this thesis, English is the same language as Pseudo-English, both reference schemes for this language being equally correct. English might, nevertheless, be said to be an ordinary language insofar as it can be correctly interpreted in terms of an intuitively ordinary reference scheme. In contrast, Contacti is a strange language because any correct reference scheme for it is intuitively strange. But the distinction between classificatory and individuative strangeness is imperiled on this view. If Contacti is the same language as Pseudo-Contacti, there is apparently no basis to regard this language as involving individuative strangeness, since any language is representable in terms of a reference scheme involving strange individuals (as is shown by English and Pseudo-English).

If we want to reject the inscrutability thesis, the most obvious additional constraint on reference schemes, beyond their yielding the right truth-conditions for a language, would be the following "demonstrative constraint": Other things being equal, a language is correctly interpreted as containing demonstrative terms that are typically used to denote something a speaker either perceives or is pointing in the direction of.[32] It seems clear that the demonstrative constraint is compatible with the truth-conditional thesis, insofar as this constraint renders various reference schemes impossible. If we accept the demonstrative constraint, then we immediately regard as impossible the reference schemes in terms of which I introduced Pseudo-Contacti and Pseudo-English. These schemes require the demonstrative term "that cdog" (or "that dog") to refer in many typical circumstances not to the thing being looked at or pointed at, but at something in contact with it, which violates the demonstrative constraint. The constraint implies, in a sense, that Pseudo-Contacti and Pseudo-English are not possible languages, in that there are no possible languages whose terms have the denotations specified in the reference schemes by which these languages were introduced.

One might attempt to extend the demonstrative constraint into a more general "causal constraint," something roughly to the following effect: Other things being equal, a language is correctly interpreted as containing many terms such that the process of learning the term typically involves perceiving or pointing in the direction of things denoted by the term.[33] This constraint, too, seems to be compatible with the truth-conditional thesis, for roughly the same reasons that applied to the demonstrative constraint.[34] Even this generalized constraint, however,

---

[32]Compare with Wallace 1977, pp. 158–60. Wallace's reason for rejecting (or at least doubting) this constraint—i.e., that it cannot be rigorously formulated—seems to me inadequate; the constraint remains highly plausible.

[33]See Field 1975, p. 398.

[34]One may view the matter in the following general terms. In order for the sentences of a language to have certain truth-conditions, there must obtain certain causal relations between utterances of the sentences and conditions in the world. Those causal relations may suffice, via the causal constraint on reference, to determine a uniquely correct reference scheme for the language. Hence, the truth-conditions determine a uniquely correct reference scheme.

does not seem able to eliminate all inscrutability. If there are truth-conditionally equivalent schemes such that "rabbit" is assigned rabbits by one and rabbit-stages by the other, the constraint will apparently not disqualify the latter scheme.

Lewis's preferred solution to the inscrutability problem is to appeal to the following constraint: The correct reference scheme is the one that maximizes assignments of natural properties and things.[35] This constraint seems obviously to be compatible with the truth-conditional thesis, at least if we assume that it is a matter of necessity whether a given property or thing is natural. Lewis's constraint would seem to eliminate almost all cases of inscrutability. A kind of case that may not be eliminated is the choice between the reference scheme for Contacti and that for Pseudo-Contacti. Both of these schemes assign unnatural items but in different ways. However, I do not know of any examples that would not succumb to a combination of Lewis's constraint and the demonstrative (or causal) constraint.

We should, I think, accept these constraints and reject the inscrutability thesis. The thesis implies that English has no uniquely correct reference scheme. Therefore, there will be examples of statements such as "'rabbit' denotes rabbit-stages," which will be as correct as "'rabbit' denotes rabbits." That is, there will be examples which violate the following disquotation schema for English terms:

"———" denotes something if and only if it is ———.[36]

But this seems patently absurd. It seems that if we know anything at all, we know that the disquotation schema must be satisfied.

The obviousness of the disquotation schema might be reinforced by considering the following point. Suppose someone asserts

(a) "Rabbit" denotes something that is not a rabbit.

The standard recursive rules for English entail

(b) A sentence of the form "a is R to something that is not F" is true if and only if "R" denotes an ordered pair consisting of something that is denoted by "a" followed by something that is not denoted by "F."

Let us assume that

---

[35]Lewis 1983b, pp. 370–77. See Putnam 1981a, pp. 35–38, which suggests interestingly that Putnam's only reason for rejecting Lewis's constraint is that he is an egalitarian. Note that (perhaps unlike Lewis himself) I am here confining Lewis's constraint to the determination of reference schemes *given* truth-conditions. See section 4.3.d. on the determination of truth-conditions.

[36]In the literature, one seems to find philosophers who espouse the inscrutability thesis while at the same time accepting the disquotation schema as trivially correct. But if it is trivially true that "rabbit" denotes rabbits then it is trivially false that it is inscrutable what "rabbit" denotes.

(c) An expression together with surrounding quotation marks denotes that expression.

Then (c) implies that the quotation at the beginning of (a) denotes "rabbit." Now, the truth of the sentence (a), conjoined with (b) and (c), entails

(d) "Denotes" denotes an ordered pair consisting of an expression followed by something that the expression does not denote.

Note that (d) might be put by saying that "denotes" does not express the relation Denotation. In other words, if the disquotation schema fails, "denotes" cannot express Denotation (assuming the standard function of quotation marks). Conversely, we are assured that so long as "denotes" expresses Denotation the disquotation schema must hold.

It seems clear that part of the reason why the inscrutability thesis is taken seriously in some literature is that it is conflated with other views that deserve to be taken seriously. One such view, which I am inclined to accept, is the truth-conditional thesis. Another view is that denotation is in some sense not a real relation.[37] This might mean that denotation cannot be analyzed in physicalistic terms. Or it might mean that denotation is not a natural relation, in the sense of naturalness discussed in the last chapter. Or it might mean that it is in some sense merely a matter of convention which constraints on correct reference schemes are adopted, since any scheme truth-conditionally equivalent to the one counted correct would accomplish the purpose of yielding the right truth-conditions for the language.[38] I offer no judgment on these various claims, except to emphasize that they do not entail the inscrutability thesis.

d. Interpretive Charity

My procedure in this section, indeed throughout this entire book, has been to assume as given the truth-conditions of the sentences of the various languages under consideration. I think this is a perfectly reasonable procedure. The languages are fantasies of my own creation; I have the right to stipulate the content of these fantasies. Of course, it is open to someone to argue that these fantasies are somehow incoherent, that it is impossible for there to be a language under the given truth-conditional description. I am quite interested in such arguments; they will be the main topic of chapters 6 and 7. However, I think it should be clear where the burden of argument lies: the burden is on the person who wants to claim that a language with certain stipulated truth-conditions is impossible.

[37]See Davidson 1977.
[38]See Field 1975.

Although this claim is a topic for later chapters, I want to make a few preliminary remarks about it now, especially with the aim of clarifying how the issue of assigning truth-conditions relates to some of the issues of inscrutability that I have addressed in this section.

The predominant view in the literature seems to be that truth-conditions can be assigned essentially on the basis of the "principle of charity." The principle requires us to interpret people's languages in such a way as to maximize the rationality of their assertions. (In many typical cases, rationality will coincide with truth, but there are many other cases in which the charitable interpretation would ascribe false but rational assertions, rather than true but irrational ones.)

Certainly there appears to be no problem in applying this interpretive principle to yield the truth-conditions I imagined for such languages as the Gricular language and Contacti. We need only imagine that people consistently utter certain strange sentences in the same epistemic and pragmatic contexts in which we would rationally utter certain ordinary sentences. This is evidence that the strange sentences are equivalent to the ordinary ones, that is, that they have the same truth-conditions. Of course, it has often been claimed that even for the ordinary sentences there is an element of indeterminacy of truth-conditions. I need not address that claim now. The important point is that there appears to be no special problem for the imagined strange languages.

It is true that if we accept the Joints Principles (or some other division principles), we regard it as being in some sense irrational for people to employ strange languages. It is not clear how this should affect the interpretive principle of charity. In its standard form the principle appeals to the rationality of the use people make of the language at their disposal (especially the rationality of the beliefs expressed in the language), not the rationality of their having such a language at their disposal. But suppose that an "extended" (as opposed to "standard") principle of charity does take the latter consideration into account. All that might follow (given the Joints Principles) is that there would be a presumption against interpreting a language as being strange. This presumption might surely be defeated by considerations coming under the standard principle. A simple image here is that of people who, in optimal perceptual circumstances, assent to the sentence "That is gricular" if and only if the perceived object is either green or circular. It should perhaps be added that, if the perceived object is either green or circular, they assent to "That is gricular" without also assenting to "That is not gricular (in another sense)"; this excludes the possibility that "gricular" is ambiguous as between "green" and "circular." Surely, any principle of charity would eventually have to assign to their language the truth-conditions I was imagining.

There may be an impulse to resist this point with respect to Contacti. Imagine people who utter sentences that, in accordance with the standard principle of charity, would be interpreted as having the truth-conditions stipulated for Contacti. Might we not say instead that they are speaking ordinary English but have crazy views about how things causally interact during contact, which leads to other crazy views about "transmigration of entity-souls" during contact, or some such thing? I can see no reason why we should be tempted to abandon standard charity to this extent. But I think the question might be put to rest decisively by the following consideration: We can *ask* them whether they have any such crazy views. Of course, we will then have to interpret their answers, but we can surely imagine answers of a sort that would provide overwhelming evidence that they are speaking Contacti rather than English. Suppose, for example, that they—or the philosophers in their midst—spell out the whole story at the level of stage-talk, and that this story sounds exactly like what we—or our philosophers—would say in terms of stage-talk. Then they obviously hold no crazy views, and it is just their language that is strange.

It is essential in this connection to bear in mind how the perspective of the division problem differs from that of other problems often treated in the literature. In imagining the strange languages, we allow for various *asymmetries* between ordinary utterances and strange utterances, and these asymmetries may provide decisive clues that we are in fact dealing with strange languages. Where we project "green," they project not "gricular," but "gricular and grincular." Green things strike us as more similar to each other than to other things, but gricular things do not strike them that way. Where we predict that a dog's intrinsic properties are likely not to change precipitously, they make no such predictions about cdogs. We, or at least the inegalitarians among us, say that dogs are genuine entities, but they have no inclination to assign any such special status to cdogs. Needless to say, these asymmetries may strike us as quite absurd, for reasons that the division principles purport to explain.

This point can be underscored by contrasting the treatment of the Grue example in the context of the division problem with its treatment in Shoemaker's well-known paper "On Projecting the Unprojectible."[39] He argues that (for complicated reasons that I will not attempt to summarize) one cannot coherently imagine a case in which people systematically project "grue" in a manner paralleling our ordinary projection of "green." Either they must really be speaking an ordinary language (with "grue" meaning "green") or some asymmetry must appear between their projective policies and ours.[40] If Shoemaker is right, he has shown that a certain version of the Grue example—a version without asymmetries—is impossible. This may go far toward answering some of Goodman's questions about the projectibility of "grue." But it would not touch the question that primarily concerns me: the question why it seems absurd to speak the Grue language without projecting "grue."

---

[39]Shoemaker 1975.
[40]See especially ibid., pp. 196–98.

It follows from what I have just been saying that I do not regard the various constraints on reference schemes as imposing any limits on possible *truth-conditional descriptions* of languages. Given a reference scheme, we can form the equivalence class of schemes truth-conditionally equivalent to it. Any scheme within the same equivalence class determines the same truth-conditional description of a language. The constraints on reference schemes tell us how to choose the correct scheme from within an equivalence class. The constraints do not tell us that we must sometimes discard as impossible a whole equivalence class of schemes, and thereby discard as impossible a truth-conditional description. This is what we would be doing if we claimed that the Gricular language and Contacti are not possible languages.

I remarked earlier that the constraints on reference schemes might be taken to imply that Pseudo-English and Pseudo-Contacti are not possible languages. But we can see now that it would be misguided to conclude that, since we already have arguments against the possibility of these languages, arguments against the possibility of the Gricular language and Contacti cannot be far behind. The cases are essentially different. In saying that Pseudo-English is impossible, we do not claim that a certain truth-conditional description is impossible. We only claim that the reference scheme implied by the name Pseudo-English is incorrect and must be replaced by the reference scheme implied by the name English. In a sense, we are saying that Pseudo-English is English but is being misdescribed. But if we tried to claim that the Gricular language or Contacti is impossible, we would not merely be saying that a language is being misdescribed in terms of the wrong reference scheme. We would be saying that a certain truth-conditional description cannot possibly apply. The attempt to find arguments in defense of such a claim is the task projected for chapter 6, and that task ought to appear daunting.

But before turning to this, I want to consider in the next chapter a pragmatic response to the division problem.

5

The Pragmatic Response

1. *Extreme Relativism versus Pragmatism*

Extreme relativism was defined in section 1.5 as the view that the strange languages are as reasonable and good as ordinary languages, even for people in essentially our life situation. It should now be clear that this view with respect to the division problem need not imply any form of relativism with respect to various other issues of metaphysics or epistemology. An extreme relativist may be a staunch metaphysical inegalitarian, and may also regard the projectibility of terms as a function of how they relate to objectively natural properties and things. One is an extreme relativist in the intended sense only because one rejects any division principle. I will sometimes use "extreme *division* relativist" to emphasize this point.

This extreme position must be distinguished from the pragmatic response to the division problem. I want to isolate in this chapter a *pure* pragmatic response, as opposed to various eclectic positions that may attempt to mix (and may therefore easily confuse) pragmatic and nonpragmatic arguments. Both extreme relativism and pure pragmatism eschew arguments for division principles which rely essentially on considerations of metaphysics or epistemology. But the latter position accepts some division principles that rely on pragmatic considerations. The view would then be that there is a rationale for our division practices, but these are entirely of a practical nature. As before, it is essential to be clear that our "division pragmatist" need not be a pragmatist about any other issues of truth or knowledge. Division pragmatists may in fact accept all of the division principles formulated in chapters 2 through 4, but, if so, they defend these principles with purely pragmatic arguments.

I think that many people will consider it immediately evident that there are pragmatic reasons for us not to use the strange languages, and would assume that the only serious question is whether there are also other kinds of reasons. I believe that this attitude is mistaken. However, a major part of the issue here consists in clarifying what qualifies as a "pragmatic argument" against the strange languages.

I take the pragmatist to be attempting to interpret and defend our initial intuition about the strange languages. The initial intuition says that these languages are in some sense bad. The pragmatist attempts to defend the intuition at least on its minimal interpretation: The languages must be bad at least for people who are essentially in our life situation. And this is because the languages could not work well for such people; they would not be practical; they would lead to people's desires not being adequately satisfied.

An essential point is that certain kinds of doctrines of cognitive psychology cannot provide pragmatists with the argument they seek. Suppose there were a doctrine saying that human beings are innately disposed to use languages containing projectible words, or words denoting similarity classes of predictable things, or words representing objectively natural properties and things; suppose, that is, the doctrine said that humans are innately disposed to use languages satisfying the previous division principles. The doctrine might even imply that if we tried to raise our children on the strange languages, they would become mentally retarded or suffer other forms of cognitive disorder. Then, it might be said, speaking the strange languages obviously could not work for us.

But this must not count as a genuine pragmatic argument against the strange languages. For there is no argument here suggesting why people in our life situation could not fare well with the strange languages, so long as their cognitive dispositions were different from ours. Certainly the initial intuition, which the division pragmatist is attempting to defend, says at a minimum that it would be bad for people in our life situation to have cognitive structures that lead to their employing the strange languages. Therefore, simply to say "We are cognitively structured not to employ the strange languages," and to leave it at that, is to accept extreme relativism. Extreme relativism, in the relevant sense, can thus be combined with various *innatist* doctrines about our division practices. An extreme relativist need not be a *conventionalist* about these practices, where conventionalism implies not only that there are no arguments against employing the strange languages in our life situation but also that we are not innately disposed against employing them. Assuming the truth of innatism, the issue between the extreme relativist and the pragmatist is whether there is any pragmatic virtue to our possessing innate cognitive structures that disincline us to use the strange languages.[1]

---

[1]The issue between the extreme relativist and the pragmatist must not be conflated with the famous question over Whorfian "linguistic relativity." The latter is essentially the question whether (or to what extent) there are universal or innate division tendencies. Both the Whorfian and the anti-Whorfian seem typically to take it for granted that there are pragmatic arguments in behalf of the division practices operative in a given culture. Furthermore, it is doubtful that the alien languages described by Whorf qualify as "strange languages" in the sense of the present discussion. See, e.g., Rosch 1977a and 1977b and Tversky 1977.

Another rather clear example of what I would regard as a pseudo-pragmatic argument against strangeness is one that derives from a certain sense of the doctrine that we have an innate quality space or innate sense of similarity. Recall my distinction between three senses of "sense of similarity" in section 2.2.b. If the claim is that we have an innate sense of similarity in the sense of innate projective tendencies, or in the sense of innate tendencies to make certain similarity judgments, then one obviously still needs a pragmatic argument to show why such tendencies should lead to ordinary languages rather than strange ones; that is, one still needs a pragmatic argument in support of the Projectibility or Similarity Principle. It is far from obvious what such arguments could be. (I will consider a few pragmatic arguments related to projectibility later in this chapter.) But suppose the claim is that we have an innate sense of similarity in the sense of an innate tendency to group certain things but not others under a common word. Then the argument is in effect: "We are cognitively structured not to use the strange languages; therefore, it is good for us not to use the strange languages." This is vacuous.

It is true, however, that the notion of "our life situation," which is being used to explicate the minimal interpretation of the initial intuition, is not completely clear, and whether we have a genuine pragmatic argument against strangeness will depend in some cases on how one sees fit to clarify this notion. Let me first give an abstract characterization of such cases, before turning to illustrations.

The pragmatist wants to find some feature F of our life situation such that it is substantively (non-vacuously) correct to claim that people whose lives have F should not use the strange languages. The claim must be substantive; otherwise, it could not capture the initial intuition, which seems clearly to be substantive. This is why F cannot simply include the fact that we are disposed not to use the strange languages, for then it would be utterly vacuous to say that people with F should not use the strange languages. Surely that vacuity is not the initial intuition. The pragmatist thus seeks a feature F that is related in the following way to our disposition not to use the strange languages: F must not be so close to this disposition as to seem to render the initial intuition vacuous, but F must be close enough to the disposition to sustain it pragmatically. Certain cases may occur in which it is unclear whether F is too close, or unclear whether F is close enough.

In section 1.5, I defined "our life situation" in terms of four kinds of ingredients: (1) the descriptive content of our language, (2) our physical environment and physical capacities, (3) our sensory apparatus, and (4) our motives and beliefs. My assumption was that if the pragmatist can find an appropriate feature F, it will be located within these four ingredients. I assumed, that is, that the initial intuition implies at a minimum that people whose lives contain (1) through (4) should not employ the strange languages. That assumption may be questioned in some cases;

arguably, some other kind of pragmatically relevant feature may show up. But that feature must not be too closely identified with the very disposition against strangeness which it is alleged to justify. In the next section, I will try to illustrate some of these issues by looking at a couple of pragmatic arguments involving the notion of "salience."

2. Salience

a. Salience and Ostensive Learning

Argument I

1. Many ordinary properties such as Green and Circular are innately salient for us.[2]

2. Such properties as Gricular and Grincular are not innately salient for us.

3. Other things being equal, it is harder to ostensively learn to use words that express properties that are not innately salient than to ostensively learn to use words that express properties that are innately salient.

4. Therefore, it would be harder, other things being equal, for us to ostensively learn strange words like "gricular" and "grincular" than to ostensively learn ordinary words like "green" and "circular."

5. Therefore, an ordinary language is, other things being equal, pragmatically better than a strange language like the strong Gricular language.

Argument I is confined to the strong version of the Gricular language because in the weak version there would be no need to learn "gricular" ostensively. Our innate sense of salience is functioning in the argument as the relevant feature F. Is this a successful pragmatic argument against strangeness? Let us accept 1 and 2 as empirical truths. It seems fairly plausible, I think, to accept 3 as a kind of a priori truth—properties that are less salient are less readily observed, hence their connection to the utterance of words are less readily observed. Certainly 1 through 3 entail 4. And it may seem that 4 entails 5.

One potential problem with the argument is that the feature of innate salience may seem too close to our propensity to eschew strangeness. A property P is said to be salient to the extent that:

- We tend to perceive the presence of P.
- We tend to perceive something as having P.
- We tend to judge on the basis of sense experience that something has P.

[2]See Quine 1973, pp. 24–27; Rosch 1977a, pp. 9–18.

- We tend to assert on the basis of sense experience that something has P.
- We tend to assert on the basis of sense experience a sentence in which a term that expresses P is applied to something.

If we allow ourselves to slide down this series of explications of salience, we wind up saying at the end that the relative salience of the property Green as compared to Gricular is a function of our propensity to make perceptual judgments or assertions applying a term for Green rather than a term for Gricular. This seems very close to saying that we are cognitively disposed not to employ any such word as "gricular." There is, to be sure, a distinction between saying, "We are cognitively disposed not to have a word for Gricular" and saying, "We are cognitively disposed not to apply a (simple or complex) term for Gricular to a perceived object." The latter statement implies that Gricular is non-salient and the former statement is what we want a pragmatic justification for. Still, the connection here is rather tight. And it seems, therefore, to border on vacuity to say that people with our innate sense of salience should not employ the strange languages. Argument I seems only to shift us slightly from the question "Why would it be bad to have a word for Gricular?" to "Why would it be bad for Gricular to be salient?" In the absence of an answer to the second question, it seems that little has really been done to answer the first question, or to sustain the initial intuition.

It may be worth trying to reformulate the "too close" objection to Argument I, since this general form of objection is critical to my anti-pragmatist stance in this chapter. Let us ask which of the following claims the division pragmatist is making:

> (i) It would be pragmatically bad for people, otherwise like us, to employ the strange languages if they are cognitively disposed to employ ordinary languages, but there need be nothing bad about their employing the strange languages if they are cognitively disposed to employ such languages.

> (ii) It would be pragmatically bad for people, otherwise like us, to employ the strange languages if they have our ordinary sense of salience, but there need be nothing bad about their employing the strange languages if they have a correspondingly strange sense of salience.

> (iii) It would be pragmatically bad for people, otherwise like us, to employ the strange languages, and bad for them to be cognitively disposed to employ such languages, and bad for them to have a correspondingly strange sense of salience.

It seems immediately clear that the division pragmatist is not saying (i). Division pragmatism is (by definition) an attempt to defend at least our minimal intuitions about the strange languages. Surely those intuitions extend at least to saying that it would be somehow absurd for people, otherwise like us, to be cognitively disposed to employ the strange languages. Now, if we accept the series of explications of salience, our ordinary sense of salience must be viewed as essentially an aspect of our disposition to think and speak in ordinary ways. (ii) seems, therefore, very close to (i), and seems no more intuitively plausible than (i). Division pragmatists must be claiming (iii). But then they obviously cannot present an argument that appeals to our ordinary sense of salience.

The "too close" objection arises if we allow ourselves to slide down the series of explications of salience. Suppose, instead, that we try to reject these explications. Perhaps we take salience to involve "perceiving the presence of *P*" in some narrowly behavioral or even physiological sense. Then the feature of salience seems too far away from our anti-strangeness propensities, for it is not clear how any narrowly interpreted behavioral or physiological propensity could pragmatically support any fact about the structure of our language.[3]

Before going on, let us note that Argument I may also apply to cases of individuative strangeness. This would obviously be so if it is correct to say that ordinary individuative properties like Dog and Table are innately salient for us, whereas strange individuative properties like Cdog and Ctable are not. Even if this contrast at the level of individuative properties could not be sustained, psychologists talk not only about the innate salience of properties but also about the innate salience of things.[4] If ordinary things like dogs and tables are innately salient for us, but strange things like cdogs and ctables are not, this seems sufficient to apply Argument I to individuative strangeness. In place of step 3, we would now have the plausible claim that, other things being equal, it is harder to ostensively learn to use words that denote things that are not innately salient than to ostensively learn to use words that denote things that are innately salient. But the application of Argument I to the individuative case seems even more vulnerable to the "too close" objection. For it is difficult to formulate any narrowly physiological or behavioral notion of salience which could make sense of the claim that the dog Fido is more salient than the cdog Cfido. This claim seems clearly to invoke conceptual or linguistic propensities, such as the propensity to employ a term that denotes Fido rather than a term that denotes Cfido.

There is another serious problem with Argument I, which already came out in my discussion of ostensive learning in section 2.3. In fact, statement 5 of the argument does not follow from statement 4 unless

---

[3]On the narrow interpretation, Argument I fails because Premise 3 will be at most a contingent fact of human psychology. Hence, Premise 3 will be unable to support the general claim that, if people have our ordinary sense of salience, they ought to employ ordinary languages: this will depend on what their cognitive dispositions are like. (And, again, it is vacuous to add that, if they are cognitively disposed to employ ordinary languages, they ought to employ ordinary languages.)

[4]For a classic discussion, see Kohler 1947, pp. 136–205. See also Hirsch 1982, chapter 8.

one has the additional premise that such words as "green" and "gricular" are to be learned ostensively. The argument does not apply, therefore, to any imaginable language (such as, perhaps, a non-public language of thinking) in which words are not learned ostensively. Now it might be answered that the pragmatically relevant feature *F* required for Argument I consists of the salience of certain properties in conjunction with the fact that we do need to learn such words as "green" ostensively; it is that complex feature of our life situation which provides the pragmatic rationale for our eschewal of strangeness. But, as I pointed out in section 2.3, this answer implies that the badness of the strange languages is essentially due to the difficulty in acquiring them rather than something bad about possessing them. And this, it seems to me, does very little justice to the initial intuition.

b. Salience and Perceptual Speed

There is a second version of an argument from salience worth looking at. It avoids the acquisition-possession problem just mentioned but highlights even further the "too close" problem.

Argument II

1. Many ordinary properties such as Green and Circular are innately salient for us.

2. Such properties as Gricular and Grincular are not innately salient for us.

3. Therefore, in the presence of a green object, we have the innate capacity to be able to judge that the object is green prior to the time that we are able to judge that the object is gricular, and prior to the time that we are able to judge that the object is grincular.

4. Therefore, in the presence of a green object, we have the innate capacity to be able to assert "The object is green" prior to the time that we are able to assert "The object is gricular and grincular."

5. Therefore, in the presence of a green object, we have the innate capacity to be able to make an assertion in English prior to the time that we are able to make any equivalent assertion in the Gricular language.

I will not draw the argument to its conclusion, but I assume there is some plausible way of maintaining that it is pragmatically virtuous to be able to make assertions as quickly as possible about what one perceives.

The tricky step in this argument is the move from 3 to 4. I am now assuming that the notion of salience applies in the first instance to (coarse-grained) conditions, either of things or of the world. (I will question this assumption later.) Since equivalent terms express the same condition, one might initially have supposed that we could in principle learn to perceptually ascribe any pair of equivalent terms with the same degree of speed, so that at any moment when we are able to assert in English, "The object is green," we would be able to assert in the Gricular language the equivalent sentence, "The object is gricular and grincular." However, the move from 3 to 4 seems to show that this is not so. To assert the sentence in the Gricular language would seem to imply that we are judging the object to be gricular (to assert a conjunction would seem to imply that we judge each conjunct to hold). But, by 3, we may be unable to judge that the object is gricular at the time when we first judge it to be green. So 4 does indeed seem to follow.

The move from 3 to 4 depends upon the condition that the equivalent of the ordinary word "green" in the strange language is a conjunction. It is, therefore, not obvious how to generalize Argument II to strange languages that do not fit this condition (for example, "grue" is equivalent not to an ordinary conjunction but to an ordinary disjunction). Another limitation of Argument II is that it (like Argument I) can work only against a strong version of the Gricular language, in which "gricular" would have to be used in perceptual assertions. (If speakers of a weak version used "green" in perceptual assertions, there is nothing in Argument II to show that it need be bad for them to use "gricular" in some other contexts.)

The fundamental weakness in the argument, however, is the "too close" problem. Obviously Argument II is at least as vulnerable to the "too close" objection as Argument I was, but a further point now emerges. Earlier I noted that there seems to be a close connection between

(a) the propensity to have words for a particular set of properties

and

(b) the propensity to make perceptual assertions in which terms for a particular set of properties are applied to things.

It now seems to emerge that the connection here is indeed so close that, as a matter of a priori necessity, certain (a)-propensities must go together with certain (b)-propensities. Suppose that people have the ordinary (b)-propensity to make perceptual assertions applying terms for Green but not terms for Gricular. Then it follows a priori that they cannot possibly have the strange (a)-propensity to employ the (strong) Gricular language. For the strange (a)-propensity would require them to apply the word "gricular" in expressing the perception of a green object, and this is precluded by the ordinary (b)-propensity. It is clear at least in this kind of case that one cannot justify the (a)-propensity by appealing to the existence of the (b)-propensity. Rather, in asking for a justification of either propensity, one is at the same time asking for a justification of the other.

I have been assuming that the notion of salience applies to conditions, either of things or of the world. Might one hold instead that it applies to fine-grained properties or propositions? If so, one might attempt to simplify Argument II (and to bypass the tricky move from 3 to 4). The idea would be that the relative non-salience of the fine-grained property of being gricular and grincular (or of the fine-grained proposition that a presented object is gricular and grincular) directly implies that we can more readily make the ordinary perceptual assertion "The object is green" than the strange equivalent assertion "The object is gricular and grincular." A corresponding argument would apply to Grue or to any other strange language. But it seems all too clear that salience in this fine-grained sense is virtually indistinguishable from the anti-strangeness propensity it is being invoked to justify. We surely have no serious pragmatic argument that simply takes us from the premise "We are innately disposed in perceptual situations not to express the fine-grained propositions expressible in the strange languages" to the conclusion "We should in general eschew the strange languages."

c. The Salience Principle

Arguments I and II suggest the following division principle:

> *The Salience Principle.* A general word ought to express a salient property and denote salient things.

In Arguments I and II, reference was made to innate salience, but it is surely not plausible to suppose that all, or even most, ordinary words express properties that are innately salient.[5] Salience, however, may be acquired as well as innate. Moreover, the notion of salience need not be restricted to perceptual situations; properties may be salient in the more general sense of being properties that we tend to pay attention to, either in perception or in thought. It may be quite plausible to suppose that virtually all ordinary words express properties that are significantly salient in this general sense, at least as compared to the non-salience of properties expressed by words of the strange languages. So it may well be that ordinary languages satisfy the Salience Principle to a much higher degree than the strange languages do.

Arguments I and II, adapted to salience in the general sense, might be used to defend the principle, at least in some of its applications. We have seen that both arguments are open to the "too close" objection. The objection will evidently be heightened for salience in the general sense, since it seems even more obvious that the latter is closely connected to our conceptual and linguistic resources. This objection challenges not the truth of the Salience Principle, but its effectiveness in

---

[5]It may, however, be plausible to suppose that most ordinary words denote things that are innately salient, since any ordinary body, for instance, might be said by gestalt psychologists to be innately salient to a significant degree (at least as compared to strange things such as cdogs).

sustaining our intuitions about the strange languages. Apart from this fundamental objection to Arguments I and II, the arguments were also seen to be restricted in certain ways. These restrictions render the arguments incapable of sustaining the truth of the Salience Principle in all of its applications (e.g., as it applies to words in weak strange languages). So these arguments do not seem to support either the effectiveness of the Salience Principle in sustaining our intuitions or its truth in all relevant applications.

These reactions to Arguments I and II and to the Salience Principle illustrate the dialectic between the extreme division relativist and the division pragmatist. A spectrum of positions runs from the former extreme to the most optimistic versions of the latter. If one reacts to Arguments I and II by saying, "There is nothing here to support the intuitive feeling that the strange languages are absurd," then one is, so far, an extreme relativist. A somewhat less extreme reaction would be that the arguments may support our intuitive feelings a bit, but not much. To get to the optimistic pragmatic end of the scale, one's reaction would have to be something like this: "There is nothing very counterintuitive here at all, for the arguments show why the strange languages are absurd just as we intuitively think." I doubt that this latter reaction ought to tempt anyone with respect to Arguments I and II. I will henceforth use "relativism" *simpliciter* to mark a position at the less optimistic end of the scale (even if not at the "extreme" end). So my conclusion thus far is that Arguments I and II do not offer a successful pragmatist rebuttal of relativism.

3. Important Properties and Things

The feature of our life situation that is pragmatically most central is our motivational tendencies. One might hope to find a pragmatic argument propelled by that feature. And it may seem obvious that there is such an argument. When we compare the properties and things represented by the words of ordinary languages with those represented by the words of the strange languages, do we not see that the former properties and things are the ones that matter to us, that interest us, that we care about, that are in one way or another *important* to us? Many people will, I think, find the following division principle immediately convincing:

> *The Importance Principle.* A general word ought to express an important property and denote important things.[6]

I shall argue that this principle is highly problematical, and in two separate ways. One problem is to explain what is meant by an "impor-

---

[6]Variations of the Importance Principle seem to be implicit in many discussions. See James 1890, pp. 284–90; Lewis 1929, pp. 49–52; Hampshire 1959, pp. 20–21; Shoemaker 1963, pp. 37–38.

tant" property or thing. The other is to defend the normative claim made by the principle. Let me begin by discussing the second problem.

a. Importance and Salience

There is a peculiar temptation, I think, to suppose that the pragmatic virtue alleged by the Importance Principle is self-evident. The principle might be put in the form "It is important for words to represent what is important," and that may seem virtually tautologous. But it is not, of course. If we spoke the strange languages, important properties and things might have to be represented by complex expressions rather than by words. One needs a careful argument to explain why that would be pragmatically worse.

One argument might be that if words rather than expressions represent what is important to us, this enables us to say in fewer words what it is important to us to say. This argument points to considerations of economy, which I will take up in the next section.

There is another argument that I think has some interest. We may attempt to defend the Importance Principle by connecting the notion of importance to the notion of salience and then relying on the Salience Principle. An argument might run as follows:

Argument III

1. The Salience Principle.

2. It is pragmatically good that all salient properties and things should be important to us.

3. Therefore, the Importance Principle.

Statement 3 does seem to follow from 1 and 2. If a general word ought to express a salient property and denote salient things, and if salient properties and things ought to be important to us, then a general word ought to express an important property and denote important things.

Premise 2 may initially seem plausible. If a property or thing is salient, we more readily notice it, and hence more readily remember it and think about it. It may seem obvious that we are better off if we more readily notice what is important to us rather than what is not important to us.

It may be supposed that Argument III, because it presupposes the Salience Principle, will inherit all of the problems of Arguments I and II if the latter are used to defend the Salience Principle. But this is not so. The most fundamental problem for those arguments was that, even if the Salience Principle is shown to be true, the principle does not effectively support our anti-strangeness propensity because our ordinary sense of salience is too close to that propensity. But that problem does not apply to Argument III. Assuming that the Salience Principle is true, and that Premise 2 is true, we wind up supporting our anti-strangeness propensity by appeal to the motivational tendencies that define what is important to us. This gives us just the right kind of pragmatic argument.

Arguments I and II were indeed restricted in various ways (e.g., as applying only to strong strange languages), and these restrictions may be inherited by Argument III. But I want to show that the argument fails in a more fundamental way.

There are a number of serious but easily missed problems with Premise 2 of the argument. To begin with, the premise says that it is good for all salient properties and things to be important. What really seems plausible, if anything, is the converse: that it is good for all important properties and things to be salient. The former premise implies, not very plausibly, that it is good for us not to notice any unimportant properties and things, whereas the latter implies, more plausibly, that it is good for us to notice any important ones. But the latter could not get us from Premise 1, that it is good for any general word to represent a salient property and salient things, to the conclusion, that it is good for any general word to represent an important property and important things. (One might be tempted to try to derive the converse of the Importance Principle, namely, that any important property or thing ought to be represented by a general word, from the converse of Premise 2 in conjunction with the converse of the Salience Principle, namely, that any salient property or thing ought to be represented by a general word. But these converse principles seem to have no initial plausibility, and certainly the converse of the Salience Principle is not supported by Arguments I and II.)

b. Which Properties Are Important?

There are deeper difficulties with Premise 2 but, before I can explain these, I must first turn to the other general problem for the Importance Principle. This is the problem of understanding what can be the relevant notion of an "important" property or thing. In order for the principle to justify our anti-strangeness propensity, it must be possible to say that the properties and things represented by ordinary words are more important to us than those represented by the words of the strange languages. I believe that there is in fact no relevant sense in which this is so.

Let me begin by discussing the case of properties. One preliminary point is critical. I am assuming that the Importance Principle is not simply to throw us back to previous principles, such as the Projectibility or Joints Principle. We are not allowed to say that a property is important simply because it is (expressed by a term that is) projectible or simply because it is natural. Rather we are now looking for a sense of "important property" which relates to human concerns other than seeking knowledge or explanations.

We do sometimes talk of properties being important to us. For instance, humor is important to me. By this I seem roughly to mean that, other things being equal, it is better for me that there be people around with humor rather than without humor. Reliability in appliances is important to me, by which I seem roughly to mean that it is better for me that appliances that I own be reliable rather than not. Illness is important to me, by which I seem roughly to mean that it is worse for me that certain people be ill rather than they not be. These examples suggest the following rough definition:

> The property *P* is important to person *x* at time *t* if and only if it is better (or worse) for *x* at *t* that certain things should have *P* rather than not.

A property might then be said to be important in general to the degree that it is important to many people at many times. Notice that we are not here distinguishing between intrinsic and instrumental importance. That distinction could be made by qualifying the word "better," as intrinsic or instrumental, in the definiens.

This definition is deliberately ambiguous in a certain respect. The expression "it is better that certain things should have *P* rather than not" has two readings. The first is "it is better, with respect to certain things, that those things should have *P* rather than that they should not have *P*." The second is "it is better that there should exist things having *P* rather than that there should not exist such things."

If the Importance Principle is to work, we must be able to say that properties expressed by ordinary nouns are important. However, many of these properties are essential to the things that have them. Therefore, it is not clearly meaningful to say, for example, that it is better, with respect to certain things, that those things should be apples rather than that they should not be apples. In such cases, we can fall back on the second reading: It is better that there should exist apples rather than that there should not exist apples. Or perhaps even in such examples we could squeeze in the first reading: It is better that those things should be apples rather than not apples, in the sense that it is better that those things should exist rather than not exist.

I am not going to attempt to sharpen this notion of an "important property." I think it is clear enough that the notion is ordinarily used only in highly restricted examples. Moreover, as I will argue more fully in what follows, any attempt to generalize from such examples in behalf of the Importance Principle should not depart in any crucial way from the rough suggestions I have made.

Let us compare now the importance of Green and Gricular. If I want to eat a banana, then it may be worse for me that it be green rather than not green. Since a banana, being non-circular, is (as a matter of physical necessity) green if and only if it is gricular, it is equally worse for me that it be gricular rather than not gricular. This reasoning will not apply to every case. If I want to go through a (round) traffic light, it is better for me that it be green rather than not green. But I cannot say that it is better for me that it be gricular rather than not gricular, for it must always be gricular, even when it is red. What I can say in this case, however, is that it is better for me that it be grincular rather than not grincular.

It seems, then, that in many though not all cases Gricular is as important as Green. By the same token, there are many cases in which Gricular is as important as Circular. If we count up all those cases (all the cases in which either Green is important or Circular is important and Gricular is also important), it seems not unlikely that Gricular is important in *more* cases than Green or in more cases than Circular. It seems untenable, in the face of these observations, to maintain that Green and Circular are important but Gricular is not.

Since I expect this conclusion to strike some people as surprising, let me reinforce it by considering another kind of example. We recall that "carple" applies to anything that is either a car or an apple. I think it seems almost immediately obvious that the property Carple must be at least as important to us as either the property Car or the property Apple. Assuming that it is better for us that certain things should be cars and better for us that certain things should be apples, surely it is better for us that certain things should be carples.

Consider, indeed, the following list of terms:

car or apple or ocean

car or apple

apple

ripe apple

big ripe apple

This is a list of increasingly informative terms. There seems to be a temptation to suppose that only the last three terms on the list express properties of practical importance. Reflection seems to reveal, however, that this temptation is misguided. The first two properties seem on reflection at least as important as the others.[7]

Part of the confusion here may stem from the following argument: "If a property is important, this must be because of its effects. But only natural properties have causal powers. Therefore, unnatural properties can have no importance." This argument does not simply equate importance with naturalness, which I warned against earlier, but attempts to argue for a necessary connection between the two notions.

However, the causally loaded notion of importance offered up by the argument cannot be the notion that is relevant to the Importance Principle. In section 3.4, I did not oppose the view that only natural properties can rightly be said to have causal powers. But I stressed there that even unnatural properties have *nomic consequences*, for they figure in

---

[7]That is, on the assumption that Apple is no more important than Car or Ocean. It seems that a disjunction of properties is at least as important as the least important disjunct.

physical necessities as much as natural properties do. Very roughly, causality equals physical necessity plus naturalness. Only the physical necessity part of this equation has pragmatic significance. Naturalness as such has no pragmatic significance; nor, therefore, does causality as such. Pragmatically speaking, all that matters to me is a property's nomic consequences; whether these be called "effects" or not is irrelevant. It is a property's nomic consequences that determine whether it is better or worse for me that things have the property. The nomic consequences make a property "important" to me in the only sense that can relate to the Importance Principle. The pragmatist intuition behind this principle is that my words ought to express properties such that it matters to my well-being whether things have those properties. This is the notion of an "important" property which my earlier definition brought out. That seems to be the correct definition for the purposes at hand.

Ultimately, of course, the question is which definition of importance has a better chance to sustain the Importance Principle. In fact, I think it doubtful that the principle can be sustained in any fashion. However, the causally loaded definition abandons the principle from the start by bringing in metaphysical factors that have no pragmatic relevance.

c. The Attention Claim

Nothing that I have said implies that there is no distinction between (relatively) important and unimportant properties. The difficulty for the Importance Principle is, rather, that this distinction seems not even remotely to correspond to the distinction between ordinary and strange words. A question that is worth considering in its own right is what the connection is between importance and salience. I have already questioned the direction of that connection in Premise 2 of Argument III. But let us now consider the connection in the most favorable direction. We are considering the notion of salience in the most general sense in which it relates to our propensity to *pay attention to* something, where this propensity need not be innate or exercised in a perceptual situation. The question I want to consider is whether the following *attention claim* is correct:

> It is good for people to pay attention to any properties that are important to them.

The attention claim is to be understood as implying that, although there may be nothing bad about paying attention to unimportant properties, there is something especially good about paying attention to important ones. It seems clear that the Importance Principle tacitly derives from the attention claim by way of some steps that turn out on examination to be problematical. But let us put that principle aside for a moment and try to assess the attention claim itself.

I will assume that we "pay attention" to a property if and only if we tend to use a term that expresses the property. This would seem to be the notion of paying attention to a property that is most relevant to the issues being discussed.

The attention claim must be false if strange properties like Carple are important, since we evidently pay no attention to such properties, and it would seem absurd to suggest that we ought to. But I am afraid that some will take this to show that Carple is not really important. It is, therefore, worth considering what might be an argument for the attention claim.

One might reason as follows: "If a property P is important to us, it is better (or worse) for us that the condition obtain in which certain things have P. Certainly, we will often need to talk about this condition, to talk about how to bring it about (or avoid it). So we will often need to use a term for P; that is, we will need to pay attention to P."

But this argument is misguided, I think, in several ways. First of all, the world-condition that consists in certain things having P can be expressed in an indefinite number of ways. It need not be expressed by a sentence containing a term that expresses P. For instance, if the existence of apples is important to us, this condition could be expressed in the Carple language by saying, "Some carples are apceans" or by saying, "Not every carple is not an apcean" (where, we recall, "carple" applies to any car or apple and "apcean" applies to any apple or ocean). This seems to show that in principle the condition that consists in there existing apples can be expressed without paying any attention to the property of being an apple. Perhaps it is not entirely clear how to generalize this point to other kinds of examples. But there is a more decisive point to be made.

Let us say that a world-condition is important if it is better (or worse) that it obtain rather than not obtain. And let us say that we pay attention to a world-condition if we tend to utter sentences that express that condition. The point I have just made is that, if the existence of things having the property P is an important world-condition, we could pay attention to that world-condition without paying any attention to the property P. But the second and more fundamental point I want to make is that there is no pragmatic necessity to pay attention to important world-conditions. This point follows from many of the examples already considered. The existence of carples is evidently important to us (it is evidently better for us that this condition obtain rather than not), but we seem to have no reason to pay attention to the condition. It seems enough for us to pay attention to the existence of cars and the existence of apples.

What seems roughly correct is the following *entailment principle*:

> For any world-condition C, if C is important to people, it is good for them to pay attention to a set of conditions that necessarily entail C.

In other words, important conditions ought to be entailed by conditions paid attention to. Even this is probably too strong a requirement, but it seems to be roughly on the right track. This entailment principle does not imply that important world-conditions ought to be paid attention to; even less does it imply the attention claim (i.e., that important properties ought to be paid attention to); even less does it imply the converse of the attention claim (i.e., Premise 2 of Argument III, which says in effect that only important properties ought to be paid attention to); even less does it imply the Importance Principle (i.e., that only important properties ought to be expressed by words). The last seems to be several steps removed from anything that is genuinely plausible.

d. Attention and Projectibility

I stipulated that, in discussing the Importance Principle, we should not simply equate importance with projectibility. But I want to consider now how the notion of projectibility might relate to the principle via the attention claim. Let us say that a property is projectible if it is expressed by a projectible term. A modified version of the attention claim would be this:

> It is good for people to pay attention to any projectible properties.

The argument for this would be that unless people pay attention to projectible properties, they could not know that these properties are projectible and hence could not know which hypotheses to project. Moreover, projectible hypotheses include projectible terms, so that in stating these hypotheses one necessarily pays attention to projectible properties.

This argument fails, I think, for we could in principle pay attention exclusively to non-projectible properties and still rationally project hypotheses equivalent to the ones we ordinarily project. To illustrate this, let us say that two properties are "coprojectible" if their conjunction is projectible. Now consider an incompatibility language such as one in which "carple" applies to cars or apples, "apcean" applies to apples or oceans, "cubound" applies to things that are cubical or round, and "ronrical" applies to things that are round or cylindrical (so that "apple" is equivalent to "carple and apcean" and "round" is equivalent to "cubound and ronrical"). Note that "All things that are A and B are C" is equivalent to "All A are either C or non-B." Speakers of the language might be willing to project the sentence

H_1: All carples are either cubound or non-apceans

on the basis of observations of instances of "carple" that are instances of both "cubound" and "apcean," and to project the sentence

H_2: All carples are either ronrical or non-apceans

on the basis of observations of instances of "carple" that are instances of both "ronrical" and "apcean." When asked why they project these sentences in this manner, they (or their philosophers) reply, "Because the property Carple is coprojectible with the property Apcean, and the property Cubound is coprojectible with the property Ronrical." The rule they implicitly follow is this: "If P is coprojectible with Q, and R is coprojectible with S, project both 'All P are either R or non-Q' and 'All P are either S or non-Q' on the basis of, respectively, observations of instances of 'P' that are instances of both 'R' and 'Q', and observations of instances of 'P' that are instances of both 'S' and 'Q.'"[8] The conjunction of H_1 and H_2 is of course equivalent to

H_3: All things that are both carples and apceans are both cubound and ronrical,

which is in turn equivalent to "All apples are round." But speakers of the language might standardly favor H_1 and H_2 over H_3. Hence, they project hypotheses equivalent (in conjunction) to the ones we project, though they pay no attention to—they tend to use no terms that express—any projectible properties.

e. Important Things

In discussing the Importance Principle, I have focused primarily on the classificatory case rather than the individuative case. With respect to the latter case, we have the same two major problems: first, to explain what it can mean to say that strange things are less important to us than ordinary things and, second, to explain what the pragmatic virtue is of having words that denote important things. Though there are, perhaps, some new complications with regard to the first question, much of the previous discussion, especially with respect to the second question, carries over straightforwardly. I will, therefore, be brief.

What can it mean to say that some particular thing, say the car c, is important to me? Perhaps that it is better for me that c should (continue to) exist. If so, the Contacti-thing cc that generally coincides with c is also important, for c cannot exist unless cc does.[9]

Perhaps c is important because it has many important properties. But so, surely, does cc. Perhaps c is important because it has important individuative properties, notably the property Car. But I suppose that the Contacti individuative property Ccar is important too, for, as things are, there could not be cars unless there were ccars.

There is the following apparent difference between c and cc: I care about c's intrinsic properties at future times but not necessarily about

---

[8]As I indicate in appendix 1, the connection between projectible terms and projectible hypotheses is actually quite obscure. So, of course, is the equivalent connection between coprojectible pairs of terms and projectible hypotheses. The rule in the text may therefore require additional refinements.

[9]This has been my usual assumption about the relationship between Contacti-things and their ordinary correlates; see note 10 in section 1.2.a.

cc's. For instance, I do not care whether *cc* will have a scratch at any future time when it is in exclusive contact with another ccar (rather, I care about the ccar it will be in contact with). So it may be suggested that a thing is important only if its *intrinsic future* is important. But this seems to be a somewhat nebulous point. Really, I may not care even about *c*'s intrinsic future at times when I no longer own it, in which case the general contrast between my concern for *c* and my concern for *cc* is unclear.

I will not belabor this definition of "important thing" any further, because the question that anyway remains is what the pragmatic virtue is of having words denote important things. There does not even appear to be any definite pragmatic virtue in paying attention especially to important things, or in their being salient. (If paying attention to a property can be associated with the tendency to employ a term that expresses it, paying attention to a thing might be associated with the tendency to employ a singular term that denotes it.) Perhaps it is obvious that in *some* sense persons are more important to us than cpersons. But, as far as the present argument has gone, we can apparently imagine persons in our life situation who do perfectly well without paying any attention to persons, so long as they pay attention to suitable properties of cpersons.

f. Summary of the Argument Thus Far

Before going on, let me summarize the main points that emerge from the last two sections. We would have the right sort of pragmatic argument against strangeness if we could show that:

(a) it is good for words to represent salient properties and things,

in conjunction with

(b) it is good for salient properties and things to be important,

in conjunction with

(c) the properties and things represented by the strange words are not important.

We found a couple of qualified arguments for (a) but virtually no defense of (b) or (c). The pragmatic response, up to this point, does not seem credible.

4. Economy

a. The Economy Principle

It may still seem obvious that if we spoke the strange languages we could not express ourselves as economically as we do. The appeal now is to this division principle:

The Economy Principle. The words of a language ought to divide the world economically.

Throughout this discussion, we assume that the languages under consideration have the same descriptive content. The Economy Principle says that a given level of descriptive content should be achieved as economically as possible.

Let us distinguish between *type-economy* and *token-economy.* One language L_1 has more type-economy than another language L_2 if L_1 has fewer (general) word-types than L_2. L_1 has more token-economy than L_2 if speakers of L_1 can say what they want to say using fewer word-tokens than speakers of L_2 require in order to say what they want to say.

Two points should immediately be noted. First, the notion of type-economy must presuppose my stipulation in section 1.1 that "word" is to mean "word taken in a particular sense." Obviously, we do not want to count homonymy or ambiguity as a gain of economy. Second, there is the following difference between the two sorts of economy: whereas type-economy is an intrinsic property of a language, token-economy is a property relative to a given life situation within which people want to say certain things rather than others.

b. Economy and Incompatibility Languages

What may seem initially obvious (but will presently be questioned) is that the strange languages would have less token-economy than ordinary languages relative to our life situation. It needs to be stressed, however, that some strange languages are superior in type-economy.

We have already seen in a number of examples how incompatibility languages yield gains in type-economy (replacing three words by two words).[10] The general principle is the following:

> *The word-reduction principle.* For any set S_1 containing 2^n-1 mutually incompatible words, there is a set S_2 containing n words such that any word in S_1 is equivalent to an expression constructed out of words in S_2 (together with logical constants).[11]

The word-reduction principle makes it immediately difficult to see how the Economy Principle will support a pragmatic argument against incompatibility languages. Presumably, the relevant notion of economy must include both type and token considerations. The evidence that token-economy ordinarily counts for something is that it sometimes seems reasonable to introduce an abbreviation, thereby token-

[10]As I noted in section 1.4.a, some of the examples of incompatibility that I consider might have to be refined or qualified. I take this not to affect the overall thrust of my argument.

[11]A proof of this is given in my "Economy and Vocabulary Reduction" (unpublished manuscript).

economizing at the expense of type-economy. The evidence that type-economy ordinarily counts for something is that it sometimes seems reasonable *not* to token-economize by introducing an abbreviation (if type-economy counted for nothing, we ought to add abbreviations virtually without limit). So if economy is a pragmatic virtue, it evidently involves some kind of balancing between these two factors. Given the large number of mutually incompatible sets of words in ordinary language, a quite enormous gain in type-economy may be achieved by the incompatibility languages. There seems no evident basis to claim that, all things considered, those languages are less economical than ordinary ones.

One may be tempted to discount the type-economy that could be gained by incompatibility languages. Part of the reason for this may be the idea that it is too hard to learn words like "carple" and "apcean," and type-economy is a virtue only if it leads to greater ease of language acquisition. But, as I argued in section 2.3, if we can imagine people who naturally think in terms of "carple" and "apcean," the acquisition of these words may be quite simple for them. It seems clear at least that acquiring the two words "carple" and "apcean" need be no more difficult than acquiring the three words "car," "apple," and "ocean." The virtue of type-economy would have to do with the memory or storage of words, which ought (other things being equal) to be easier for two than for three.[12]

Here it is essential not to slip into the kind of pseudo-pragmatic argument discussed in the first section of this chapter. It may be obvious that, given our innate cognitive predisposition, we could gain nothing but headaches from using such words as "carple" and "apcean." The relevant question, however, is whether it would be pragmatically bad for people in our life situation to be predisposed to use such words. We are, of course, talking about strong versions of the incompatibility languages; weak versions would obviously yield no gain of type-economy. In imagining strong versions of a strange language, we imagine people for whom that is the only language; if they think in a language, they think in *that* language. These are not people who say the word "carple" and think "car or apple." It would appear that for such people to have the two words "carple" and "apcean," instead of our three words "car," "apple," and "ocean," would constitute a genuine gain of type-economy.

Slipping into the pseudo-pragmatic argument is related to another confusion that it is necessary to see through. It might be said that a word like "carple" cannot be type-economical because its meaning is complex, indeed as complex as that of "car or apple." Here one must distinguish between metaphysical (or logical) complexity and psychological (or semantic) complexity. As an inegalitarian, I would indeed say that the

---

[12]This must really be the virtue of type-economy in the ordinary case, since introducing an abbreviation imposes virtually no strain at all on (momentary) acquisition, but only a strain on memory.

property Carple is unnatural and, in that sense, metaphysically complex, being merely a disjunctive construction of the (more) natural properties Car and Apple. The pragmatist, I allowed, might be an inegalitarian. But the point is that no pragmatic argument flows from these metaphysical considerations. The fact that the property Carple is metaphysically more complex than the property Car does not obviously imply that understanding the word "carple" need be in any sense psychologically more complex an operation than understanding the word "car." The pragmatist must not say: "But the semantic rule for 'carple' is a complex rule relating that word to cars and apples." The only pragmatically relevant question is how the speakers of the language represent the rule to themselves, that is, how they express and think of the rule. And what we should be imagining is that the speakers express and think of the rule like this: "The word 'carple' stands for carples." This may be for them as psychologically simple as our rule for "car" is for us.

The pragmatist has no right to assume that it need be in any sense *harder* to think in terms of "carple" than in terms of "car." In the next chapter, I will be considering a view that it is metaphysically impossible (harder than hard) to think in terms of "carple." If we had such a metaphysical position at our disposal, we might still need a pragmatic argument to show why, for example, weak versions of strangeness are bad. But the "pure" pragmatic response we are examining in the present chapter obviously cannot depend upon any such metaphysical position.

To pursue this further, not only would the strange incompatibility languages type-economize but it is not even clear to what extent they would have to token-uneconomize. In virtually any case in which a carple is talked about, the physical or linguistic context is likely to make it clear whether the carple is also an apcean or not. We can even imagine the relevant context being described in terms of equally crazy disjunctive words. For instance, if a person drites (drives or writes) a carple, then it is clear that the carple must not be an apcean. Hence, it would suffice for me to say (and to think), "That person is driting a carple." This judgment might in turn justify the inference that the person had enckled (entered or suckled) the erage (eraser or garage), and so on. It seems that in many such ordinary cases a suitably constructed incompatibility language need not adversely affect token-economy.

Perhaps this point will not apply to more theoretical levels of discourse. This is not immediately clear. In any case, the possible absence of token-economy at the theoretical level does not have overriding importance. (Indeed, it may have little importance, as I will bring out later in this section.)

c. Scopes of Attention

The notion of token-economy in the Economy Principle may seem deceptively simple when actually it is fraught with many difficulties. The most general question to ask about it is this: Given a life situation S and a language L, what is it about the relationship between S and L that determines whether L will be token-economical in S? I can offer only a few fragmentary suggestions about this.

According to the "entailment principle" of the last section, people in S ought to express world-conditions that entail those that are important to them; that is, they ought to assert sentences that express such world-conditions. As noted before, not all important world-conditions tend to get expressed in a given language. For instance, English-speaking people in our life situation are not heard to say, "Cars or apples exist" or any equivalent sentence, though this expresses an important condition. A critical question is what determines which conditions ought to get expressed, in that there are obviously an indefinite number of sets of conditions that would entail the important ones. This question might be recast in slightly different terms. I have been assuming that people pay attention to conditions that they tend to express. We have a certain "scope of attention," this scope consisting of the conditions we tend to express. What determines this scope of attention?

Imagine people in our life situation who want to express every condition entailed by the conditions they express (that is, they want their scope of attention to be closed under entailment). If they start out expressing the conditions we do, they will also want to express the condition that someone drives or writes a car or apple, and the condition that certain things are green or non-circular, and the condition that a person with certain specified properties comes into exclusive contact with another person having certain other specified properties. Evidently, they could express these conditions more token-economically in the Carple language, or in the Gricular language, or in Contacti. This indicates that we can make no intuitive sense of the idea that ordinary language is more token-economical for them than various strange languages. To put it another way, we have no intuitive idea of how to assess the token-economy of the different languages relative to the totality of conditions entailed by those we express.[13] The notion of token-economy can be meaningfully applied only to people whose scope of attention is quantitatively restricted in some manner comparable to ours.

Even if people's scope of attention is restricted in this manner, we can imagine it to be very peculiar from our point of view. We can imagine people in our life situation whose scope of attention is such that relative to it Contacti, say, would be far more token-economical than English. The division pragmatist who appeals to token-economical con-

---

[13]Of course, I do not mean to deny that introducing abbreviations enhances token-economy even with respect to the totality of conditions. I mean only to deny that we can make an intuitive judgment about the relative token-economy of ordinary and strange languages with respect to the totality.

siderations must claim that such a scope of attention cannot be as *bene-ficial* as ours.

The pragmatist who appeals to the Economy Principle must there-fore be making the following claim:

> (C) If A_1 is our ordinary scope of attention, there cannot be people in our life situation whose scope of attention is A_2 (where A_2 may or may not be identical with A_1) such that A_2 is quantitatively restricted in a manner comparable to A_1, and A_2 is as beneficial as A_1, and the overall economy of some strange language relative to A_2 is as high as that of English relative to A_1.

In assessing the claim (C), it would be worthwhile to have a clear analysis, first, of what the nature is of the quantitative restrictions on our scope of attention and, second, what the criteria are for determin-ing how beneficial a scope of attention is. Unfortunately, I am unable to provide either of these. I did suggest, as one criterion for assessing the utility of a scope of attention, that it ought to entail important world-conditions, but it remains unclear what other criteria may be brought to bear on this assessment.

Intuitively, the claim (C) does appear to be correct with respect to some of the strange languages. Certainly it is hard to imagine a benefi-cial scope of attention in our life situation, which is quantitatively restricted in the ordinary manner, for which Contacti would have a com-petitive level of token-economy. (C) also seems to hold for the Gricular language, against which considerations of type-economy may also be brought to bear. Given that our scope of attention must be quantita-tively restricted to the degree that it is, English seems to be economi-cally better than both of these languages, in that it is better with respect to one dimension of economy without being worse in the other respect.

Nevertheless, (C) seems highly doubtful for incompatibility languages such as the Carple language. It seems that we can imagine a scope of attention A containing conditions about driting and carples and erages such that A is virtually as beneficial as our ordinary scope of attention, and such that the Carple language is not (much) less token-economical relative to A than English is relative to the ordinary scope. Furthermore, the (generalized) Carple language is far more type-economical than English. It appears that a pragmatist who relies on the Economy Prin-ciple might actually be led to argue that the incompatibility languages are *superior* to English for people in our life situation. I take this to be a kind of reductio ad absurdum of this form of pragmatism.

d. How Fundamental Is Economy?

If the Economy Principle threatens to lead to absurdity, we ought to begin to wonder whether there may be something inherently wrong with the idea of appealing to this principle in criticizing any of the strange languages. I suspect that economy in a language, whether of the type or token variety, is not that fundamental a virtue, at least within limits. In none of the strange languages under consideration are we talking about very great losses of type or token-economy. (Even Contacti may contain the notion of "contact-F," which would substantially ameliorate the token-uneconomical effect of the language.[14]) Relatively small differences may really not matter. Certainly, it seems to me unlikely, even apart from the conclusions it may imply with respect to the incompatibility languages, that the Economy Principle, taken by itself, could go very far toward substantiating our initial intuition about any of the strange languages. The intuition seems to be that these languages are somehow *absurd*. But that could not plausibly be because they require some extra word-types or word-tokens.

Consider that in English the word "puppy" expresses the property of being a young dog, but there is no (familiar) word that expresses the property of being an old dog. One may speculate that it is beneficial for us to pay somewhat more attention to the former property than to the latter, and that having a word for the former property is therefore somewhat more token-economical than having a word for the latter. But I doubt that anyone—at least after a bit of reflection—will want to suggest that it would be seriously irrational to have no word for either property, or to have words for both, or even to have a word for the latter but not the former. Even if there are many such examples in a language, I doubt that anyone who reflects on the matter will want to say that the language is irrational in any serious way. A division relativist might jump in here and say, "That's the way it is with our intuitions about the irrationality of the strange languages: on reflection they fade away." That is one view. My own inclination is to think that the intuitive absurdity of the strange languages remains vivid even after the most prolonged reflection. But if that is so, it probably has little or nothing to do with considerations of type or token-economy.

This point can be brought out in another way. We are all familiar with the fact that natural languages contain many peculiar quirks of spelling, or pronunciation, or syntax, or even lexicon. Some natural languages may have relatively few such quirks and may therefore be, in some rather straightforward sense, more efficient than various other languages that have significantly more quirks. This does not make us regard the latter languages as absurd, surely not in the sense in which we are inclined to regard the strange languages as absurd. To defend our intuitions about the strange languages (i.e., to reject division relativism) we must uncover a contrast between natural languages and the strange languages which is fundamentally different from any contrast that may exist between natural languages. It seems doubtful that considerations of economy can provide the required contrast.

[14]See section 4.3.a.

e. Stylistic Econony versus Inductive Simplicity

I mentioned a few paragraphs back that the incompatibility languages may be token-uneconomical in theoretical contexts. In fact, it seems often to be implied that in just such contexts token-economy counts for nothing. Goodman has discussed the economy of the primitives of a theory.[15] His view implies that if we have two sets of monadic terms applying to individuals then if the smaller set has the same defining power as the larger, it is the more economical primitive basis for a theory.[16] In other words,

> (G) If S_1 and S_2 are sets of monadic terms of lowest logical type and each term in S_2 is definable on the basis of terms in S_1, then, if S_1 has fewer members than S_2, S_1 is a more economical set of primitives than S_2.

It is clear that the notion of economy in (G) ignores token-economical consideration.

(G) is restricted to monadic terms of lowest logical type to avoid certain complications that I need not go into. But it is clear that if we confine ourselves to such terms, Goodman imposes no additional constraints on their content. He states explicitly that

> The number of words in the predicate and the complexity of what it expresses are not [relevant considerations]. For example, "P" and "Q" may be equally simple for our present purposes even if "P" means "is crimson" while "Q" means "is crimson and metallic and exhibits fluorescence in a degree equal to the square of its electric charge."[17]

Goodman evidently considers economy in the sense of (G) to be an important virtue of a set of primitives. In the light of the word-reduction principle, however, this is extremely doubtful. I think it possible that no theory in the history of the world has been put forth with a set of primitives satisfying the condition that no three of them be mutually incompatible. Certainly the vast majority of familiar sets of primitives seem to violate this condition. One need only think of the species of biology, the elements of chemistry, or the figures of geometry to get a sense of the pervasiveness of this. If economy in the sense of (G) were an important virtue then, given the word-reduction principle, the primitives in all of these theories could be improved in an important way. This seems implausible. Of course, I do not mean to imply that what is wrong with (G) is that it ignores token-economical considerations. Rather, I doubt that economy in any relevant sense is very important here.

---

[15]Goodman 1977, pp. 45–84; see also "The Test of Simplicity" and "Condensation versus Simplification" in Goodman 1972.

[16]See especially Goodman 1977, p. 49.

[17]Goodman 1977, pp. 48–49.

It must be stressed that neither the Economy Principle nor Goodman's (G) (as I am understanding it) pertains to the case in which the relative credibility of conflicting theories are assessed on the basis of considerations of "simplicity." Let us use "theory" in the coarse-grained sense, so that a given theory can be formulated in a number of ways. And let us distinguish between the "inductive simplicity" of a theory and the "stylistic economy" of how it is formulated. Type-economy and token-economy are two aspects of stylistic economy. Neither the credibility of a theory nor its inductive simplicity, upon which its credibility is based, can depend on how it is formulated. The inductive simplicity of a theory depends upon such considerations as the following:

- How many irreducibly new properties does the theory introduce?
- How many irreducibly new laws does it posit?
- How similar is it to other theories we already accept?

The answers to these questions are often suggested more by looking at a picture, graph, or physical model of the theory than by looking at the sentences used to express the theory. In any case, the sentences and their degree of stylistic economy are irrelevant to the theory's inductive simplicity.

I argued in section 2.2 against the "epistemological claim" that speaking a strange language would make it impossible to correctly evaluate the projectibility of hypotheses. I am making essentially the same point with respect to the inductive simplicity of theories. If we attempt to formulate rules of projectibility or rules of inductive simplicity, it may happen that these rules are more type or token-economical when formulated in one sort of language rather than another. (Compare, for example, the rule in terms of coprojectibles given in the last section with the equivalent rule in terms of projectibles.) But then we are back again merely to these stylistic considerations; nothing deeper than that comes into play, even when we are talking about formulating rules of inference. If rules can be formulated in ordinary terms, equivalent rules can be formulated in strange terms.

f. Heuristic Devices

In section 2.2.d, I mentioned what might be regarded as a limiting case of token-economy as applied to rules of inference. In ordinary language, there is the presumption that a word will be projectible, and on this presumption one can build what I called the System S for determining when a term or hypothesis is projectible. So, one might say, in ordinary language it requires utterances of zero length (i.e., no utterances) to communicate that certain terms (i.e., the words and their equivalents) are projectible; this information is built into the very structure of the language. In ordinary language we get this information token-free, whereas in the strange languages it would be token-costly. Similar points may be made about the presumption in ordinary language that words represent natural properties and things, or salient properties and things, or important properties and things. These presumptions can be seen as valuable heuristics whereby some essential cultural assumptions are passed on token-free.

It seems to me that this point does carry some weight, enough, possibly, to rebuff the most extreme form of division relativism. But its significance must not be exaggerated. First, and perhaps most fundamentally, we are still dealing with nothing deeper than token-economy; there is no deeper compulsion to allow the structure of the language, rather than utterances made in the language, to carry the cultural assumptions. Second, as I already brought out in section 2.2.d, the heuristics in question are highly imperfect and must be supplemented and qualified in token-costly ways. Third, it is not obvious that the strange languages could not avail themselves of corresponding heuristics. For instance, coprojectible words might be revealed as such by some phonetic relation between them. Finally, there are many possible heuristics absent from ordinary language. Imagine a language in which one can tell by how a pair of words are phonetically related whether they (are culturally assumed to) express species of the same genus, or whether they denote things that have closely related functions, or whether one entails the other. There are an indefinite number of such possibilities. Would speakers of such a language have the right to regard our language as absurd because it lacks such heuristics? We have no greater right to regard the strange languages as absurd simply because they lack some heuristic devices available in our language.

5. The Pure Pragmatic Position

Let me summarily list some of the main points that I have tried to make in this chapter.

1. If (and only if) salience is explicated in terms of certain cognitive dispositions, then there may be (at least with respect to many examples) an obvious pragmatic virtue in having words express salient properties; but that merely shifts the question slightly to what the virtue is of having our ordinary sense of salience.

2. It is by no means obvious what the pragmatic virtue is of having words rather than complex terms express important properties.

3. Indeed, there does not even appear to be any pragmatic virtue in paying attention to important properties, so long as important world-conditions (or conditions entailing them) are paid attention to.

4. Moreover, the properties expressed by strange words seem often to be as important as properties expressed by ordinary words.

5. At least in some central examples, strange languages seem to be virtually as economical as ordinary languages.

6. In any case, it seems that relatively modest differences of economy cannot account for the kinds of intuitions that we have about the strange languages.

In the general literature, there appears to be virtually no inkling of the problems and questions I have discussed in this chapter. One can scarcely look into a work on metaphysics, or epistemology, or cognitive psychology without expecting to find some casual remarks about the essential pragmatic virtue of this or that ordinary feature of our language and thinking. The ubiquitous assumption seems to be that there are obviously compelling pragmatic reasons at least for the most ordinary features of our division practices. As I implied at the beginning of this chapter, the blindness in the literature to the genuine problems in this area stems partly from a tendency to confuse empirical psychological claims with normative pragmatic claims, and partly from the related failure to discern the vacuity of pseudo-pragmatic arguments of the form "It is good for our language and thinking to have such-and-such features because we would find it unnatural to talk and think in any other way."

In concluding this chapter, let me emphasize that my arguments have been directed against a "pure" pragmatic position. Division pragmatism holds that our ordinary division practices are rationally constrained *solely* in terms of pragmatic considerations. My view is that if we have nothing to appeal to but pragmatic considerations, then there are virtually no rational constraints on our division practices, at least none that would render the strange languages absurd. However, as will immediately emerge in the next chapter, I think that there may be non-pragmatic constraints on our division practices. And it may turn out that these other constraints can combine with pragmatic considerations in certain ways. So the intuitive feeling that it must be in some sense impractical for people in our life situation to employ the strange languages may yet be sustainable, but not on the terms envisioned by the pure pragmatic position.

6

The Order
of Understanding

1. The Impossibility Claim

In this chapter, I want to consider various claims to the general effect
that the strange languages cannot possibly function in ways that ordinary languages function. The notion of possibility in these claims is to
be understood in the sense of metaphysical possibility. The most fundamental claim of this sort is the following:

> *The Impossibility Claim* (*IC*). It is impossible for people to have as
> their only language a strong version of one of the strange languages.

It seems obviously possible for people's only language to be a weak version of a strange language, and also for people's second language to be
a strong version of a strange language. IC, therefore, makes the strongest claim of this general sort that one might hope to defend.

Before considering the plausibility of IC and various associated claims,
I want to say something about how they relate to our initial intuitions
about the division problem. From the outset of this book, I expressed
these intuitions as being normative in nature. IC should be viewed not
as simply repudiating these intuitions, but as reinterpreting and elabo-
rating them. It is quite common to view modal assertions as closely
related to normative assertions. In the present case, the intuition says,
"One must not employ such languages." IC reinterprets this modally
rather than normatively. To put it from a slightly different angle, when
one hears a description of a strange language, the intuitive reaction is
"That's crazy (absurd, unthinkable)." IC reinterprets this to mean that
it is crazy (absurd, unthinkable) to suppose that people speak such a
language.

Moreover, the overall response to strangeness may still include a normative element. As I just remarked, IC does not apply to weak versions of strangeness or to strangeness in secondary languages. A proponent of IC who wishes to sustain our negative intuitions about these cases would have to do so in normative terms. What those normative terms might be is something that I will come back to later.

If IC has any immediate attraction, I assume that this derives from the intuitive plausibility of a related claim about thinking or conceptualization. It seems intuitively plausible to suppose that one could not have the concept "gricular" without having the concept "green" and the concept "circular"; that one could not have the concept "cdog" without having the concept "dog" and the concept "touching"; in general, that one could not have the concept signified by a strange word without having the concepts signified by ordinary words in terms of which the strange word is explained.[1] Perhaps the general point might initially be formulated (subject to modifications) as follows:

> IC1. Necessarily, for any strange word "*F*," if people have the concept "*F*," there is an ordinary expression "*E*" equivalent to "*F*" such that for any general word "*G*" in "*E*," they have the concept "*G*."[2]

In the individuative case, there is the possible complication that one may regard strange individuative terms like "cdog" as not equivalent to any ordinary expression if one holds that no ordinary expression denotes the class of cdogs.[3] If so, IC1 would have to be recast for the individuative case in terms of strange sentences being equivalent to ordinary sentences. For example: Necessarily, if "*F*" is one of the strange individuative words and "*S*" is a strange sentence of the form "Some *F* is at place 1 at time 1 and at place 2 at time 2" then, if people have the concept "*F*," there is an ordinary sentence "*T*" equivalent to "*S*" such that, for any general word "*G*" in "*T*," they have the concept "*G*."

It seems clear that there is some important connection between IC and IC1. It is important to appreciate, however, that IC1 by itself (with-

---

[1] I adopt a notation in which "the concept" followed by a quoted expression refers to the concept that is in some sense signified by the expression. I will indicate presently how I intend concepts to be individuated.

[2] For stylistic convenience, IC1 is formulated in terms of "necessity," whereas IC was formulated in terms of "possibility"; obviously this could be altered.

IC1 is not to be understood as implying that, if people have the concept "*F*," there must be people who employ an ordinary expression "*E*" equivalent to "*F*." At present, we are not assuming that having a concept need involve employing any expression. Nor, of course, do we want IC1 to be refuted by the trivial possibility that the ordinary or strange expressions under consideration might have been used differently. In this principle and subsequent ones, it is assumed that the expressions under consideration have their uses fixed in abstract languages that need not be employed in the worlds being imagined.

[3] Alternatively, one may hold that "cdog" is equivalent to a necessarily inapplicable ordinary expression, such as "square and circular" (see section 1.3.c), which would again render IC1 inept for the individuative case.

out IC) offers no obvious critique of the strange languages. Granted that speakers of the Gricular language must have the concept "green," it is not immediately obvious how that would imply a fault in their language.

Though there seems evidently to be an intimate connection between IC1 and IC, this is not straightforward, insofar as the connection between thinking and language is not straightforward. In section 1.3.b, I outlined a number of different views about thinking and language. One view was that thinking always takes place within a language. A modal version of this view is that necessarily thinking takes place within a language. Let me call this the "thesis of the necessity of language." Now the following may seem to be a promising line of argument: Given IC1, and given also the thesis of the necessity of language, we can arrive at a linguistic version of IC1, in which concepts are replaced by words; and this linguistic version of IC1 will imply IC. Take the Gricular language as an example. People who speak this language must have the concept "gricular." By IC1 there must be some ordinary words that signify concepts these people have, out of which concepts they can construct the concept "gricular." Given the thesis of the necessity of language, this may be tantamount to saying that they must employ in thinking ordinary words in terms of which an expression can be constructed equivalent to "gricular." But if the strong Gricular language is their only language, they would have no such words. Hence, it is impossible that this is their only language.

There appears to be no argument from IC1 to IC unless one appeals to the thesis of the necessity of language. The argument just sketched is evidently very rough; I will attempt to work it out carefully in a later section. Before pursuing this, I want to dwell on IC1 itself. Certainly this is an important philosophical claim in its own right, whatever its precise bearing on the strange languages.

2. Concept-Dependence Claims

IC1 is a particular instance of a general kind of philosophical claim: a claim about *the necessary order of understanding* or, as I shall also put it, a *concept-dependence* claim. Such claims are, I think, prevalent throughout philosophy, at least implicitly, though I suspect that many current philosophers who implicitly make such claims might recoil from an explicit formulation in the manner of IC1.

a. The Interpretation of the Claims

A perennial example of a concept-dependence claim is the following:

(a) It is impossible for people to have the concept "the average plumber" without having the concept "plumber."

The overwhelming intuitive inclination, surely, is to accept this claim. Might this be because of some ambiguity in the modal operator in (a)? Someone might say: "What seems clear is that it is *psychologically* impossible to have the concept 'the average plumber' without having the concept 'plumber'. But when you shift to metaphysical possibility, (a) becomes false." But why would the psychological possibilities seem so clear if this were not at bottom an a priori metaphysical point? (Would anyone dream of trying to experimentally test (a)?) I agree, of course, that when the modal operator in (a) is interpreted in the metaphysical sense (which is always the interpretation I intend for an unqualified modal operator), philosophical difficulties arise. But it seems clear that our intuitive inclination is to accept (a) in this sense. Intuitively, it seems difficult to conceive of a situation in which someone has the concept "the average plumber" without having the concept "plumber."

If it is wrong to psychologize the import of (a), it is also wrong, I think, to trivialize it by making it depend upon the syntactic relation between "the average plumber" and "plumber." The trivializing interpretation of (a) would say the following: "To understand the expression 'the average plumber' necessitates that one understand the constituent word 'plumber,' for, in general, to understand a complex expression necessitates that one understand its constituent words. That is the reason why (a) is true."

To see how this trivializes (a), imagine someone who uses the sentence "The shlumber has 3.4 children" with the same truth-conditions as we assign to "The average plumber has 3.4 children." On the trivializing interpretation, this might be possible even if this person did not have the concept "plumber," since "shlumber" does not contain "plumber" as a constituent. Surely the intuition behind (a) is to deny this.

(a) should, therefore, be understood to imply

(a') It is impossible for people to understand sentences equivalent to those of the form "The average plumber is *F*" without having the concept "plumber."[4]

(a') says, in other words, that one cannot possibly grasp the truth-conditions of sentences of the form "The average plumber is *F*" without having the concept "plumber."

One must also avoid a trivializing interpretation of the concept-dependence claim made in IC1. Assuming that any ordinary expression equivalent to "gricular" must contain a word equivalent to "green," IC1 implies

---

[4]We might formulate (a') more simply as "It is impossible for people to understand an expression equivalent to 'the average plumber' without having the concept 'plumber'" but, since "the average plumber" is not properly a term ("The average plumber is *F*" does not entail "Something is *F*"), it is problematical whether any expressions can properly be said to be equivalent to it.

(b) It is impossible for people to have the concept "gricular" without having the concept "green."

A trivializing interpretation of (b) might go like this: "The word 'gricular' was introduced by way of the expression 'green or circular' and is (not merely equivalent to but) synonymous with that expression. Now it seems to be a general principle that if the expression '*F*' is synonymous with the expression '*G*' and the latter contains the word '*H*,' then one cannot understand '*F*' without having the concept '*H*.' This is why (b) is true."

Since this interpretation appeals to the synonymy of "gricular" with "green or circular," it in effect denies that (b) entails

(b') It is impossible for people to understand an expression equivalent to "gricular" without having the concept "green."

As I explained in section 1.3.c, an important feature of the strong Gricular language is that one may suppose that in it "gricular" is not synonymous with "green or circular" (or any other ordinary expression). Might it then be possible to employ "gricular" within the strong Gricular language without having the concept "green"? Certainly, we want to understand IC1 as implying a negative answer to this question. (b') implies this, but the trivializing interpretation of (b) does not. We should, therefore, reject that interpretation and understand (b) to amount to (b').

b. "Having a Concept"

I am pushing for a certain interpretation of concept-dependence claims, one that I think properly captures their intuitive import. On this interpretation, such claims depend on neither syntactic nor synonymy relations. Concept-dependence claims lend themselves to various interpretations in part because of the extreme obscurity of the notion of "having a concept." For the purpose of understanding concept-dependence claims, I suggest that we adopt a fairly liberal reading of "having a concept." On this reading, a sufficient condition for people's having the concept "*F*" is that they understand expressions equivalent to "*F*" (or, as in the case of "the average plumber," that they understand certain sentences equivalent to those containing "*F*"). At least as a first approximation, this does seem to be a sufficient condition for one sense of having a concept. We are, I think, prepared to say that, at least in one sense, any normal adult has the concept of a first cousin once removed, in that any normal adult might be expected to understand an expression equivalent to "first cousin once removed." (Readers who feel reluctant to say that normal adults must *have* the concept should ask themselves whether they would feel more comfortable saying that normal adults might *lack* the concept.)

If we were presupposing the necessity of language thesis, we might also say (as a first approximation) that a necessary condition for people's having the concept "*F*" is that they understand expressions equivalent to "*F*," hence making that linguistic condition both necessary and suffi- cient for having the concept. Indeed, one of the great appeals of the necessity of language thesis is that it condones the conversion of talk about concepts into much more tractable talk about bits of language. However, if we are not presupposing that thesis, we cannot offer as a necessary condition for people's having the concept "*F*" that they understand expressions equivalent to "*F*." It may still be elucidating to say the following: If we are dealing with people who can express all of their concepts in words, then a necessary and sufficient condition for them to have the concept "*F*" is that they understand expressions equivalent to "*F*." This implies that the concept "*F*" can be identified with the con- cept "*G*" if and only if "*F*" is equivalent to "*G*."

As I have indicated, I offer this account only as a rough approxima- tion to one ordinary sense of having a concept. The account seems to fit more comfortably in some contexts than others. (For instance, it may seem highly strained in mathematical contexts, where hidden equivalences are the rule.) I think it fits many ordinary examples well enough to be useful for our present purposes. I have no doubt that there are less liberal (more fine-grained) notions of having a concept, but I think that I have indicated one viable notion that seems especially well suited to capture the intuitive import of concept-dependence claims.[5]

c. Analysis and Concept-Dependence Claims

In order to highlight the centrality of concept-dependence claims in many philosophical discussions, we should note that one context in which such claims are often implicitly made is philosophical analysis. An analysis is often rejected as "(viciously) circular." I think that what this means is that one of the analysans concepts (the concepts figuring in the analy- sis) is such that having it necessarily depends on having the analysandum concept (the concept to be analyzed).

Here is an example: In discussions of identity, a central question is whether the transtemporal or transworld identity of a thing can be analyzed. Now, one can trivially introduce a relationship and call it, say, "kinship," such that, by definition, momentary thing-stages, or world- bound thing-slices, are kindred if and only if they are stages, or slices,

[5]A somewhat more restrictive notion would require that, in order for the concept "*F*" to be identified with the concept "*G*," "*F*" and "*G*" must have the same analysis (i.e., they must have the same analytic expansion in the sense explained in appendix 3.4). The most restrictive notion would require that "*F*" be synonymous with "*G*." If either of these more restrictive notions are insisted on, then I would have to recast my suggested interpretation of concept-dependence claims by saying that these claims ought to be put in the form "It is impossible for people to have the concept '*F*' or an equivalent concept without having the concept '*G*' or an equivalent concept." Along similar lines, all of the arguments that follow could be recast to suit the more restrictive notions.

of the same thing.[6] Why would this procedure not trivially demonstrate the analyzability of identity? The obvious answer, I think, is that, given the way that the concept "kinship" has been explained, it seems to depend on the prior concept of transtemporal or transworld identity, so that the analysis seems circular.[7] Circularity claims of this sort are frequently made in the literature and should, I think, generally be understood to imply concept-dependence claims.

I am assuming that analysis, in at least one important sense, aims at a metaphysical insight, rather than at something essentially epistemological or psychological.[8] It should follow, I think, that the success or failure of an analysis depends on metaphysical considerations. For an analysis to be successful, the analysans concepts must be metaphysically more "basic," more "simple," than the analysandum concept.[9] It seems that a necessary condition for one concept to be more metaphysically basic than another is that having the former does not necessarily depend on having the latter. Circularity condemns an analysis because it reveals that the analysans concepts are not more metaphysically basic than the analysandum concept.

d. The Intuitiveness of the Claims

In this section I have not considered any argumentative defense of such concept-dependence claims as IC1. I will turn to that in later sections. But I think it quite important to highlight the intuitiveness of many such claims. It is a remarkable feature of many current discussions that these claims and the intuitions that support them are wholly ignored. Strange words abound in the literature on projectibility, on inscrutability and indeterminacy, on the "Kripkenstein paradox." Rarely is it so much as mentioned that it seems intuitively impossible that anyone should understand these words without having the concepts signified by the ordinary words that the strange words are imagined as replacing.

Of course, one would like to have some arguments to bolster these intuitions. Moreover, we may have to worry about there being arguments against them; I will consider that later, too. But there can be no good reason simply to ignore these intuitions.

3. Fine-Grained Propositions and Concept-Dependence

There is a certain philosophical doctrine that may seem ready-made to provide the arguments we seek in defense of concept-dependence claims.

---

[6]This is essentially Quine's procedure in Quine 1961, p. 66.

[7]But I leave it open here whether the analysis might eventually be made good by explaining kinship in a non-circular fashion (e.g., in terms of similarity, or causality, or spatiotemporal continuity).

[8]This way of viewing analysis has been stressed in Kripke's lectures on identity.

[9]Cf. appendix 3.2.

This is the *fine-grained doctrine* to which I have previously alluded a number of times.

Let me indicate in a preliminary way how a certain version of this doctrine may yield the concept-dependence claims. A basic tenet of the doctrine is that propositions are structured entities made up of various constituents. It may be held that there are metaphysically necessary constraints on what these constituents must be like. One such constraint might be that propositions must be ultimately built up out of natural properties and things.[10] Let me call this the *natural-constituents principle*. Moreover, it may seem immediately plausible to hold the following *concepts-of-constituents principle*: People can think a proposition only if they have concepts of the proposition's constituents. From these two principles, it seems to follow that people must have concepts of the natural properties and things that are the ultimate constituents of propositions. And this seems to imply IC1 and the other concept-dependence claims.

In this section, I will try to develop the argument just sketched.

a. The Fine-Grained Doctrine

Let me begin by articulating the relevant version of the fine-grained doctrine in terms of five claims.

1. Necessarily, to think is to think a fine-grained proposition.

2. Necessarily, any fine-grained proposition is made up of certain constituents arranged in a specific way. The constituents of a proposition may be other propositions, logical operations, properties, and perhaps particular things. Some constituents may themselves be built up in a proposition as a complex arrangement of other constituents. *Ultimate* constituents are those that are not built up of other constituents.

The next claim is the aforementioned natural-constituents principle.

3. Necessarily, if a property is an ultimate constituent of a fine-grained proposition, the property is natural and belongs to some (possible) natural things; and if a particular thing is an ultimate constituent of a fine-grained proposition, the thing is natural.

In the next claim it should be understood that to think a proposition, in the sense intended, is not necessarily to think that the proposition is true. It is to entertain the proposition, to address it in one's thinking.

---

[10]I want to temporarily ignore the notion of *degrees* of naturalness (discussed in section 3.6); the relevance of that notion to the present argument will be taken up later (see section 7.3.d). Until then, "natural property (or thing)" should be understood to mean roughly a property (or thing) that is natural to a (sufficiently) high degree.

4. Necessarily, if people employ a sentence (in a certain context), they think the fine-grained proposition that the sentence expresses (in that context).

The next and final claim is a somewhat embellished formulation of the concepts-of-constituents principle mentioned earlier. The principle attempts to establish certain connections between thinking propositions and having concepts. The basic idea is that thinking a proposition requires having concepts that represent the proposition's constituents. To simplify matters, let us limit this principle to constituents that are properties.[11] A certain complication must first be noted in saying that a concept *represents* (or is *of*) a certain property. Suppose that, as a matter of necessity, a thing is hot if and only if it has (a lot of) molecular motion.[12] Then the property of being hot is the same (coarse-grained) property as the property of having molecular motion.[13] Nevertheless, since "hot" is not equivalent to "has molecular motion," the concept "hot" cannot be identified with the concept "has molecular motion." These are distinct concepts that represent the same property. In general, if "F" and "G" are not equivalent, but the (coarse-grained) property of being F is identical with the property of being G, then the concept "F" and the concept "G" might be said to be distinct concepts that represent the same property.

The concepts-of-constituents principle says, most basically, that thinking a proposition requires having concepts that represent the proposition's constituent properties. But the principle should also be understood to require a certain kind of logical relationship between concepts of a proposition's ultimate constituents and concepts of its non-ultimate constituents: the latter concepts must be *constructible from* the former. For example, the concept "green or circular" is in an obvious sense constructible from the concept "green" and the concept "circular." The relevant notion of constructibility can be defined as follows: Suppose that "F" is (equivalent to) an expression whose only general words are "F_1," "F_2," . . . "F_n." Then the concept "F" will be said to be constructible from the concept "F_1," together with the concept "F_2," . . . together with the concept "F_n." "F" may of course contain logical operators, and perhaps also demonstratives, proper names, or other singular terms, but let us stipulate that only the general words in "F" will figure in describing how the concept "F" is, in the relevant sense, constructible from other concepts.

[11]It is doubtful that we ordinarily talk of the concept of a particular thing. Perhaps we do talk of concepts of logical operations ("logical concepts"), and these would not be, in the relevant sense, concepts of properties. In any case, in formulating the concepts-of-constituents principle, I want to concentrate on concepts of properties.

[12]See Kripke 1980, p. 136.

[13]Throughout this discussion, I will assume that the properties under consideration are coarse-grained. The effect of bringing fine-grained properties into the discussion is considered in appendix 3.4.

The concepts-of-constituents principle can now be formulated as follows:

> 5. Necessarily, if people think certain fine-grained propositions, they have concepts representing every constituent property of these propositions, such that their concepts representing non-ultimate constituent properties are constructible from their concepts representing ultimate constituent properties.

The principle implies that, in order to think a proposition, people must have concepts that are in a sense isomorphic to the constituent properties of the proposition. The relevant notion of isomorphism is easier to bring out at a linguistic level. Let us say that a sentence "S" *expresses a proposition* p *isomorphically* if "S" expresses p and there is a one-to-one correspondence between the general words in "S" and the ultimate constituent properties of p (and, hence, a one-to-one correspondence between the complex terms in "S" and the non-ultimate constituents properties in p). What the concepts-of-constituents principle amounts to is that in order to think a proposition, it is necessary to have the concepts that would be needed in understanding some sentence that expresses the proposition isomorphically.

b. Natural Constituents

The most distinctive feature of the fine-grained doctrine just outlined is the natural-constituents principle. I adapt this principle from George Bealer's work.[14] The principle may be viewed as a kind of compromise between two extreme positions. One position would be that there are no metaphysical constraints of any sort on which properties and things can be ultimate constituents of propositions. At the other extreme is the position held by Russell and the other logical atomists, who claimed that the ultimate constituents (or "components") of propositions (or "facts") must be in some sense *simple*.[15] Certainly, such natural properties as Dog or Spherical would not have been regarded by the atomists as simple in the relevant sense, and these properties would have been disqualified as ultimate constituents. But, on the natural-constituents principle, these properties are eminently eligible as ultimate constituents.

Russell's claim that a proposition's ultimate constituent properties must be simple does not cohere with the concepts-of-constituents principle. It seems clear that many of our ordinary concepts do not depend on their being constructible from concepts we have of Russellian simples.

---

[14]See Bealer 1982, pp. 177–90. Though I am not aware of any other philosopher who explicitly formulates this principle, I suspect that it is tacitly (or, perhaps, subversively) assumed in many contemporary discussions.

[15]See Russell 1918.

(For example, people can have the concept of a complex melody without having any concepts of the notes that make up the melody; the notes, or perhaps even simpler ingredients, would be the Russellian simples.) This is in itself a kind of weakness in Russell's position, for the concepts-of-constituents principle seems inherently plausible. It seems obvious that the propositions we entertain require us to have certain conceptual resources; we need to have certain concepts to think certain propositions. It is difficult to see how to explain this connection between propositions and concepts except by reference to the concepts-of-constituents principle.[16]

Nevertheless, the atomists' requirement of simple ultimate constituents is in a way easier to appreciate than the natural-constituents principle, for the former requirement appeals to the immediate intuitive connection between "ultimacy" and "simplicity." A proponent of the natural-constituents principle, however, must have some way of explaining why an unnatural property such as Gricular is ineligible as an ultimate constituent, while a "natural complex" such as Spherical is eligible. Note that we do not want to answer this question by appealing to intuitions about concept dependence, for we are rather seeking an argument that goes in the opposite direction. That is, we do not want to derive the natural-constituents principle from IC1; rather, we are trying to derive IC1 from the natural-constituents principle (together with the other claims in the fine-grained doctrine).

It is tempting to suggest that the natural-constituents principle can be defended on ontological grounds. The view that may seem most congenial to the principle is ontological inegalitarianism, discussed in chapters 3 and 4. This is the view that an unnatural property or thing is merely a set or function, whereas a natural property or thing is a universal or entity distinct from any set-theoretical construction. On this view, the natural-constituents principle can be construed as simply saying that a set, or function, or other set-theoretical construction cannot be an ultimate constituent of a proposition. This may seem immediately plausible; the very notion of a set-theoretical *construction* suggests something that is necessarily built up in a proposition. (Note that the natural-constituents principle need not imply that the word "set" cannot express an ultimate constituent of set-theoretical propositions. This word can be viewed as expressing a logical operation or property that, it may be

---

[16]It is unlikely that the logical atomists typically held a concepts-of-constituents principle. As Urmson remarks, they seemed to allow that their "logical constructions" could be psychologically basic; see Urmson 1956, p. 38. More is said in appendix 3.1 about the relationship between the fine-grained doctrine under consideration and logical atomism. As I suggest there, it may be that there are different senses of "proposition"; Russell's requirement of simple ultimate constituents may hold for one sense, while the natural-constituents principle together with the concepts-of-constituents principle may hold for another sense.

allowed, can be an ultimate constituent. What cannot be an ultimate constituent, however, is a set that derives from this logical operation, such as the set that is the unnatural property Gricular.)

In the next chapter I will want to criticize the ontological defense just given of the natural-constituents principle. But if one accepts this defense, the whole fine-grained doctrine under consideration may seem quite compelling. The doctrine consists of several major putative insights: first, an insight into the necessary structure of a certain domain of entities, the "propositions"; second, an ontological insight into which properties and things have the status required to occupy various positions within that structure; and, third, an insight into the necessary connection between the activity or process of thinking and the domain of propositions. On this view, the structure of propositions imposes necessary constraints on the activity of thinking, and this is why our concepts have a certain order of necessary dependence. I now want to examine a bit more carefully how concept-dependence claims derive from the fine-grained doctrine.

c. Derivation of Concept-Dependence Claims

Let us henceforth assume that an "ordinary" language is one whose general words express natural properties and denote natural things. The "strange" words are then words that do not express natural properties or that do not denote natural things.

In order to see how IC1 follows from the fine-grained doctrine, let us first consider what the doctrine implies about the concept "gricular." If people have the concept "gricular," they must be able to employ this concept in thinking propositions, for example, the proposition that is expressed in their language by the sentence "Something is gricular." We are assuming that Gricular is an unnatural property. Let it be assumed, further, that the unnaturalness of Gricular is a necessary truth (more generally that it is a matter of necessity which properties are natural and which unnatural).[17] By the natural-constituents principle, the ultimate constituent properties of the proposition expressed by "Something is gricular" must be natural, and hence cannot possibly include Gricular. Therefore, by the concepts-of-constituents principle, people who have the concept "gricular" must necessarily have concepts representing these natural properties such that the concept "gricular" is constructible from these concepts.[18] But this is precisely what IC1 implies about the concept "gricular." Since the same argument evidently applies to any other concept of an unnatural property, we see that IC1 has been established.

---

[17]See section 3.4.a.

[18]The above argument may not be fully rigorous but I think it is sufficiently clear. I am relying on a sympathetic interpretation of the five principles that make up the fine-grained doctrine.

The claim about the concept "gricular" that has just been derived is this:

> It is impossible for people to have the concept "gricular" unless they have a set of concepts representing natural properties such that the concept "gricular" is constructible from that set.

This is the claim that corresponds to IC1. This claim is weaker than the claim (b) discussed earlier, that is, the claim that it is impossible for people to have the concept "gricular" without having the concept "green." What I had said earlier about (b) is that it follows from IC1 on the assumption that any ordinary expression equivalent to "gricular" must contain a word equivalent to "green." In other words, the weakened version of (b) follows directly from IC1, which in turn follows directly from the fine-grained doctrine. To arrive at (b) itself, some further assumption is required.

The weakened version of (b) stands to (b) in the way that IC1 stands to the following stronger claim:

> For any strange word "F," there is an ordinary expression "E" equivalent to "F" such that, for any general word "G" in "E," necessarily, if people have the concept "F" then they have the concept "G."

Let a general concept be called an N-concept if it represents a natural property of natural things and otherwise be called a U-concept. The strengthened version of IC1 says that there is a particular way of constructing any U-concept from N-concepts such that if people have the U-concept they must have those particular N-concepts; IC1 makes the weaker claim that if people have a U-concept it must be constructible from some N-concepts or other that they have. It seems quite clear that IC1 does follow from the fine-grained doctrine, for this doctrine implies that U-concepts can represent only non-ultimate constituents of propositions and must therefore be dependent on N-concepts that represent ultimate constituents. But the strenghtened version of IC1 does not follow from the doctrine unless some further assumptions are made. And it is the strengthened version that corresponds to (b).

It should be noted that, if we try to defend (b), we are not defending the even stronger claim that having any concept that represents Gricular must depend on having a concept that represents Green. This claim is immediately implausible, at least if we confine ourselves to coarse-grained properties. Suppose that a certain kind of event Z is caused only by the presence of a green thing or by the presence of a circular thing. Let "B" abbreviate "something that has a property that in this (actual) world causes Z." Then, necessarily, anything is B if and only if it is gricular. Hence, the concept "B" represents Gricular, though this concept surely need not depend on any concept that represents Green. But the claim made by (b) is only that a *certain* concept that represents

Gricular must depend on a *certain* concept that represents Green; that is, the concept "gricular" (which is the same as the concept "green or circular") must depend on the concept "green." This does follow from IC1 (and from the fine-grained doctrine) on the assumption that any ordinary expression—any expression made up of words for natural properties of natural things—which is equivalent to "gricular" contains a word equivalent to "green." For that assumption amounts to saying that there is no way to construct the concept "gricular" from concepts of natural properties unless one of the latter concepts is the concept "green."

The assumption may seem initially plausible, but it is in fact problematical. Suppose we take "A," "B," and "C" to be words that express, respectively, "dark green," "light green," and "medium green." Then it seems that "green" is equivalent to the disjunction of "A," "B," and "C," and, arguably, all of these words express natural properties. "Gricular" would then be equivalent to the disjunction formed of those three words together with "circular," where none of these words are equivalent to "green."[19]

Earlier, I took (b) to be an example of a highly intuitive concept-dependence claim. Do we have to retreat to the weakened version of (b)? I think we can still defend (b) if we adopt the following charitable assumption: People may be said to have the concept "*F*" so long as they have concepts from which the concept "*F*" can be constructed. At the linguistic level, this assumption seems quite straightforward, for if one understands a set of general words, one would normally have all the concepts required to understand any expression constructible from the words. Now, the weakened version of (b) says that if people have the concept "gricular," this concept must be constructible from some concepts of natural properties which they have. It seems clear that these latter concepts must then also be such that the concept "green" can be constructed from them. (If the latter concepts include the concept "green" then the concept "green" will be trivially constructible from itself.) Hence, on the charitable assumption, if the weakened version of (b) is true, so is (b). (Generalizing on this, we have an argument for the strengthened version of IC1.)

(This conclusion might be drawn even if we somewhat restricted the charitable assumption. It might be held that having a set *S* of concepts qualifies one as having a certain concept constructible from *S* only if it is already established that one has the capacity to perform the logical operations required to construct that concept from *S*. It seems fairly clear that (b) will follow from the fine-grained doctrine even on this more restricted assumption. If people are able to employ the concept "gricular"

---

[19]More extreme examples come out of my discussion in section 3.3.c. If, as I there in effect suggested (vis-à-vis the property P^*), any sufficiently limited stretch of the spectrum answers to a natural property, "green" can certainly be defined in terms of other natural properties.

in thinking a proposition, then they must have the capacity to construct the concept "gricular"—and, hence, the concept "green"—from concepts of the proposition's ultimate constituents.)

Even if (b) is held not to follow from the fine-grained doctrine, we need not retreat to the weakened version of (b). From what I have said in the last two paragraphs, it seems clear that the fine-grained doctrine implies at least the following "intermediary" version of (b):

> It is impossible for people to have the concept "gricular" without having either the concept "green" or some other concepts from which the concept "green" is constructible.

This version of (b) may come close enough to capturing our intuition about the dependence of "gricular" on "green," even if it falls somewhat short of (b) proper.

The intermediary version of (b) corresponds to an intermediary version of IC1. This says that there is a particular way of constructing any U-concept from N-concepts such that if people have the U-concept they must have either those particular N-concepts or some other N-concepts from which the former N-concepts are constructible.[20]

d. Asymmetric Concept-Dependence

The intermediary version shares with the strongest version of IC1 a certain important virtue: These versions seem to sustain the intuitive idea that there is an *asymmetric* (one-way) dependence of U-concepts on N-concepts. It seems clear (at least in general) that if a U-concept depends on a particular N-concept in the way specified by one of these versions, the latter will not depend in the same way on the former. For instance, if having the concept "gricular" necessarily depends on having either the concept "green" or some other concepts in terms of which the concept "green" is constructible, it surely does not seem to be the case that having the concept "green" necessarily depends on having either the concept "gricular" or some other concepts in terms of which the concept "gricular" is constructible. It is less clear that the straight (i.e., weakest) version of IC1 sustains an asymmetric dependence. In order for N-concepts to depend on U-concepts in the way that, according to the straight version, U-concepts depend on N-concepts, all that is required is that if people have an N-concept, it must be constructible from some U-concepts or other that they have. This requirement will

---

[20]The formulation of the intermediary version in the style in which IC1 was initially formulated is a bit complicated:

> For any strange word "F," there is an ordinary expression "E" equivalent to "F" such that, for any general word "G" in "E," necessarily, if people have the concept "F," either they have the concept "G," or there is an ordinary expression "E'" equivalent to "G" such that, for any general word "G'" in "E'," they have the concept "G'."

be satisfied by, for example, the N-concept "green" so long as people who have the concept "green" must have two U-concepts of the form "green or F" and "green or non-F," for some term "F" unrelated to "green." Perhaps this requirement need not be satisfied if we are sufficiently uncharitable in our attribution of concepts to people, but the point is hazy. It is an improvement on IC1, therefore, to restate it in the intermediary version (or the strongest version, if that too is held to follow from the fine-grained doctrine).

Even these versions, however, may fail to satisfy fully the demand for an asymmetric dependence. It seems arguable that having any concept "F" necessarily depends on also having the concept "non-F" (for example, having the concept "green" necessarily depends on also having the concept "non-green"). (This seems arguable even if one rejects the earlier "charitable assumption" that people have whatever concepts are constructible from the concepts they have.) If the former is an N-concept and the latter a U-concept then, at least in this special case, particular N-concepts and particular U-concepts seem to be mutually dependent.[21] It is tempting to answer, I think, that whereas the concept "green" and the concept "non-green" are mutually dependent (and mutually constructible from each other), the latter depends on the former in the special sense of *containing* the former. The problem with this answer, however, is that to talk of one concept containing another seems to attribute to concepts a syntactic structure, which is tantamount to treating concepts as bits of language. It appears, therefore, that until we bring the thesis of the necessity of language into the story and formulate a linguistic version of IC1, we may not have a fully satisfactory way of capturing the asymmetric dependence of N-concepts on U-concepts.[22] The thesis of the necessity of language will be discussed in the next section.

e. Further Applications

Let us briefly consider how the fine-grained doctrine relates to the concept-dependence claim (a), that is, the claim that it is impossible for people to have the concept "the average plumber" without having the

---

[21]In appendix 2.4, I argue that the complements of many N-concepts such as "green" are U-concepts. Probably there are also other kinds of prima facie examples of mutual dependence of particular N-concepts and particular U-concepts.

[22]Let C-dependence be the relationship that holds between the concept x and the concept y if having x necessarily depends on having either y or some other concepts from which y is constructible. Then we can at least say the following:

> In almost every case of a U-concept, the concept is C-dependent on some N-concept that is not in turn C-dependent on it, but it is never the case that an N-concept is C-dependent on a U-concept that is not in turn C-dependent on it.

But it is doubtful that this fully captures the intuitive idea that *every* U-concept (including complements of N-concepts) must be asymmetrically dependent on N-concepts.

concept "plumber." The argument is complicated slightly here because "the average plumber" is not properly a term.[23] We should, therefore, shift attention to sentences of the form "The average plumber is *F*." One has the concept "the average plumber" only if one has the concepts needed to understand such sentences or their equivalents. Without entering into the details, I think it is sufficiently clear that, on a reasonable interpretation of the fine-grained doctrine, we can arrive at the result that, in order to understand a sentence equivalent to one of the form "The average plumber is *F*," it is necessary to have the concept "plumber" (or concepts from which the concept "plumber" is constructible).[24]

There are a number of other complicated questions about the fine-grained doctrine which I think it best to put off for appendix 3. I have tried here to explain the doctrine's basic import and to show that it does imply IC1, as well as the intermediary version of IC1 (and perhaps even the strongest version of IC1). I now want to continue to lay out the overall response to strangeness which IC1 is intended to support.

4. Derivation of the Impossibility Claim

As I indicated earlier, a critical step in this response is the impossibility claim IC, that is, the claim that people could not possibly have a strong strange language as their only language. In this section, I want to try to formulate an argument that will take us from the fine-grained doctrine to IC.

a. Strange Propositions

I have already made the point that in order to derive IC one must appeal to the thesis of the necessity of language. Neither the fine-grained doctrine nor IC1 implies IC in the absence of the thesis. In order to reinforce this point, let me now indicate two further principles, in addition to IC1, that seem to follow from the fine-grained doctrine but still fall short of IC.

I am in effect completing an argument that was begun in section 1.3. It was suggested in 1.3.c that the most provocative example of a strange language would be a strong strange language in which the strange words

[23]The same complication might apply to strange individuative words like "cdog," if one's ontological position leads one to regard "cdog" in Contacti as not functioning properly as a term (as not really denoting anything).

[24]To allow the fine-grained doctrine to apply to this sort of example, we can take a proposition to be itself a limiting case of a non-ultimate constituent of that proposition. The concepts-of-constituents principle then implies that in order for one to have, e.g., the concept "the average plumber's having three children," this concept must be constructible out of concepts one has of the ultimate constituents of the average plumber's having three children. From this point, the argument proceeds essentially as before.

are not synonymous with any ordinary expressions; and it was suggested in 1.3.d that sentences of the strange languages might express "strange propositions" that could not be expressed in an ordinary language. Both of these fantasies, however, seem to be excluded by the fine-grained doctrine. The latter fantasy is immediately excluded so long as we continue to assume that an "ordinary" language is one whose general words express natural properties and denote natural things ("ordinary" sentences and expressions are then those that belong to an "ordinary" language). The fine-grained doctrine immediately implies that "Something is gricular" must express an ordinary proposition, that is, a proposition whose ultimate non-logical constituents are natural properties of natural things. More generally, the following principle is implied:

> *IC2*. It is impossible for people to employ a language containing strange sentences that express propositions not expressible by ordinary sentences.

The former fantasy seems to involve a closely related point. On the simplest view of propositional identity, two sentences (or at least two sentences not containing any singular terms) express the same proposition if and only if they are synonymous.[25] Given this simple view, it would seem to follow that if the strange word "gricular" is not synonymous with any ordinary expression, then strange sentences containing "gricular" would express propositions that are not expressible by ordinary sentences. Since this possibility has been excluded by IC2, it seems that we also have the following principle:

> *IC3*. It is impossible for people to employ a language containing strange general words that are not synonymous with ordinary expressions.

An immediate corollary of IC3 is that strange words cannot be semantic primitives (i.e., words that are not synonymous with any complex expression in any language). IC3 would have to be adapted, in the by now usual manner, to the case of individuative strangeness if one holds that a word like "cdog" is not equivalent to, and hence not synonymous with, any ordinary expression. The idea would then be that it is impossible for people to employ sentences containing strange individuative words if these sentences are not synonymous with ordinary sentences.

IC2 and IC3, however, do not immediately imply IC, for the latter excludes the possibility of people having as their only language a somewhat less provocative strong version of a strange language, in which the strange sentences *do* express ordinary propositions and the strange words *are* synonymous with ordinary expressions.

Suppose it were possible for people to think without a language. Then it seems that IC must be false. If people could think without a language,

---

[25]More complicated views of propositional identity are considered in appendix 3.1 and 3.3.

they could intend at the non-linguistic level to employ the sentence "Something is gricular" to express the proposition that something is either green or circular. The fact that their language contains no words for Green or for Circular would apparently be no impediment. Even given the fine-grained doctrine, this appears to hold.

b. The Derivation of IC

IC can be defended only if we hold the thesis of the necessity of language, which I shall now understand to imply the following:

> Necessarily, if people think certain fine-grained propositions, they have a language that contains general words expressing every ulti-mate constituent property of these propositions, such that terms for non-ultimate constituent properties are (equivalent to expressions) built up from words for ultimate constituent properties (together with logical constants and singular terms).

One can perhaps imagine a weaker thesis that requires people who think the proposition p to be able to express p in a language without specify-ing any special relation between the words of the language and the con-stituents of p. But an essential part of the thesis under consideration is an *isomorphism* claim, that is, the claim that, in order to think p, people must have the wherewithal to express p isomorphically. This isomorphism claim is the linguistic counterpart of the similar claim made in the con-cepts-of-constituents principle.[26]

In the way that the fine-grained doctrine was shown to imply IC1, it seems fairly clear that the doctrine in conjunction with the thesis of the necessity of language implies:

> *IC4.* Necessarily, for any strange word "F," if people employ "F," there is an ordinary expression "E" equivalent to "F" such that for any word "G" in "E," they employ "G."[27]

(I assume the relevant reformulation for the individuative case if this is required.) One may view the derivations of IC1 and IC4 in the follow-ing light: Since the thesis of the necessity of language is the linguistic counterpart of the concepts-of-constituents principle, replacing the prin-ciple by the thesis in the fine-grained doctrine results in a linguistic coun-

---

[26]The thesis of the necessity of language might be taken to imply that the language in which people think must admit of a standard truth-conditional semantics; see sections 4.2.a and 4.2.b. Whereas in the earlier chapter the demand for this sort of semantics was supposed to derive from purely semantic considerations about the infinite richness of language, the demand in the present argument would be rooted in a metaphysical story about the structure of fine-grained propositions.

[27]As in the previous derivation of IC1, the derivation of IC4 may not be fully rigorous but follows on the most obvious interpretation of the import of the thesis of the necessity of language.

terpart of the doctrine. And IC4 is the linguistic counterpart of IC1. So, just as IC1 is derivable from the fine-grained doctrine, the linguistic counterpart of IC1 is derivable from the linguistic counterpart of the fine-grained doctrine.

The intermediary version of IC1 discussed earlier applies as well to IC4, and possibly the strongest version does too.[28] I will not enter into these details again. It should be noted that IC4 as stated is enough to establish a clear asymmetric dependence of strange words on ordinary words (i.e., ordinary words obviously do not depend on strange words in the way that, according to IC4, strange words depend on ordinary words).

IC4 implies that any strange word in a language is necessarily parasitic on an ordinary expression to which it is equivalent, in the sense that people could not possibly employ the strange word without employing an equivalent ordinary expression. A more extreme position would seem to follow if we accept the simple view that sentences (without singular terms) express the same proposition if and only if they are synonymous. IC4 could then be strengthened by substituting "synonymous" for "equivalent" (the argument for this is essentially the same as that given earlier to show that IC3 follows on the simple view of synonymy).

Given IC4 (whether in the extreme form or not), IC seems to follow immediately. If it happened that people's only language were a strong version of a strange language, they could not employ the ordinary words required by IC4. Hence, this could not possibly happen. (I temporarily suppress a minor difficulty in this argument stemming from an ambiguity in the notion of a strong strange language.[29]) So IC seems derivable from IC4, which is in turn derivable from the fine-grained doctrine supplemented by the thesis of the necessity of language.[30]

c. The Thesis of the Necessity of Language

This thesis is of course highly controversial. On its most radical interpretation, the language it refers to must be a public language. Such an interpretation might be encouraged by Davidson's view that "a creature cannot have thoughts unless it is an interpreter of the speech of another."[31] However, the interpretation that most interests me is less radical and has as its point of departure the observation that any complex system of mental representations must be sufficiently like a language to constitute a "language of thought," where it is left open whether someone's language of thought might sometimes be a public language. This sort of observation is elaborated by Harman as follows:

[28]See section 6.3.c.

[29]See section 6.5.c.

[30]It should be noted that, since we are now assuming that an "ordinary language" is one whose general words express natural properties and denote natural things, IC is closely related to (a modal version of) the Joints Principles discussed in chapters 3 and 4.

[31]Davidson 1975, p. 9.

What a mental state represents must surely be determined by the way in which certain elements are combined in that state, just as what a sentence represents is determined by the way in which certain words are combined in that sentence. Just as a finite stock of words can be combined in an infinite number of possible ways to form an infinite number of sentences, so too, it seems, a finite stock of mental elements must be combinable in an indefinite number of ways to form an indefinite number of mental representations. Mental states must have elements and structure in a way that is analogous to the way in which sentences have elements and structure. There must be, as it were, mental words, mental structure, mental names, mental predicates, mental connectives, and mental quantifiers.[32]

One may object to Harman's position on the grounds that, even if internal representations must be languagelike in the weak sense of being related by logical entailments, there is no necessity that they be languagelike in the critical sense of having an analogue of syntactic structure and of having constituents corresponding to the semantic constituents of sentences.[33] However, I think it is plausible to hold that there is that necessity, at least for the mode of representation that is properly called thinking.

It may help first to distinguish between the representation$_c$ of coarse-grained world-conditions and the representation$_f$ of fine-grained propositions. We may allow that the objector is right with respect to representation$_c$; the internal states required for a thing to represent$_c$ various world-conditions need not be languagelike in any important sense. Even simple devices such as thermometers might be said to represent$_c$, though such devices surely contain nothing that should be viewed as an internal language. The thesis of the necessity of language, however, is about thinking, which is a form of representation$_f$. It seems quite plausible to suggest that representation$_f$ does require a language.

Part of what I want to appeal to is a rather immediate intuition. Consider the fine-grained difference between thinking, say, that something is green and thinking that it is either green and hard or green and not hard. Certainly the inclination is to say that this is a difference that could arise only within language, or within a structure so akin to language that we can justifiably call it an "internal language" or "language of thought."

It is essential to be clear that the thesis of the necessity of language need not imply that what propositions people think is wholly determined by what is "in the head." The words of thought may have a contextual component, on analogy to the words of speech. Even the intralinguistic context, much emphasized by Burge, can be accommodated by the thesis.[34] The thesis formulates a general condition on the linguistic

---

[32]Harman 1978, p. 58.
[33]This objection is made in Stalnaker 1987, p. 23.
[34]See Burge 1979.

resources "people" require in order to think a proposition, not a condition on what must be in the head of some particular person who thinks a proposition on some particular occasion. In order for people to think p, some of them—perhaps only the "experts"—must understand a sentence that expresses p isomorphically. Others may then be said, perhaps, to think p (and to have the concepts involved in thinking p) in virtue of their being related to the experts in some suitable way. The thesis leaves this open.

For much the same reason, the thesis can easily accommodate Fodor's plausible suggestion that abbreviations are employed in thinking.[35] Consider what happens when one hears and understands the sentence "The average plumber has three children." On one view, when this happens, one must employ in thought a longer sentence containing an expression like "ratio of the number of plumber's children to the number of plumbers." Fodor's view, which seems more plausible, is that, when one hears and understands "The average plumber has three children," one employs in thought a structurally similar sentence (perhaps the same sentence), which functions in thought as an abbreviation for a longer sentence. The essential point to note about this view is that the presence of an abbreviation in a language necessarily depends on the presence of what it abbreviates; an abbreviation must in some sense stand proxy for what it abbreviates. Therefore, people's capacity to think a proposition in an abbreviated way necessarily depends on their (some of them) having the capacity to think it in an unabbreviated way. Hence, Fodor's view is fully compatible with the claim made by the thesis, that to think a proposition people must have in their language the wherewithal to express it isomorphically.[36]

In short, the thesis under consideration implies that the primary way of thinking p is to employ in thought a sentence that expresses p isomorphically. The thesis does not rule out various parasitic ways of thinking p.

Moreover, the thesis is not committed to any particular view about what it means to "employ a sentence in thinking," beyond the sort of abstract characterization given by Harman. As far as the thesis goes, the language of thought may be identified with a public language or it may not be. If it is not, its mode of representation may be viewed as differing greatly or not so greatly from that of a public language. For my immediate purposes, these sorts of issues can be left open.

The argument for IC appeals to the thesis of the necessity of language only in this highly abstract sense. It might be objected that at

---

[35]See Fodor 1975, pp. 152–53.

[36]I assume that if "*F*" abbreviates "*G*," then "Something is *F*" expresses the same proposition as "Something is *G*." On the simplest view of propositional identity, this would imply that "F" and "G" are synonymous. If synonymy is held to depend on obviousness of equivalence, the point may be made that, if "*F*" abbreviates "*G*," it must be obvious at least on the occasion of "*F*"'s introduction into the language that "*F*" and "*G*" are equivalent.

this level of abstraction there is really no difference between the thesis and the concepts-of-constituents principle, that is, the principle that thinking *p* requires having concepts that are related in a certain isomorphic way to the constituent properties of *p*. This is almost correct, except that there is one essential way in which the thesis goes beyond the concepts-of-constituents principle. Philosophers have often talked about concepts without feeling that they could distinguish between cases in which concepts are signified by simple mental words and cases in which concepts are signified by complex mental expressions. But that distinction is essential to the idea of a "mental structure" comparable to the structure of a language.[37] That there is this kind of structure is implied by the thesis.

The thesis of the necessity of language in conjunction with the fine-grained doctrine entails IC when the latter is understood in the following sense: It is impossible for people to have as their only language, and hence as their language of thought, a strong version of one of the strange languages. In what follows, I will often restate IC in this way: It is impossible for a strong strange language to function as the language in which people think.[38]

It is obvious that my remarks in this section about "thinking in a language" are quite shallow and perfunctory. This is not because I regard this notion as sufficiently clear. Quite the opposite, it seems to me that the notion and the issues surrounding it are impenetrably obscure and difficult. I pass quickly over these issues only because I have nothing of interest to say about them. I am, however, inclined to accept the thesis of the necessity of language in some form or other, at least for the sake of pursuing the present argument.[39] It will emerge in the next chapter that even when the thesis is assumed there are serious problems with the argument. But let me first complete the argument.

5. A "Solution" to the Division Problem

An adequate solution to the division problem would defend at least some of our strongest intuitions about strangeness while in some manner explaining, even if not fully defending, some of the other intuitions. In

---

[37]Compare with Fodor's discussion of "lexical" and "phrasal" concepts in Fodor 1981. If we continue to view equivalent concepts as identical, we should say that only some of our concepts are *had* (or realized) *lexically*, while all of our concepts are had phrasally (i.e., any concept we have answers to some complex expressions in the language of thought).

[38]This is a legitimate way of restating IC because, given the thesis of the necessity of language (which says that people must think in a language), the claim made by IC (that a strong strange language could not possibly be people's only language) is true if and only if a strong strange language could not possibly be the language in which people think.

[39]It is possible that a weakened form of the thesis might support a weakened version of IC, where the latter suffices to resolve the division problem. See note 46 later in this chapter. However, the cleanest version of the argument of this chapter derives from the thesis in the form stated.

this section I will outline a solution that flows from IC. I postpone until the next chapter a further critical evaluation of IC. I want to show that *if* IC is correct, we do seem to have the basis for a satisfactory response to the division problem.

a. The Fundamental Case

It seems quite plausible to maintain that our deepest intuitions about the strange languages concern strong versions rather than weak, and concern thought rather than communication (points I already made in chapter 1). IC sustains these intuitions in an extreme modal form. Confronted with a strong version of a strange language, and given IC, we can say: It would be impossible for that language to be the language in which people think. Or, more simply put: It would be impossible to think like that.

Might we not be able to make the latter remark even without IC? It is important to be clear how much needs to be presupposed in this response. It might seem that even IC1, which does not presuppose the thesis of the necessity of language, would allow us to say, "People couldn't possibly think like that." But I believe this is not so. Although IC1 implies that concepts of unnatural properties necessarily depend on concepts of natural properties, IC1, taken by itself, does not exclude the possibility that people may have the concept "green" while having as their only language the strong Gricular language. On IC1, their concept "gricular" necessarily depends on their concept "green," but that point does not in itself give any sense to the idea that (with respect to the strong Gricular language) "they couldn't possibly think like that." That idea has sense only if we add to IC1 some strong assumptions about their necessarily thinking in a language, assumptions tantamount to the thesis of the necessity of language.

It may still seem that once we bring in the fine-grained doctrine then, even without the thesis of the necessity of language, we would have an adequate basis to criticize, even if not to exclude the possibility of, people having as their only language the strong Gricular language. There are two suggestions that might be made. First, the fine-grained doctrine implies that the proposition that something is green is distinct from the proposition that something is both green or circular and green or non-circular (since these propositions contain different constituents). The sentence "Something is gricular and grincular" might express the latter proposition, but (and this is the key point) there would be no sentence in the Gricular language to express the former proposition. In this respect, English is superior, for the proposition that something is green is evidently expressible in English. Moreover, given the natural-constituents principle, there is no proposition containing Gricular as an ultimate constituent, and hence there is no proposition expressible in the strong Gricular language that is not expressible in English.[40]

One reaction to this suggestion might be to ask why it would be a defect in a language not to contain a sentence that expresses the proposition that something is green when the language contains an equivalent sentence that expresses the proposition that something is both green or circular and green or non-circular. I have been assuming from the outset of this book that the burden of argument is on someone who wants to claim that, where we have two equivalent sentences, it is better to assert one rather than the other. Admittedly, the present situation is different: First of all, we are now comparing (fine-grained) propositions rather than sentences; and, second, the claim is not necessarily that one proposition is better than the other, but that it is better to be able to express both rather than only one. However, the basis for this claim remains unclear. (From a purely pragmatic standpoint, what seems important is which world-conditions are expressed; it does not seem to matter which, or how many, fine-grained propositions are expressed answering to a given world-condition).[41]

The second suggestion completes an argument begun in section 3.7.d. Let us say that a proposition p contains superfluous constituents if there is a necessarily equivalent proposition p' such that every constituent of p' is a constituent of p (and occurs as many times in p), but some constituent of p is not a constituent of p' (or occurs fewer times in p').[42] It might be claimed that an explanation is somehow inadequate if its explanans is couched in terms of a proposition containing superfluous constituents. Suppose, now, that we would ordinarily explain something by reference to a thing's being green. Then, in the strong Gricular language we should have to couch this explanation in terms of a sentence that contains "gricular and grincular" (or some other constructions to the same effect). Given that the proposition expressed by this sentence must contain only natural constituents, the proposition must evidently contain superfluous constituents. Hence, employing the strong Gricular language would prevent us from giving adequate explanations.

The second suggestion might be combined with the first in the following way: It might be said that the only way to explain why something is both green or circular and green or non-circular is by reference to its being green. In this kind of case, a reduction to the more basic proposition provides the proper explanation. Since in the strong Gricular

[40]This suggestion, together with some of its limitations, was expressed by Bealer in correspondence.

[41]Cf. section 5.3.c.

[42]I limit the relation between p and p' to necessary equivalence because it is not obvious how to define a priori equivalence among fine-grained propositions (insofar as a given proposition may, on some views, be expressible by sentences that are not a priori equivalent).

language people could not express the basic proposition, they would have no way of properly explaining why something is gricular and grincular.

An immediate (and, I am inclined to think, fairly compelling) reaction to the second suggestion is that the notion of an adequate explanation being invoked is problematical. But there is a more fundamental and perhaps less obvious objection that applies to both suggestions. Both suggestions take it for granted that the sentence "Something is gricular and grincular" in the strong Gricular language will express a complex proposition such as the proposition that something is both green or circular and green or non-circular, rather than the simpler proposition that something is green. Why is this being assumed? If we believe in fine-grained propositions, we must suppose that the semantical rules for a language do not just determine the truth-conditions of sentences but also assign to sentences (relative to contexts of use) the propositions they express. It seems that we can easily imagine a version of the strong Gricular language that incorporates a "superfluous constituent deletion" rule. The rule would in effect block some of the other rules in the language from assigning to sentences propositions with superfluous constituents. The rule might imply, in part, something like this:

> If the sentences "Something is *F*" and "Something is *G*" express, respectively, the proposition that something has *P* and the proposition that something has *Q* (where *P* and *Q* may be non-ultimate structured constituents), the sentence "Something is *F* and *G*" expresses the proposition that something has *P* and *Q*, unless that proposition has superfluous constituents; in the latter case, "Something is *F* and *G*" expresses the proposition that results from deleting the superfluous constituents.

Given this rule, "Something is gricular and grincular," in the strong Gricular language, expresses the proposition that something is green (assuming that other rules assign to the sentences "Something is gricular" and "Something is grincular," respectively, the proposition that something is green or circular and the proposition that something is green or non-circular). This immediately neutralizes the second suggestion's claim that, in the strong Gricular language, explanations would have to be couched in terms of superfluous constituents. The first suggestion may still stand on the rather peculiar complaint that in the strong Gricular language one could now not express the propositions containing superfluous constituents that one can express in English. But it seems clear that some suitable restriction on the deletion rule could cancel even this complaint.

If the deletion rule strikes us as absurd—and I think it does—this reinforces the thesis of the necessity of language. The latter thesis implies that sentences in the language of thought—or, at least, the primary, non-parasitic sentences in the language of thought—must necessarily be structurally isomorphic with the propositions they express. In the language of thought, there could not possibly be any superfluous-constituent-deletion rule, and therefore, a sentence of the form "Something is gricular and grincular" could not possibly express the proposition that something is green. But if the two suggestions presuppose the thesis of the necessity of language, they are gratuitous, at least as regards the fundamental case of a strong strange language that is employed in thinking. What should be said about that case, given the presupposition, is not that it would be *bad* for one reason or another, but that it is *impossible*.

b. Secondary Strange Languages

Let us turn now to the case of a strong strange language being employed as a secondary language of communication, the language of thought being ordinary. There are a couple of obvious, even if not very strong, pragmatic arguments against this. To begin with, we may appeal to pragmatic problems in learning the strange language. Part of my reason for slighting such considerations in previous chapters is that the notion of (ostensive) learning seems not to apply to the language of thought, and, given a strange language of thought, it seems that it would be simple to learn a strange language of communication. However, given our present assumption that the language of thought must be ordinary, it would be harder to learn a strange language of communication than an ordinary one. This seems virtually a priori.[43] This consideration is still open to the objection that it makes the badness of the strange language a matter of acquisition rather than a matter of possession. But even at the level of possession, one may try to make a point about the relative difficulty of communicating in a strange language. Given that people think in an ordinary language, understanding a strange sentence in a public language must involve a relatively complex act of decoding.

These pragmatic arguments are rather flimsy, but perhaps one need not demand more at the secondary level. The arguments could be strengthened in a very dramatic way, however, if we accepted the following hypothesis put forth by Harman: The primary function of a natural language is to serve as a language of thought.

> It can be argued that a natural language like English or German will be part of the system of mental representation possessed by someone who speaks that language. For one thing, there is the experience familiar to second language learners of no longer having to translate between their first language and the language they are learning, when they come, as we sometimes say, to be able to "think in" the new language. Second, when we learn a new theory of some sort, . . . learning the language of the theory and learning to think in the new

---

[43]Perhaps what is strictly a priori is this: The hypothesis that the sentence "S" has the same truth-conditions as "T" is, other things being equal, more inductively simple and easier to confirm the more structurally similar "S" is to "T," where "S" is in the language of communication and "T" is in the language of thought.

way required by the theory seem impossible to separate. Third, giving arbitrary labels to aspects of the natural environment seems to have an immediate effect on the way we perceive that environment. Fourth, in most conversations we do not plan our remarks ahead of time but, as it were, simply "think out loud."[44]

The view that the primary use of language is in thought has roughly the following implications for the theory of communication. Linguistic communication is the communication of thought. The parties involved typically communicate with the language they use in thinking. The words used to communicate a thought are the same as or similar to those one "says to oneself" when one has that thought. Linguistic communication does not typically require any *complicated* system of coding and decoding. . . . Words are used to communicate thoughts that would ordinarily be thought in those or similar words.[45]

On Harman's hypothesis, if we try to imagine a strong strange language being employed only for communication, we are imagining a language that is not serving the primary function of our natural languages. If we accept Harman's hypothesis, in conjunction with the various metaphysical claims of this chapter, we can say the following: It is metaphysically impossible for a strong strange language to serve what is in actuality the primary function of a natural language, that is, the function of a language of thought. This would be an enormously powerful pragmatic argument against strong strange languages, an argument of a very different sort from any considered in the last chapter.[46]

c. Weak Strange Languages

Finally, let us turn briefly to the case of weak strangeness. Even with respect to this case, our current perspective is significantly different from that of the last chapter. In the last chapter, we thought of "gricular" as just a word in a language, perhaps a word that one could easily do without. This seemed to lead to rather inconclusive considerations of type and token-economy. On our present perspective, we see the employment

---

[44]Harman 1978, pp. 58–59.

[45]Harman 1975, pp. 270–71.

[46]If we accept Harman's hypothesis, then our present pragmatic argument against strangeness may not require metaphysical claims quite as strong as those made in this chapter. Instead of IC we might have the following weaker claim:

> It is impossible for people to have as their only language a strong version of one of the strange languages, if their language is to function as a language of thought.

This weakened version of IC could be derived from the fine-grained doctrine in conjunction with the following weakened form of the thesis of the necessity of language:

> Necessarily, if people's language is to function as a language of thought, it must satisfy the isomorphism condition specified in the thesis of the necessity of language.

It seems questionable, however, whether the weakened from of the thesis of the necessity of language could seem plausible to anyone who does not already accept the stronger form.

of "gricular" as being necessarily parasitic on the employment of some equivalent ordinary expression. Indeed, on the extreme version of IC4 (which substitutes "synonymous" for "equivalent" in IC4), "gricular" must be a mere abbreviation of some synonymous ordinary expression. To simplify matters a bit, let me assume the extreme version in this paragraph and the next. The pragmatic objection to "gricular," then, is that in our life situation this word is a *useless abbreviation*, an abbreviation for an expression that we almost never have need to use. Perhaps this consideration is not overwhelmingly strong, but I think it is a significant advance on those of the last chapter. It is one thing to have words in a language which could in principle be replaced by a more economical set of words, but there seems to be something especially perverse and pragmatically unreasonable about having abbreviations that are useless.

Let me now fill in a gap left in a previous argument. In chapter 1, I introduced the notion of a "strong" strange language as one in which ordinary words are replaced by strange words. This formulation is somewhat ambiguous. Suppose that "puppy" is synonymous with "young dog" and "bachelor" is synonymous with "unmarried man." Imagine a strange language that does not contain either "puppy" or "bachelor" but contains the three words "puchelor," "punchelor," and "npuchelor," which stand to "puppy" and "bachelor" the way that "gricular," "grincular," and "ngricular" stand to "green" and "circular." If this were to count as a strong strange language then the claim IC, that a strong strange language could not be the only language people employ, would not follow from (the extreme version of) IC4, which says that any strange word people employ must be synonymous with some ordinary expression made up of words they employ. In the Puchelor language, every strange word may be synonymous with some ordinary expression in the language. Let us stipulate, therefore, that a strange language does not count as "strong" unless it contains strange words that are not synonymous with any ordinary expression in the language. The Puchelor language may be only weakly strange. It can be criticized, however, as containing perversely useless abbreviations.[47]

(We can, I think, draw the following moral: It is harder to pragmatically criticize strange primary—i.e., non-parasitic—words than strange parasitic words. Hence, unless strange primary words can be excluded on metaphysical grounds, it is unlikely that a pragmatic response to strangeness will have much force.)

Let me add that there may be examples of weak strangeness which are harder to criticize than the examples that I have considered. But perhaps I have already said enough about this case to indicate, first, that there are pragmatic objections at least to many examples of weak strange-

---

[47]If one rejects the extreme version of IC4, a strong strange language should be defined as one containing strange words not equivalent to any ordinary expression in the language. Weak strange languages can be criticized as containing perversely useless *parasitic* words.

ness and, second, that our firmest intuitions ought to be reserved for strong strangeness.

d. *The Lexicon of a Natural Language*

The modest aim throughout this book has been to find a justification for the strong negative intuitions we seem to have about certain extreme examples of strange languages. But if we now have a basis to hold that, at the level of thought, words must either express natural properties of natural things or be parasitic on such words (as in the case of abbreviations), it may be possible to argue further that, in our life situation, there is a practical need for words with essentially the force of many of the words we actually have. I suggested in the last chapter that, for any world-condition C, if C is important for people, it is good for them to pay attention to—and to be able to express—C, or at least conditions that necessarily entail C. Consider, for instance, the various important conditions revolving around what people eat or do not eat. Assuming that our primary, non-parasitic words are restricted to words for natural properties of natural things, it seems arguable that, in order to express the important conditions or conditions entailing them, we would need a word for Eating, or at least words for some closely related natural processes; we would also need words that denote people, and words that denote various foods, or at least words that denote natural things closely related to these. On the assumption that our primary words must express natural properties of natural things, therefore, it seems that it may be possible to reach the conclusion that much of our ordinary lexicon is more or less required by our life situation. I think I showed in the last chapter that, without the assumption, no such conclusion can be reached.

It seems clear on reflection, I think, that many specific details of the lexicon of any natural language are not rationally constrained. These details result from brute (i.e., non-normative) facts of psychology or culture. My remarks in the last paragraph imply, however, that once strange primary words are excluded as possibilities, at least the rough general contours of a natural lexicon might be seen as rationally compelled by people's life situation.

e. *The Altered Perspective*

If there is an intuitively satisfactory solution to the division problem, I believe it must be along the general lines sketched in this section. In particular, the solution must be grounded in IC, which in turn depends on some very strong metaphysical assumptions about the nature of thinking, the nature of language, the nature of properties and things, and about how all of these are necessarily interrelated. I want especially to emphasize the shift of perspective that IC brings. The perspective that I deliberately attempted to adopt throughout this book till the present chapter might be put like this. There are an indefinite number of languages that have the same descriptive content as a given language. People confront a world that could in principle be described by any of these languages. What, then, could possibly select some of them as more rational than others, or negatively select some of them as being completely absurd? Given IC, the picture is very different. The ordinariness of the primary words in which we think is metaphysically necessary. At this most basic level, there is no relevant latitude. Strangeness could only be injected at a more shallow level, and this seems pointless, at least in our life situation. I think this new perspective gets much closer to some of our strongest immediate intuitions about the division problem.

Unfortunately, I also believe that the solution to the problem given here is seriously flawed. This leads me to be skeptical about whether it is possible to formulate an intuitively satisfactory solution to the division problem. In the final chapter of this book, I will discuss some of the difficulties the solution seems to face.

7

Ontology and
the Division Problem

1. Ontology and the Order of Understanding

Perhaps the single most important insight required to understand the nature of the division problem is that there is no obvious way in which ontology can solve the problem. One must constantly struggle against the temptation to deny this. One is tempted to say, for example: "It's obvious why Contacti is an unthinkably crazy language. It's simply because there are no such things as cdogs, ctables, and so on." But the assumption that there are no such things does not explain in any obvious way why it would be unreasonable or impossible to speak a language containing sentences with the specified truth-conditions of Contacti. A corresponding remark applies to the ontological claim that there is no such universal as being gricular. This claim does not in any obvious way condemn the Gricular language. These are points that were already made in chapter 1 and elaborated in various ways in subsequent chapters.

The argument in the previous chapter attempts to show that there is a *non-obvious* way in which ontology condemns the strange languages. Ontological commitment enters the argument at two crucial points in the defense of IC. First, there is the commitment to "fine-grained propositions." These are the objects of thinking, and their structure necessarily determines the structure of thinking, that is, the structure of the language of thought. Second, there is the commitment to ontological inegalitarianism. The claim that unnatural properties and things are merely set-theoretical constructions is supposed to justify the natural-constituents principle, that is, the principle that unnatural properties and things cannot possibly occur as ultimate constituents of propositions.

I do not want to discuss the merit of these ontological commitments right now; I will say something about them in the next section. My immediate worry is that they make no real contribution to the defense of IC. To the extent that this defense is tenable, it can be formulated without these ontological commitments. They may do little more, ultimately, than contribute to the discussion a certain air of hocus-pocus, as if a rabbit is being pulled out of a hat. It may also turn out, however, that once the defense of IC is set forth in more austere terms, its force will seem diminished.

a. Propositions as Individuals

Let us begin with the ontological issue about the existence of fine-grained propositions. For expository convenience, let me stipulate that henceforth the word "individual" will be used as a synonym for "non-set." It seems clear that for many semantical purposes a fine-grained proposition can be construed as a certain kind of set-theoretical construction, for example, a sequence whose elements are properties, things, and logical operations.[1] But I take it that such a construal would not work within the fine-grained doctrine of the last chapter, if that doctrine is to function in the intended way. The main function of the doctrine in the overall argument of the last chapter was to put us in the position of saying that we cannot possibly think in strange ways because there do not exist any strange propositions to think; that is, we cannot possibly think in (strong) strange languages because there do not exist any propositions containing unnatural properties or things as ultimate constituents. But if a proposition is a certain kind of sequence (e.g., of properties, things, and logical operations), there obviously will be such sequences containing unnatural properties and things as elements, for example, a sequence containing Gricular as an element. There will be such sequences even if unnatural properties and things are merely set-theoretical constructions. Our only basis for not counting such sequences as propositions would be that they cannot figure as objects of thinking. We must, therefore, begin with the belief that it is impossible to think in strange languages, and from this we conclude that certain sequences do not count as propositions. There appears to be no semblance of an argument here that derives the impossibility of our thinking in strange languages from the ontological unavailability of certain kinds of propositions.

To put this point in a slightly different way, if fine-grained propositions are defined as those sequences that figure as the objects of thinking, then the natural-constituents principle seems to reduce in effect to the claim that thinking about unnatural properties and things must be dependent on thinking about natural properties and things. But that is essentially the concept-dependence claim IC1 that the natural-constituents principle (in conjunction with the rest of the fine-grained doctrine) was supposed to justify.

[1]See Lewis 1986, pp. 57–58.

Propositions in the fine-grained doctrine must be construed as individuals, if the doctrine is to function in the intended way. The picture presented by the doctrine is that of a domain of non-mental and non-linguistic individuals that necessarily impose their structural stamp on the language of thought. It is within the context of this picture that ontological inegalitarianism is supposed to enter as a vindication of the natural-constituents principle. The idea is that we have an insight into the essential nature of these individuals, the propositions, to the effect that their ultimate constituents cannot be sets. I now want to consider whether we really do have any such insight.

b. The Relevance of Ontological Inegalitarianism

The question that must be pressed is this: Why would it be impossible for a set to figure as the ultimate constituent of a proposition? The internal structure of sets differs in well-known ways from the internal structure of individuals. The parts of any part of an individual must themselves be its parts, but the members of a member of a set need not be its members. Moreover, it seems that sets must be grounded in individuals, in that one could not have a hierarchy of sets of sets of sets . . . , without hitting bottom at the level of individuals. Arguably, there is no corresponding principle for the part-whole relation (pace Leibniz). These are familiar points. But how do they show, or even suggest, that a set could not be an ultimate constituent?

The tempting answer is that sets are *constructions*. We do, of course, talk about "set-theoretical constructions." Since I want to assume a realist attitude toward sets—I will indicate in a moment why it would seem only to complicate the argument further, and to no special end, to look at alternatives to set realism—the notion of a set-theoretical construction must not be taken to imply that thinking literally constructs sets, in the sense of bringing them into existence. But it may be taken to imply that a concept that represents a particular set must be reached via a construction in which some logical operations are applied to concepts representing individuals. Hence, if Gricular is merely a set, the concept "gricular" must be constructed by applying, for instance, the logical operation of disjunction to the concepts "green" and "circular," the latter representing individual universals.

The essential point to note about this argument is that its weight has now come to rest entirely on the notion of a "construction." Compare the position of the ontological inegalitarian in this argument with the following position of an elitist inegalitarian. To fix our ideas, let us henceforth suppose that we are dealing with the sort of elitist who thinks that even unnatural properties and things are individuals. The elitist may maintain, however, that unnatural things like cdogs could not possibly be ultimate constituents because they are merely "mereological constructions," and that unnatural properties such as Gricular could not possibly be ultimate constituents because they are merely "logical constructions." By calling these unnatural individuals "constructions," the elitist means that thinking cannot possibly reach them except by way of concepts of natural individuals. One must conceive of a cdog as, for example, "the sum of temporal parts of dogs interrelated in such-and-such a way," and one must conceive of Gricular as, for example, "the universal that is the disjunction of Green and Circular."

The elitist, we are supposing, agrees with the ontological inegalitarian that unnatural properties and things cannot possibly be ultimate constituents. It is difficult to see why the latter is better placed to defend this principle than the former. Both philosophers can appeal to the intuition that thinking must begin with natural properties and things, and both seem hard-pressed to answer a skeptic who demands to know why this is so.

Why are we tempted to suppose that the ontological inegalitarian is better placed to defend the natural-constituents principle? I think it seems to us that the distinction between sets and individuals is *deep*, and that this element of depth is what is needed to explain why the order of understanding is such that thinking necessarily begins with natural properties and things. But, surely, there may be a deep distinction within the domain of individuals (consider the distinction between particulars and universals). And it is not obvious that the distinction between sets and individuals need strike us as relevantly deep with respect to every issue.

One may be tempted to suggest that the doctrine of propositions as individuals directly implies that sets cannot be ultimate constituents of propositions. "If propositions are individuals," it may be argued, "they cannot be built up out of sets. Sets can contain other sets as members, but individuals cannot contain sets as parts." But this argument is fallacious. Perhaps it is plausible that no set can be part of an individual.[2] It would follow that, if propositions are individuals, no sets are parts of propositions. But one ought not identify a proposition's *constituents* with its parts. When a proponent of "singular propositions" claims that Mont Blanc itself is a constituent of the proposition expressed by "Mont Blanc is more than 4,000 meters high," surely this claim is not meant to imply that any part of the mountain is a constituent of that proposition; but this would follow if one identified constituents with parts.[3] Even if propositions are individuals, they may have no parts, strictly speaking, or their parts may be related in various ways to their constituents (e.g., the members of any set of individuals that is a constituent of a proposition might be said to be parts of the proposition). There is no argument here to prevent sets from being (ultimate) constituents.

---

[2] But this seems to imply that there cannot be mereological sums of sets, since such sums would be non-sets, and hence individuals.

[3] See Frege 1980, p. 169.

Throughout this book, I have assumed agreement on the existence of sets, indeed, on the existence of sets of "actual and possible things," or functions from possible worlds to sets of things in those worlds. But the more essential assumption I have made is that it is possible to describe coherently the intended truth-conditions of sentences in the various strange languages. Obviously, without that assumption, the division problem cannot even be formulated. Given that essential assumption, I doubt that a version of ontological inegalitarianism which rejects sets (or rejects possible worlds) could substantially enhance the ontological defense, which I have just been criticizing, of the natural-constituents principle. So long as we can coherently describe the truth-conditions of the strange sentences, it seems that we must have ontological devices that would enable us to systematically associate some category of items with the strange classificatory and individuative words. (For example, on some views one might associate with "gricular" not a set of actual and possible things, but a set or sum of universals and logical operations.) The difficulty that then must arise is what the basis is for claiming that it is metaphysically impossible to think propositions having such items as ultimate constituents. In assuming the existence of sets (of actual and possible things), it seems to me that I only pose this difficulty in its most obvious form.

c. The Bare Argument

It has not been my aim in this section to reject the natural-constituents principle. Rather, I have wanted to question the general strategy of the argument in the last chapter. The strategy consisted in deriving IC from (a linguistic version of) IC1, that is, the claim that concepts of unnatural properties and things must necessarily depend on concepts of natural properties and things. The latter claim was supposed to be derived from the natural-constituents principle (in conjunction with the rest of the fine-grained doctrine), and the natural-constituents principle was supposed to be supported by considerations of ontology. I suggest that, first, ontology has little to do with the matter; and, second, things actually work the other way around: we will accept the natural-constituents principle only if we have *already* accepted the concept-dependence claim IC1.

Imagine we start out by doubting the claim that concepts representing unnatural properties and things must necessarily depend on concepts representing natural properties and things. Suppose we are then converted to ontological inegalitarianism and also to the general picture of propositions as individuals that impose their structure on thinking. Should this resolve our doubts? No; rather, our doubts ought to carry over to the natural-constituents principle. Propositions are individuals that have an essential structure, granted, but why assume that this structure excludes unnatural properties and things as ultimate constituents? This really seems to be the same question that was initially bothering us, recast in a slightly different way. It seems that we have no insight into the necessary structure of propositions—into what the ultimate constituents of propositions must be—that is independent of whatever insight we may have into the necessary order of understanding. Hence, any doubts and puzzles that we have about the latter ought to carry over to the former.

If what I have been saying is correct, it would be useful to formulate an argument for IC that does not appeal to the fine-grained doctrine or the ontological accouterments to that doctrine. I will call this the "bare argument."

> *Premise 1.* Necessarily, if people have concepts representing properties that are not natural or that do not belong to natural things, these concepts are parasitic on concepts representing natural properties of natural things.
>
> *Premise 2.* Necessarily, people must have a (mental) language containing terms for any concepts they have, such that any term signifying a parasitic concept is equivalent to an expression built up from words signifying primary or non-parasitic concepts.
>
> *Conclusion.* IC.

In Premises 1 and 2, a concept is parasitic if having it depends asymmetrically on having other concepts in terms of which it is constructible, just as a word is parasitic if employing it depends asymmetrically on employing other words in terms of which an equivalent expression can be constructed. These premises are closely related, respectively, to IC1 and the thesis of the necessity of language. The latter was formulated in the last chapter in terms of the notion of fine-grained propositions, whereas Premise 2 skirts that notion. The premise asserts that there must be a certain correspondence between parasitic concepts and parasitic words, and between primary concepts and primary words. This constitutes the essential connection between language and concepts which is implied by the thesis of the necessity of language. It seems clear that IC does follow from Premises 1 and 2.

It was pointed out in the last chapter that, unless one is prepared to associate concepts with language, it may be impossible to fully capture the sense in which concepts of the unnatural items are asymmetrically dependent on concepts of the natural items.[4] If this is so, Premise 1 presupposes Premise 2, which in effect defines what it means for concepts to be parasitic on other concepts. In the bare argument, on this construal, we start in Premise 1 with the vague idea that concepts of the unnatural items must be parasitic on concepts of the natural items, and then come to realize via Premise 2 that this really amounts to saying that words for the unnatural items must be parasitic on words for the natural items.

---

[4]That is, the asymmetric dependence might not be properly statable until one arrives at the linguistic version of IC1 (i.e., IC4). See sections 6.3.d and 6.4.b.

The suggestion I am making is that the bare argument captures whatever genuine force the argument in the last chapter had. I should emphasize again that I am not rejecting the fine-grained doctrine or even the ontological claims associated with it. Indeed, the picture of propositions as individuals that cast their structural shadows on thinking is in many ways highly suggestive, and it may even be a literally correct picture, for all that I have said. My immediate worry about it is that it may dazzle us into wrongly supposing that we have a defense of IC that goes substantially beyond the bare argument. This is wrong, as I have tried to explain, because we have reason to accept the picture (and, most essentially, the natural-constituents principle included in it) only if we have already accepted Premise 1 of the bare argument. (Once this point is understood, it may remain useful at times to continue to formulate the argument for IC in terms of the picture.)

We are left, I think, with the bare argument. The argument presupposes inegalitarianism, but it takes no ontological stand on which form of inegalitarianism. It also takes no ontological stand on the nature of propositions. Those ontological issues turn out not to be relevant. Thus laid bare, the argument may not seem like much. I will assume the correctness of the thesis of the necessity of language and hence of Premise 2. In Premise 1, however, we are thrown back essentially on the concept-dependence claims with which we began in the last chapter. As I said then, such claims may seem intuitively appealing, but we would like some argument to support them.

2. Soft and Hard Ontology

I want to say something more about the general irrelevance of certain questions of ontology to the division problem. In this section, I will offer some remarks about ontology which may help to explain this irrelevance. Let me emphasize that I regard these remarks as the most controversial in this book, and I place no reliance on them in my overall argument prior to and subsequent to this section. The reader should imagine that this section has an asterisk attached to it or that it is in parentheses.

a. Soft Questions and Verbal Questions

I want to draw a distinction between two kinds of ontological questions, which I will call "soft" and "hard" questions. I am going to maintain that there is a close connection, though perhaps not an outright equivalence, between a question's being soft and its being merely verbal. So let me begin by looking at a famous example of a verbal question outside ontology.

William James gives the following example.[5] A man tries to observe a squirrel that is clinging to a tree. The man moves around the tree but

[5]James 1907, pp. 43–45.

so does the squirrel, so that the man never gets abreast of it. The sentence under controversy was:

(1) The man went around the squirrel.

James suggested that the disputants were taking (1) in the following two different senses:

(1a) The man passed from the north of the squirrel to the east, then to the south, then to the west, and then to the north again.

(1b) The man was first in front of the squirrel, then on its right side, then behind it, then on its left, and then in front again.

James pointed out that the disputants both agreed that (1a) was true and (1b) false. So the only question was the verbal one whether to take (1) in the sense of (1a) or (1b).

Let us say that James offered a "reconciling hypothesis" in terms of the two "reconciling sentences" (1a) and (1b). The reconciling hypothesis implies that each disputant, in his or her own idiolect, correctly judges the controversial sentence (1) to be equivalent to one of the reconciling sentences. It appears that one condition for a dispute to be verbal might be the following:

> *The Equivalence Condition.* For any controversial sentence (C) within the dispute, there are two sentences (Ca) and (Cb) (the "reconciling sentences") such that (i) neither (Ca) nor (Cb) is controversial, and (ii) one disputant believes that (C) is equivalent to (Ca) and the other believes that (C) is equivalent to (Cb).

Clearly, however, the equivalence condition is not sufficient for a dispute to be verbal. Suppose that two people count out fifteen rows and eighteen columns of coins on the table. They may disagree about the truth of

(2) There are 120 coins on the table,

because they disagree about which of the following two sentences is equivalent to (2):

(2a) There are 18 × 15 coins on the table.

(2b) There are 8 × 15 coins on the table.

Both parties agree that (2a) is true and (2b) false, and one party believes, because of an arithmetical blunder, that (2) is equivalent to (2a), whereas the other party believes that (2) is equivalent to (2b). So the equivalence condition is satisfied. Yet it would be absurd to suggest the reconciling hypothesis that both parties correctly assert (2) in their own idiolects.

It seems to be important that in the disagreement about (2) the person who believes that (2) is true can be made to see that this is wrong (either by counting the coins or by going over the multiplication again). Certainly we should hesitate to say that someone asserts the truth in her own idiolect if she can be made to retract her assertion by further observation, or discussion, or calculation, or examination of examples. Even in the controversy about (1), this condition must be taken seriously. James is perhaps obliquely mindful of it when he mentions that "discussion [about (1)] had been worn threadbare. Everyone had taken sides, and was obstinate."[6] We might suggest that a condition for a dispute to be verbal is that neither disputant can be made to retract a position by further observation or argument.

There is one kind of argument that must be excluded in applying this condition. In a verbal argument, one of the disputants may be making a "verbal mistake"; that is, his idiolect may diverge from the conventional language.[7] In this case the disputant may withdraw his remark in the face of empirical evidence about the conventions of language (e.g., evidence from a dictionary). A disputant satisfies the condition if he cannot be made to withdraw his remark on the basis of further observation, logical or mathematical computation, reflection on further examples, and so on—arguments *other* than an appeal to empirical evidence about how people conventionally use language.

The relevant condition might then be formulated as follows:

> *The Consistency Condition.* Each disputant's position with respect to the controversial sentences is consistent with what the disputant would say after further observation or argument, discounting empirical arguments about the conventions of language.

I will say that a question or disagreement is "soft" if and only if it satisfies both the equivalence and consistency conditions. It seems clear that softness is not necessary for a question to be verbal. Imagine that we raise a child to apply the word "red" to blue things and the word "blue" to red things. When she goes out into the world, she will find herself in disagreement over such sentences as "The sky is blue." We may hope that she and her opponents will eventually come to see that their dispute is merely verbal, that they both say the truth in their own idiolects. In this case the equivalence condition may very well not hold, for it is doubtful that the disputants would regard any non-controversial sentence as equivalent to "The sky is blue." Where the equivalence con-

---

[6]Ibid., p. 43.

[7]This can be said even if one accepts the sort of view put forth in Burge 1979, p. 82. If someone mistakenly thinks that the word "arthritis" conventionally applies to a painful condition of the thigh and therefore utters "I have arthritis in my thigh," it may be correct to say, as Burge urges, that this person mistakenly believes that he has arthritis in his thigh. Burge may still allow that this mistake (about having arthritis in the thigh) is "verbal" rather than "substantive" in that it derives from a mistake about the conventions of language.

dition holds, the disputants can, as it were, find a neutral linguistic ground on which to dissolve their dispute. This they may not be able to do in every verbal dispute.

But should we say that the two conditions are sufficient for a dispute's being verbal? This may seem quite plausible when we consider why it is ever reasonable to accept a reconciling hypothesis rather than assume that one of the disputants is substantively in error. Clearly, we are applying some kind of "principle of charity." As Quine puts this principle, it requires us to interpret someone's words non-homophonically rather than regard the person as being illogical or irrational.[8] A reconciling hypothesis in effect invites each disputant to interpret her opponent charitably rather than homophonically. Where the two conditions are satisfied, it may seem that only an exceedingly *modest* principle of charity need be invoked. For we are not dealing here with the Quinean scenario in which someone's language is being interpreted from scratch. We assume that the disputants are speaking a common language containing a vast body of non-controversial sentences that are not being called into question. The reconciling sentences are among these. If a disputant claims that the controversial sentence C is equivalent to the reconciling sentence R, then, since the truth-conditions of R are assumed to be non-controversially given, she is in effect telling us what the truth-conditions of C are. If someone claims that a certain sentence has certain truth-conditions, and holds to this claim consistently (in the sense explained), it may appear to be a modest bit of charity indeed to assume that, at least in this person's idiolect, the sentence *does* have those truth-conditions.

Nevertheless, I am not prepared to make the blanket assertion that softness is sufficient for verbalness. There may be complicating factors that need to be taken into account, possibly on a case-by-case basis.[9] A dispute is verbal only if a plausible reconciling hypothesis can be formulated for it, and this may not be possible for every soft dispute. But I would make the following claim: If a dispute is soft, there is a presumption that it is verbal; one must have an open mind to that possibility.

b. Hard Ontology

Let us now consider whether any familiar questions of ontology are hard. We may note, to begin with, that in many ontological disagreements, the consistency condition is not satisfied. Philosophers often make an

---

[8] See Quine 1969b, p. 46.

[9] As an example of a complicating factor, the reconciling hypothesis may seem to imply that, while one of the disputant's positions is consistent with everything else that she believes, her arguments expressed for the position have no sensible bearing on it. It may be unclear in such cases whether or not "charity" supports the reconciling hypothesis.

ontological claim that they are forced to retract because of its inconsistency with other things they want to say.[10] However, as David Lewis has remarked, in ontology we seem eventually to reach a point when "all is said and done," when "all the tricky arguments and distinctions and counterexamples have been discovered."[11] That is the point at which the consistency condition is satisfied. Let me assume that in the examples that follow we have been around the dialectical maze enough times to be reasonably secure that this point has been reached. On the assumption that the consistency condition is satisfied, a dispute will be soft so long as it satisfies the equivalence condition.

It is essential to see that there are a number of fundamental ontological disagreements for which the equivalence condition does not hold. Such disagreements are hard. Consider a dispute between a Platonist and a Radical Nominalist who rejects any abstract items, including sets, properties, or numbers. One might initially suppose that this dispute will satisfy the equivalence condition if one focuses on a controversial sentence such as:

(3) There are (such things as) numbers.

The Platonist, it may be supposed, will regard (3) as equivalent to any trivial a priori necessary truth (e.g., the law of identity), whereas the Radical Nominalist will take (3) to be equivalent to any trivial a priori necessary falsehood (e.g., the denial of the law of identity). So it may appear that the equivalence condition is trivially satisfied.

However, people who disagree about (3) must also disagree about:

(3') There is an odd number that is the number of the planets.

There is no non-controversial sentence that the Platonist regards as equivalent to (3').[12] So the equivalence condition fails to hold.

It must be understood that, for a sentence to be "non-controversial," the disputants must agree not only about its actual truth-*value* but also about its truth-*conditions*, that is, the conditions under which it *would* be true. The Platonist and Radical Nominalist will agree on the truth of "If there are numbers, then (3')" (taking this in the sense of the material conditional), and the Platonist will regard this sentence as equivalent to (3'). But this cannot function as a reconciling sentence because only the Radical Nominalist regards it as a priori necessarily true. Or consider the sentence

---

[10]The lesson that consistency in ontology is not always easy to come by is brought home in a number of recent works. See, e.g., van Cleve 1986; van Inwagen 1981; Lewis and Lewis 1970.

[11]Lewis 1983c, p. x.

[12]This is on the assumption that the disputants do not both accept mereological sums. If they do, then there may be a non-controversial sentence that the Platonist regards as equivalent to (3'), constructible along the lines explained in Goodman and Quine 1947. The point I am making would then require a more complicated example than (3').

(3'a) If there are either numbers or golden mountains, then (3'),

which the Platonist will regard as equivalent to (3'). Both the Platonist and Radical Nominalist would regard (3'a) as an a posteriori contingent truth, but the sentence is still controversial because they evidently disagree about its truth-conditions, in that only the Platonist would allow that the sentence holds true for a possible situation in which there are golden mountains.[13]

There is a general pattern here that recurs in a number of ontological issues. If we look only at such general statements as "There are sets," "There are properties," and "There are propositions," it may be plausible to suppose in each case that the believer will take the statement to be a priori necessarily true and the disbeliever will take it to be a priori necessarily false. So it may seem that the equivalence condition is trivially satisfied. But in all of these cases one can formulate "applied" statements comparable to (3') for which the equivalence condition may not hold.

It must be noted that in applying the equivalence condition, one cannot simply look at a sentence, such as (3'). One needs to know what is being presupposed as the background of non-controversial sentences. If the non-controversial sentences include only those countenanced by the Radical Nominalist, then the condition fails for (3'), as we have just seen. Contrast this case with one in which both sides accept sets (the view assumed throughout this book), but there is a disagreement about the existence of numbers. Within this dispute, the equivalence condition *will* hold for (3'). So we cannot ask, simply, "Is the dispute about the existence of numbers soft?" We must ask, "Is the dispute about the existence of numbers soft when such-and-such is being assumed?"

c. Soft Ontology

Let us now consider the dispute between ontological and elitist inegalitarians. Within this dispute, it is assumed as non-controversial that some properties and things are genuine or natural and some are not. The first philosopher, O, takes this to imply that only the natural properties and things are individuals, the unnatural ones being sets. The second philosopher, E, is the sort of elitist who thinks that even unnatural properties and things are individuals. I want to show that this dispute is soft.

---

[13] A sufficient condition for a sentence to be controversial is that there is disagreement as to whether it is equivalent to a given non-controversial sentence (e.g., there is disagreement as to whether (3'a) is equivalent to the obviously non-controversial "There are no golden mountains"). However, I am not able to suggest any general criteria for deciding when people agree about the truth-conditions of a sentence. In order for a reconciling hypothesis to be plausible, it must seem plausible that the disputants agree about the truth-conditions of the reconciling sentences. This is clearly not plausible with respect to (3'a). In contrast, in an example such as James's, there seems no reason to raise any question as to whether the disputants disagree about the truth-conditions of the reconciling sentences.

Let us first consider the dispute with respect to things. We may assume that E countenances as individuals arbitrary spatial and temporal parts of things and arbitrary mereological sums of such parts, although E agrees with O that they are in general unnatural.

Imagine, now, that within some particular region of space p and time interval t, there is a brown dog and a white dog, and no other brown or white thing (i.e., in p and t, any brown or white thing overlaps either the brown dog or the white dog). A controversial sentence in the dispute between O and E is

(4) In p and t, there exists an individual that is first brown and then white.

O will say that (4) is false, and E will say that it is true. O will regard (4) as equivalent to

(4a) In p and t, there exists a natural thing that is first brown and then white.

We may assume that E will regard (4) as equivalent to:

(4b) In p and t, there exists a pair of (perhaps identical) natural things such that first some member of the pair is brown and then some member of the pair is white.

Here we are assuming that E will regard any unnatural thing (or, at least, any unnatural thing of the sort relevant to (4)) as a mereological construction out of parts and stages of natural things. (Sentence (4b) must be understood in such a manner as to accommodate the possibility that E will not regard every part of a natural thing as natural; E may regard (4) as true even on the assumption that no natural thing is wholly in p.) Since (4a) and (4b) are non-controversial sentences in this dispute, the equivalence condition holds.[14]

If the equivalence condition holds for (4), it seems that it will hold for any controversial sentence about the status of unnatural things as individuals. So this dispute is soft. I am inclined to say that here is an example of a soft dispute that is merely verbal. The reconciling hypothesis ought to be accepted that each disputant correctly judges that in his own idiolect (4) is equivalent to one of the reconciling hypotheses, (4a) or (4b).

On the basis of the principle of charity, O ought to say to himself:

My friend E evidently enjoys speaking a version of a strange individuative language rather than plain English. E's language incorporates a simulated quan-

---

[14]Another sentence that E would regard as equivalent to (4), is

In p and t, there exists either a natural or unnatural thing that is first brown and then white,

but this sentence is controversial, since I assume that O does not regard ordinary words of English like "brown" and "white" as denoting unnatural things.

tifier, i.e., a device that functions syntactically very much like a real quantifier but which permits simulated quantification over various "virtual individuals." But no matter: the truth-conditions of the sentences in E's language are perfectly coherent, and he is able to say in his language (things equivalent to) everything that I can say in mine, and vice versa.

E, for his part, ought to say to himself:

> My friend O apparently employs a restricted quantifier. In O's language, "there exists something such that it is . . ." is equivalent to "there exists either a natural individual or a set such that it is. . . ." In this way, unnatural individuals are effectively excluded. But no matter, for he is able to say in his language (things equivalent to) everything that I can say in mine, and vice versa.

d. Soft Semantic Questions

It might be objected that a substantive question must remain about the *semantics* of such sentences as (4). The reconciling hypothesis implies that both disputants speak the truth in their own idiolects, in their own versions of English. Let us call these versions O-English and E-English. O-English and E-English differ with respect to the truth-conditions of such controversial sentences as (4) but not with respect to such non-controversial sentences as (4a) and (4b). Now, consider the sentence

(5) In E-English, (4) is true in virtue of the fact that there exists some individual in p and t such that the expression "first brown and then white" denotes it.

E will accept (5) as true but O cannot, for there is, according to O, no individual in p and t that is first brown and then white. Even if O accepts the reconciling hypothesis and, therefore, accepts the fact that in E-English (4) is counted as true if a brown dog and a white dog are in p and t, O cannot possibly accept the semantic analysis of (4) given in (5). It appears that this substantive issue, at least, remains.

We should agree, I think, that this suggestion brings out one interesting difference between the ontological dispute and the dispute in James's example, for which no issue of semantic analysis arises. However, as an explanation of why the ontological dispute is substantive, I think this suggestion should strike us as implausible. The meta-linguistic issue posed by (5) seems to be entirely derivative of the object-level issue posed by (4), that is, the issue about the existence of unnatural individuals. It would, therefore, seem odd to uncover the true substantive content of the latter issue by being referred to the former.

Nevertheless, the challenge remains to explain how the equivalence condition is satisfied for (5). If we cannot do this, we have not fully succeeded in showing how the disputants, who do indeed disagree about (5), can be said to be telling the truth in their own idiolects. Half of the task is simple. We immediately have as one of our reconciling sentences the result of replacing "individual" in (5) by "natural thing." This

yields a non-controversially false sentence that O regards as equivalent
to (5). The difficulty is to find a non-controversially true sentence that
E would regard as equivalent to (5). But I think we can find such a
sentence:

> (5a) In E-English, (4) is true in virtue of the fact that there exists a
> set of stages of individuals such that the expression "first brown and
> then white" behaves as if it denotes an individual in p and t com-
> prised of the members of the set.

The sort of set referred to in (5a) might be the set S that contains the
stages of the brown dog up to a certain time, together with the stages
of the white dog after that time. S is the sort of set that O regards as
capturing the only reality that unnatural things can be said to have. E,
however, considers there to be an individual comprised of the members
of S.

I think that (5a) can be accepted as a non-controversial truth. Even
O, if O has accepted the reconciling hypothesis, should admit that in
E-English expressions behave *as if* they denote individuals comprised of
such sets as S.[15] And it seems that E but not O should take (5a) to be
equivalent to (5). If an expression behaves *as if* it denotes an individual
comprised of a set of stages, and if (as E holds) there necessarily *is* an
individual comprised of any such set, what more could one need to make
it the case that the expression *does* denote an individual so comprised?
The dispute about (5), therefore, turns out to be merely a mirror image
of, and no more substantive than, the dispute about (4). This is, I think,
what one should have expected.

(Note that E and O will disagree about the ontological status of
"stages"; E will regard stages as individuals, whereas O will regard stages
as set-theoretical constructions. But, on my argument, any object-level
dispute about stages can be reconciled in essentially the manner of (4).
Although E and O disagree about the status of stages, I think they should
agree about (5a). It should be borne in mind that "behaves as if it
denotes" is not a technical notion; all that we require is that the intuitive import of this notion makes (5a) acceptable to these disputants as a
reconciling sentence.)

There are other meta-linguistic issues that are more obviously parasitic on the issue about the truth of (4), and hence are no more substantive than that issue. I would regard it as wrong, for example, to
suggest that we have a substantive issue about whether E-English contains a simulated quantifier. The sentence (4) contains a simulated quantifier in E-English if and only if its truth in E-English does not imply
that there exists in p and t some individual that is first brown and then
white. But the question whether this is so is precisely the question
whether in the envisioned circumstances there exists in p and t some

---

[15]Cf. section 1.2.b.

individual that is first brown and then white. If the latter question is verbal, as I have suggested, so is the former.

e. Implications of Softness

It should be borne in mind that if we say that a certain ontological issue is soft, we say this only on the assumption that "all is said and done" (i.e., that the consistency condition is satisfied), and on the assumption that the issue is posed against a background of relevant agreement on other matters. Both of these assumptions seem plausible with respect to the issue of ontological versus elitist inegalitarianism. Let us contrast this issue with the related issue of egalitarianism versus inegalitarianism. The latter is likely to be hard, given a typical background of non-controversial sentences. A controversial sentence in the latter dispute might be

(6) There is no natural property that all and only things on Earth that are green or circular have in common.

Sentence (6) is controversial because only the inegalitarian would view it as being possibly true and possibly false; the egalitarian would regard it as either unintelligible or impossible. Is there a non-controversial sentence that the inegalitarian can put forth as equivalent to (6)? Some inegalitarians might regard (6) as equivalent to a sentence about objective similarity relations, or about the causal powers of properties.[16] The egalitarian, however, would typically not accept such sentences as non-controversial. The dispute would then be hard.

In the first section of this chapter, I mentioned two ontological issues that seemed to be critical to the defense of IC based on the fine-grained doctrine: the issue of ontological versus elitist inegalitarianism and the issue of propositions as individuals versus propositions as sequences. I have maintained that the first of these is soft and verbal. I believe that the second is probably soft and verbal too, given some reasonable background assumptions, but it might require an intricate discussion to clarify this issue. For my immediate purposes, it suffices if I have established that at least one of the supposedly critical ontological issues is in fact soft and verbal.

In a verbal dispute, it would generally seem safe to assume that the person whose remarks run counter to common sense is the one who is making a verbal mistake. In the dispute between E and O about (4), it seems quite clear that E's view runs counter to common sense. Assuming that this dispute is merely verbal, E is presumably misusing ordinary language. To put this another way, O-English rather than E-English is (closer to) ordinary English. We can confidently conclude (speaking plain English) that there do not exist any strange individuals that result from

---

[16]See section 3.3 and 3.4.

arbitrarily putting together the parts or stages of different things. But we regard this conclusion as being metaphysically trivial. And if someone finds it useful at times to speak E-English, that is okay, too.

I have been discussing the issue of ontological versus elitist inegalitarianism with respect to things. Parallel considerations would seem to show that the issue with respect to properties is also soft. In this issue, however, it does not seem that common sense or ordinary usage favors one side over the other.

The soft disagreement between the ontological and elitist inegalitarian has the following general structure: Both philosophers agree on the existence of certain sets but only one of them believes that these sets correspond to ("define") a certain range of individuals. I am inclined to think that soft ontological disputes that have this general structure are almost always verbal. (This would include the dispute about the existence of numbers, given the existence of sets.) In such cases it seems plausible to (charitably) attribute the dispute to a difference in what is meant by "the existence of an individual."

I expect there to be considerable resistance to the suggestion that soft ontological disputes are (often) verbal. The dominant attitude among philosophers seems to be not to treat any ontological disputes as verbal. David Lewis might be taken as representative of this attitude. Ontological disagreement, he tells us, eventually turns into "a matter of opinion" in which one side "is making a mistake of fact."[17] It seems clear that he intends this characterization to apply to such a dispute as that about (4). "A reasonable goal for a philosopher," says Lewis, "is to bring [one's opinions] into equilibrium."[18] Certainly that *is* a reasonable goal, but one way to achieve it might be to recognize that certain questions are merely verbal and that nothing is at stake but the words one uses.

Part of the resistance to this viewpoint stems from the difficulty in clearly separating object-level remarks from meta-level ones. Hence, I am afraid that my view will be taken to imply that really there is no difference between sets and individuals, or that what individuals exist depends on what language people speak, object-level claims that I would regard as incomprehensible. The correct meta-level claim, on my view, is that certain ontological disputes depend upon the fact that the disputants employ their "ontological vocabulary" in systematically different ways, where this vocabulary includes such words as "exists," "identity," "individual," "set," and "denotes." It seems to me a priori not surprising that ontological discussion might generate in different people a slightly different use of their ontological vocabulary—slightly different, in the sense that the difference is not likely to affect any remotely ordinary conversation.

[17]Lewis 1983c, p. xi.
[18]Ibid., p. x.

There are certain points of contact between my view and Carnap's famous position on ontology, as well as Putnam's recent anti-ontological stance.[19] But neither of those philosophers distinguish between soft and hard issues of ontology, which I regard as crucial. Moreover, unlike them, my position is intended to have no affinity to verificationist or anti-realist attitudes. In fact, I approach every topic of this book from the standpoint of robust or even naive realism. I do not take realism to be compromised by the view that people sometimes use their words differently.

f. Connections between Hard and Soft

One very important example of a hard question is the question about IC. Consider the sentence

(7) People on Mars have strong Contacti as their only language.

The philosopher who accepts IC will regard (7) as impossible, whereas the philosopher who rejects IC will regard (7) as possibly true and possibly false. The latter will evidently be unable to put forth a non-controversial sentence equivalent to (7). Hence, the question about the truth of IC is hard.

In the earlier ontologically loaded argument for IC, it was implied that the plausibility of IC is enhanced if one is an ontological rather than an elitist inegalitarian. But I would suggest the following principle:

Answers to hard questions ought never to be determined by answers to soft questions.

This seems obvious if soft questions are merely verbal, but even if they are not (always), the principle is plausible insofar as hard questions seem deeper and more serious than soft ones. The hard issue about IC must not be settled, therefore, by reference to the soft issue of ontological versus elitist inegalitarianism. I take this to reinforce my claim in the last section that a correct argument for IC must be bare of this ontological issue.

3. Prospects for the Impossibility Claim

The conclusion of all of the arguments in this book up to the present point might be put in terms of the following disjunction:

Either the impossibility claim IC is correct or a rather strong form of division relativism is correct.

Since, as I have maintained, division relativism seems acutely counter-intuitive, this disjunction is an argument in favor of IC. In addition, we

[19]See Carnap 1956; Putnam 1981a, 1987.

have the bare argument in favor of IC, which rests on the initial intuitiveness of the claim that concepts representing unnatural properties and things are necessarily parasitic on concepts representing natural properties and things.[20] So it would appear that the burden is on someone who wants to reject IC.

Let us contrast IC with another claim that came up several times in earlier chapters and that I had summarily dismissed. This was the claim that such division principles as the Projectibility Principle, the Similarity Principle, or the Joints Principles express irreducibly new intellectual virtues. The objection to this claim was that it seems clear that the only intellectual virtues are knowledge and rational belief, together with whatever may lead to (or be closely related to) these. Hence, it makes little sense to suggest that there is an irreducibly new intellectual virtue that consists, say, in having words for natural rather than unnatural properties. In contrast, it seems that shifting from normative to modal grounds, in the formulation of IC, avoids this objection. We have no short list of metaphysical necessities about which we can say: Any necessity of thinking, of conceptualization, must belong to that list (or be related to the list in such-and-such a way). There is room, therefore, to seriously entertain IC as a necessity of thinking.

a. The Mysterious Attraction

There is, however, another kind of general consideration that seems to undermine the plausibility of IC. According to IC, there is, as one might say, a *necessary attraction* between words of a language (or at least words of a language of thought) and a certain class of properties and things, that is, the natural ones. At the sentential level (which may be in a way the more fundamental level), the necessary attraction is between, on the one hand, sentences having a certain kind of structure and, on the other, a certain class of conditions of the world, for example, between sentences made up of the existential operator together with a single word, and world-conditions consisting of the existence of things having some natural property. It is important to feel how mysterious this attraction is. How could there be something about a property or thing which makes it necessary that words should in the first instance hook onto just that kind of property or thing, rather than another kind? How could there be something about certain world-conditions which makes it necessary that sentences having a certain kind of structure should initially express just such conditions? IC attempts to straddle the breach between language and the world in a way that seems baffling.

---

[20]Since, in the bare argument, IC follows from this concept-dependence claim in conjunction with (a version of) the thesis of the necessity of language, and since I am not going to worry any further about the latter thesis, in what follows I will often not scruple to distinguish between IC and the concept-dependence claim.

In the first section of this chapter, I argued that if we believe that thinking must begin with concepts of the natural items, we cannot justify this belief by appealing to the natural-constituents principle and the rest of the fine-grained doctrine. It might now be suggested, however, that even if the fine-grained doctrine cannot *justify* our belief in the conceptual primacy of the natural items, once we have the belief, the doctrine can *explain why* there is this primacy. The explanation is that thinking must have propositions as its object, and propositions cannot have unnatural ultimate constituents. What fails as a justification of our belief in IC may succeed as an explanation of why IC holds.

This suggestion seems to me unconvincing, for I think that when we look carefully at the purported explanation, we find that it seems quite empty. The reasons for this mirror the reasons given earlier for the failure of the fine-grained doctrine to provide the desired justification. How, really, is the conceptual primacy of the natural items explained by the doctrine? No explanation is given as to why propositions cannot contain unnatural items as ultimate constituents; nor (to put the point from another angle) is any explanation given as to why thinking must be related to just those "propositions," rather than to various set-theoretical structures that certainly do contain unnatural items as ultimate elements. If these matters can be accepted without further explanation, we might as well accept the conceptual primacy of the natural items without further explanation. It does not seem that any real explanatory move forward has taken place. The mysterious attraction of thinking to the natural items has simply been translated into the mysterious coincidence between ultimate constituents of propositions and the natural items. I suspect that what is partly at work in the back of our minds is a crude analogy to certain physical explanations, such as an explanation in which the essential structure of one chemical accounts for alterations in other chemicals with which it interacts. But propositions do not have essential structures in the a posteriori way in which chemicals do, and certainly propositions do not "interact" with thinking. If this sort of crude analogy is what moves us, then we are merely suffering from an illusion if it seems to us that the fine-grained doctrine helps us to understand why the structure of thinking must be what it is.[21]

b. Functionalism and the Mysterious Attraction

The situation we are faced with, it seems to me, is that, on the one hand, our intuition says that thinking cannot possibly begin with unnatural properties like Gricular or unnatural things like cdogs. In conflict with this intuition, however, is the sense that there is something excessively mysterious in the necessary attraction of thinking to natural properties

[21]Let me add that I do not regard this question as settled; perhaps the explanatory force of the fine-grained doctrine can be made to seem more impressive than I now appreciate.

and things. I suspect, on the basis of some casual remarks in the literature, that proponents of a causal-functionalist view of the mind may
regard the attraction as less mysterious, because causally based. I think
the opposite is the case: Given such a view of the mind, IC has no hope
of being defended.

A functionalist who is also an inegalitarian may be tempted to argue
as follows:

> The connection between words and the world must be, in one way or
> another, causal: a word expresses a property insofar as it is causally related in
> some appropriate way to that property. But only natural properties of natural
> things have causal powers. This establishes a presumption—if not the out-
> right necessity—that words in the first instance express natural properties of
> natural things.[22]

To see why this is wrong, one should begin by considering how easy
it would be in principle (perhaps even in practice) to construct a device
that indicates the presence of the property Gricular. The device may
consist of a light that blinks when, and only when, a green or circular
object is in the vicinity. The device may contain nothing that indicates
whether Green is present, or whether Circular is present; it only indicates whether Gricular is present. In the functionalist scheme, this would
have to approximate, at least in a rudimentary fashion, to the device's
having a concept representing Gricular without having concepts representing Green, or Circular, or any other relevant natural properties.

A functionalist may, of course, insist that in order for a device to be
said to have concepts, it must be far more complicated than a blinking
light. It seems clear, indeed, that not every causal process that might be
said to "carry information" or to "represent" something can be said to
think or to have concepts. A barometer is said to carry information about
the surrounding air pressure but surely has no concept of, and does not
think about, air pressure. The most obvious way for the functionalist to
distinguish between conceptual and non-conceptual representation is by
linking the former to languages or languagelike systems. But this does
not seem to affect my basic point that, for a functionalist, it must be
possible to have a concept or word representing Gricular without
having concepts or words representing any relevant natural properties
such as Green. Perhaps we get somewhat closer to the image of a
languagelike system if we imagine a device equipped with a great many
lights ("words"), where each light is associated with a property such that
the light blinks when and only when something with that property is
present. The device may contain a light that blinks when and only when
a gricular object is present but contain no light that blinks when and
only when a green object is present. Any additional complications
required (e.g., blinking "sentences" made up of blinking "words") will
evidently not alter the force of this argument.

[22]Compare with Shoemaker 1988, p. 208.

It must be clearly understood that I am not denying the claim that "only natural properties of natural things have causal powers." But this claim is being misapplied by a functionalist who thinks it can be used to show that concepts must initially represent natural properties and things. Insofar as the claim is accepted, the functionalist's "causal theory of reference" should be renamed the "physical (or nomological) necessity theory of reference." For what is evidently essential to the functionalist's picture is that a word expresses a property if, roughly, the presence (or the absence) of the property, together with certain other conditions, physically necessitates that the word will (or will not) be uttered. But a property need have no causal powers to enter into physical necessities (a point that has already been crucial in several previous contexts). Hence, it may be physically necessary that a certain word will be uttered by an entity when and only when Gricular is present, even if it is not physically necessary that another word will be uttered by that entity when and only when Green is present. Arguably, whenever the entity utters the word that indicates the presence of Gricular, there must be a causal process inside it, or leading into it, that carries either the information that Green is present or the information that Circular is present. (That much seems to follow from very general—if not strictly necessary—principles about the sorts of causal processes that are found in the world.) But the causal process need not be languagelike and need not, in any case, be inside the entity. Hence, on the causal-functionalist view, from the fact that an entity has a concept representing Gricular, it does not follow that anything, let alone it, has a concept representing Green or any other relevant natural property.

This argument seems to generalize to every concept-dependence claim. No such claim seems to be tenable on functionalist grounds. This applies even to so perennial and intuitively compelling a claim as that having a concept of the average plumber necessarily depends on having a concept of a plumber. We can, it seems, imagine a languagelike system containing various letters and numerals associated with properties and numbers such that if the symbols "Ave-P," "Q," "R," and "n" light up, this reliably indicates that the average P-thing is R-related to n Q-things. It may happen that in this system the only symbol associated with the property Plumber is one of the form "Ave-P." It would appear that, on functionalist grounds, this system may think that the average plumber has two children (or something equivalent) without having the capacity to think any propositions about something's being a plumber.

What these reflections show, I think, is that if it is impossible to have concepts of the unnatural properties and things without having concepts of the natural ones, this is neither for causal reasons nor for epistemological reasons. There is nothing about causality or knowledge as such which would make it impossible for a being to think and to know facts about the unnatural items without ever thinking or knowing anything about the natural ones. If this is impossible, it is because of something about the nature of *understanding*. But it seems that on a causal-functionalist view of the mind, there can be nothing in the nature of understanding that makes this impossible.

If we are functionalists, we must apparently reject the notion of a metaphysically necessary order of understanding, and with it any such metaphysical claim as IC. My own opinion is that the functionalist approach is misguided for essentially the metaphysical reasons found in Descartes and elaborated in Kripke's argument against mental-physical identity; but this is obviously not the place to enter into a general discussion of the mind-body problem.[23] If we are not functionalists, if, say, we accept thinking as an irreducibly non-physical phenomenon, then we need not abandon IC for the specific reasons that have just been applied to functionalism. But on any view of the mind, the notion of a necessary order of understanding must seem mystifying. To repeat the question that I raised earlier: How could there be something about a property or thing which makes it necessary that words or concepts should in the first instance hook onto just that kind of property or thing, rather than another kind?

c. Comparing Classification and Individuation

It might be countered that this question seems mystifying only at a distance from examples. It does in fact seem that when I concentrate on particular examples of concept-dependence claims, these claims seem sufficiently clear and evident. Moreover, at least if we are not functionalists, there appears to be no definite argument against these claims. So perhaps we can accept IC; and then we have our solution to the division problem.

Nevertheless, I doubt that we can simply ignore the sense of bafflement that arises when we move away from the level of particular examples and try to make some general sense of the notion of a necessary order of understanding. I now want to point out that this sense of bafflement is more severe for the case of individuation than for the case of classification. The reason is that, when we think about it in a certain way, we find that our concept of a natural property seems to be deeper than our concept of a natural thing. The basic argument for this has already been given in an earlier discussion;[24] I will here fill out the argument and apply it to the issue of IC.

A property is metaphysically natural insofar as the sharing of it makes things similar. I assume that this formulation will be acceptable to most property-inegalitarians, even those who decline to analyze property-naturalness in terms of some similarity condition such as (N). The for-

[23]I have discussed Kripke's argument in Hirsch 1986.
[24]See section 4.1.d.

mulation seems to give us a kind of handle on how a certain conceptual activity, the activity of classifying things, is necessarily linked to a certain kind of property in the world, namely, the natural properties. It seems easy to believe that the act of classifying is essentially the act of *comparing* things, of *noting similarities.* Classifying things as grue or gricular is, therefore, necessarily derivative, and parasitic on the primary case of picking out natural properties.

One might also try to express this point in terms of the Wittgensteinian notion of "going on the same way." If we are property-inegalitarians, we believe that there is an objective fact of the matter whether, in applying a word to different objects, one is going on the same way: one is doing this if and only if the word expresses a natural property. IC implies that thinking's entry into the world necessarily consists in "going on the same way"; this is why natural properties are necessarily the point at which thinking and the world first make contact. It seems possible to believe this.

But one cannot give a comparable account of the necessary connection between natural things and the conceptual activity of individuating things. There is no formulation of what a natural thing is which makes it appear reasonable that the act of individuating is essentially linked to natural things. To the extent that we can formulate any account of what constitutes a natural thing, we find ourselves driven to an apparent potpourri of conditions such as: various kinds of internal connections and continuities, boundaries marked by natural properties, a condition of minimizing change, additional conditions for transworld identity (such as the necessity of origins), and, worst of all, an appeal to some prior list of sortals. It seems impossible to look at these conditions and say: "This is why natural things are necessarily the things with which thinking first makes contact." The more one focuses on the conditions, the more baffling seems the claim made by IC with respect to natural things.

Let me draw a distinction between "deep" and "shallow" inegalitarianism. Inegalitarianism is the view that there is an objective distinction between the natural and unnatural items. A form of inegalitarianism is deep or shallow, depending on whether or not it holds that concepts representing unnatural items are necessarily parasitic on concepts representing natural items. I take inegalitarianism for granted with respect to both properties and things, but I have been saying that deep property-inegalitarianism seems less baffling than deep thing-inegalitarianism. This is what I mean when I say that the distinction between natural and unnatural properties seems deeper than the distinction between natural and unnatural things.

I must hasten to add that, baffling or not, deep thing-inegalitarianism remains intuitively compelling when we focus on particular examples. Because the examples that I have been discussing throughout this book may have taken on a somewhat numbing quality by now, let me momentarily switch to another kind of example, one related to transworld identity.[25] Try to imagine a language whose words denote things constituted by world-slices of different natural things, so that modal remarks of the form "This *F* might have been *G*" will have strange truth-conditions. The intuition is overwhelming that any concept of modally strange things must necessarily be parasitic on concepts of modally ordinary things. And we have roughly comparable intuitions, at least initially, about temporally strange things like cdogs and incars. Deep thing-inegalitarianism, therefore, cannot easily be rejected.[26]

d. The Difficulty of Degrees

My suggestion a few paragraphs back was that there is a way of viewing natural properties which seems to make a kind of sense of the fact that thinking must necessarily begin with such properties. Of course, no attempt was made to formulate a general theory of the mind which could accommodate, in a way that functionalism apparently cannot, the notion of a necessary order of understanding. Hence, the general sense of bafflement that I spoke of earlier is by no means fully erased, even for the case of properties. Moreover, I now need to point out that there is a more specific source of bafflement which applies to properties as much as to things. I will call this the *difficulty of degrees.*

I have been pretending throughout this chapter and the last that we are dealing with a simple distinction between natural and unnatural properties and things. But we have seen in chapters 3 and 4 that this distinction seems really to be a matter of degree. Our intuition in particular cases seems to say that some properties and things are more genuine than others and, correlatively, classificatory and individuative strangeness seems to be a matter of degree. The perplexing question that arises for IC is where a point along this spectrum of naturalness can be sensibly marked such that concepts of items on one side of the point are necessarily parasitic on concepts of items on the other side.

With respect to this question, the move away from the normative division principles of earlier chapters to the modal claims of this chapter and the last proves highly disadvantageous. Normative principles can readily accommodate matters of degree. It makes perfectly good sense to say that there ought not to be words for unnatural items and then to add that the strength of this normative prohibition increases with the degree of unnaturalness. But (metaphysical) impossibility admits of no degrees. IC evidently cannot be interpreted as implying that the degree

---

[25]I mentioned this sort of example briefly in section 1.4.b.

[26]At several points in Hirsch 1982, without yet appreciating the general nature of the division problem, I in effect tried to defend shallow thing-inegalitarianism, while taking for granted deep property-inegalitarianism (see especially Hirsch 1982, pp. 293–97). I now feel that I underestimated the intuitive force of deep thing-inegalitarianism. I still believe, however, that deep inegalitarianism is harder to defend for things than for properties.

to which an item is unnatural determines the degree to which it is impossible for thinking to begin with that item. IC seems to require that somewhere along the spectrum of naturalness there is a definite point beyond which what is possible suddenly becomes impossible. How could there be such a point? That is the difficulty of degrees.

One's first temptation is to try to deal with this difficulty by marking the point either at one extreme or the other. The first possibility is to distinguish between items that are "completely natural" and those that are "not completely natural." The second would be to distinguish between items that are "not completely unnatural" and those that are "completely unnatural." In discussing these possibilities, let me focus on the case of properties.

As regards the first possibility, I suggested in section 3.6.a that a property has the highest degree of metaphysical naturalness if it satisfies the similarity condition (N), or some refinement of this condition, where similarity is taken in the sense of intrinsic similarity.[27] For a property to have the highest degree of overall naturalness, it also had to satisfy various nomic requirements (and, perhaps, a requirement of local boundedness). If we allow these non-similarity considerations to enter into our current definition of a "completely" natural property, we immediately lose the advantage of being able to regard natural properties as uniquely the ones that figure in the act of noting similarities, or in "going on the same way." Furthermore, the argument for IC (both in this chapter and the last) assumes it to be a matter of metaphysical necessity whether a given property is natural, and that assumption holds only for metaphysical naturalness.[28] For our present purposes, therefore, it is better to confine ourselves to metaphysical naturalness and to define a completely natural property simply as one satisfying some relevant similarity condition such as (N).

However we work out these details, the major problem for the first approach is that our intuition in particular cases does not seem to say that concepts representing properties that are not completely natural must be parasitic on concepts representing completely natural properties. Many of our most elementary words, words that children are assumed to acquire as their first words, seem to express extrinsic properties, as well as family resemblances.[29] It might be held, heroically, that such words, despite superficial appearances, are not psychologically primary and that

[27]An alternative suggestion, noted in section 3.6.a, is that the highest degree of metaphysical naturalness belongs to the simplest properties satisfying the similarity condition.

[28]As I have tacitly understood IC, it not only makes the claim that, necessarily, words for unnatural properties are parasitic, but also claims with respect to each specific unnatural property such as Gricular that, necessarily, a word for that property is parasitic. The assumption mentioned in the text is required to get from the first claim to the second.

[29]Certainly many of them must express extrinsic properties if I was right in section 2.4.b to claim that all individuative words do so.

the concepts they signify must be built up from concepts of completely natural properties. But this view has no immediate plausibility.

The second approach would require us first to say what is meant by a "completely unnatural property." It would seem that there must be unnatural properties that are not (finitely) constructible from natural properties.[30] These might be called "super-unnatural." But we now seek a definition of complete unnaturalness that would include such properties as Grue and Gricular; so the super-unnatural properties are not what we want. Let us say that a property is "fairly natural" if it satisfies some relevant similarity condition such as (N) at least when the notion of similarity is allowed to include both intrinsic and extrinsic factors (so that sharing the property tends to make things either intrinsically or extrinsically similar). And let us now say that a family resemblance property is one that consists in the having of more than half of a set of fairly natural properties. Then we might say that a property is "completely unnatural" if it is neither fairly natural nor even a family resemblance property.

It does not seem intuitively difficult to hold that a concept that represents a completely unnatural property must be parasitic on concepts that represent properties that are not completely unnatural. The trouble here is on the other side: Our intuitions about concept dependence seem to apply just as much to many properties that are not completely unnatural. The point being marked along the naturalness spectrum does not seem to be the one that governs our intuitions. Consider the property of touching a red object that is touching a green object that is touching a blue object. This is not completely unnatural on the proposed definition. The property Gricular, by contrast, is completely unnatural. Does our intuition say that a concept representing the first property is in principle more independent than a concept representing the second? This is, on the face of it, doubtful. Nor does it seem that family resemblance properties, in the very weak sense defined, really differ significantly from simple disjunctions. It might be possible to formulate another definition of complete unnaturalness, one that will fit more felicitously with our intuitions. But I do not, at present, see how to do this.

One might attempt to deny that the difficulty of degrees is serious. It might be said that it seems intuitively clear that some concepts are necessarily parasitic on others. It seems clear, also, that at least many of the strange words discussed in this book signify concepts of the necessarily parasitic category. These intuitions are too strong to be denied. Hence, even if we cannot determine precisely where the point is, we do know that there must be in principle a point somewhere along the spectrum of naturalness such that concepts of items on one side of the point are necessarily parasitic on concepts of items on the other side. And, in many particular cases, we know which items belong on which side. This

---

[30]See Lewis 1983b, p. 372, and Shoemaker 1988, p. 207.

is enough to sustain IC. The fact that there is a gray area of cases about which we are uncertain is not of critical importance.

Perhaps IC can be sustained in this manner, but it cannot be denied that an air of mystery hangs over it. It seemed hard enough to find a theoretical underpinning for the claim that thinking necessarily begins with the natural items. But it is hard even to understand the claim that in principle one could mark off a point within the spectrum of natural-ness and correctly say: Up to here, concepts need not be parasitic but, beyond that point, concepts must be parasitic. Unless we can make sense of their being such a cutoff point, IC must be seen as a paradox.

4. Concluding Remarks

To summarize and conclude: Division relativism is the view that, even for people in essentially our life situation, there need be nothing absurd about employing the strange languages. Arguments to the contrary seem to amount to little, unless one accepts the impossibility claim, that is, the claim that strong strange languages are necessarily inadmissible at the level of thought. This claim, however, faces two kinds of difficul-ties. First, there is the general difficulty of providing a view of the nature of understanding which would make it seem intelligible that there should be a necessary order of understanding wherein natural items are prior to unnatural ones. Second, there is the more specific difficulty of degrees. Both of these difficulties seem to me overwhelming. If it is worth struggling with them, it is because they derive from intuitions about the strange languages which seem especially deep and insistent. I suspect, indeed, that whether or not we can deal with these difficulties, we can never really get ourselves to accept division relativism. I am inclined to regard division relativism as a kind of Pyrrhonian skepticism, a philo-sophical stance that Hume characterized as capable of generating tem-porary amazement but not real conviction. But, as Hume also implied, our inability to satisfy a skeptical demand may reveal something about the modesty of our understanding. If the present book is any indication, we may be far from knowing how to satisfy the division relativist's demands.

Appendix 1

Projectible Terms

Throughout chapter 2, I made use of the notion of a "projectible term." In this appendix, I want to try to clarify this notion.

1. Relative and Absolute Projectibility

In *Fact, Fiction, and Forecast*, Goodman spoke about the projectibility of *hypotheses* of the simple form "All F are G."[1] However, it has become commonplace in the literature (including some of Goodman's own writings) to talk of the projectibility of *terms*. What does this mean?

I will take a hypothesis to be a sentence, so that I can talk of the grammatical parts of a hypothesis. (There will then be equivalent hypotheses that are distinct.) Let it also be stipulated that a hypothesis cannot be a priori true.

One might initially guess that a hypothesis cannot be confirmed if it contains a non-projectible term either as its whole grammatical subject or as its whole grammatical predicate. But even "grue" occurs in such hypotheses as "All emeralds examined before *t* are grue" and "All grue things are either reflecters of light of type *g* and examined before *t* or blue and not so examined," where *t* is the time with respect to which "grue" is defined and *g* is the type of light reflected by green things. Since the first hypothesis is entailed by "All emeralds are green," and the second is entailed by "All green things reflect light of type *g*," there can be no problem in confirming them.

Throughout this discussion, I will assume that if the hypothesis *H* is projectible, and *H* entails *H'* (i.e., "If *H* then *H'*" is a priori necessary), then *H'* is also projectible.[2] Certainly this principle should hold if the credibility of a hypothesis is a function of its projectibility. (A trivial

---

[1]Goodman 1973. I make no use of Goodman's distinction between "unprojectible" and "non-projectible" (p. 101); by "non-projectible," I shall simply mean "not projectible." [2]Strictly speaking, given Goodman's terminology, *H'* would be projectible only if *H'* is supported and unexhausted (see Goodman 1973, p. 103). This will not affect any of the

corollary of the principle is that any hypothesis equivalent to a projectible hypothesis is itself projectible.) Given this principle, the point made in the last paragraph can be restated as follows: Although "grue" is not projectible, many hypotheses that contain "grue" as either the whole subject or the whole predicate are projectible.

This point may seem to show that one can talk of "projectible terms" only as relativized to other terms, so that "green" is projectible relative to certain terms, while "grue" is projectible relative to other terms. The basic idea would be that "F" and "G" are projectible relative to each other if "All F are G" is projectible. If the projectibility of terms had to be relativized in this manner, the Projectibility Principle of section 2.2 (which says that general words ought to be projectible) would also have to be relativized to read something like this:

A general word of a language ought to be projectible relative to (a sufficient number of) other general words of the language.

Perhaps English satisfies this principle to a high extent, or even completely, but it is not clear why the strange languages could not equally satisfy it. We can immediately see that at least one strange language does as well as English, namely, the language that inverts every English word with its complement. The complements of any words must be projectible relative to each other if the words are, since "All F are G" is equivalent to "All non-G are non-F." Obviously, therefore, this language will satisfy the relativized principle to the same extent that English does. Moreover, I cannot see any way of showing that there could not be a language with the same descriptive content as English, containing words such as "grue" or "gricular," which satisfies the relativized principle.

In section 2.2.a, I in effect suggested a way of defining a non-relativized notion of a "projectible term." The rough idea is that for a term to be projectible it must not apply to two classes of objects having no special evidential relationship to each other. Hence, "green or circular" is non-projectible because information about green things has no special evidential bearing on circular things. If we know that not all things are radioactive, and we are given the information that all green things are radioactive, this will not be evidence that all circular things are radioactive.

But this does not get the point quite right. I assume that we would like to say that "green fruit or circular fruit" is non-projectible (at least we would like to say this for the sake of the Projectibility Principle). But the reason for this cannot be that "All green fruit are radioactive" provides no special evidence for "All circular fruit are radioactive." Even if we are given that not all things are radioactive, the former sentence does provide evidence for the latter in virtue of providing evidence for "All

---

examples discussed in this appendix, however; all of the examples given of hypotheses entailed by projectible hypotheses are themselves supported and unexhausted.

fruit are radioactive." We can, however, explain the non-projectibility of "green fruit or circular fruit" as follows. Let us say that one sentence is *stronger* than another if the first entails the second but not vice versa. The reason why "green fruit or circular fruit" is not projectible is that a hypothesis referring to the class of green fruit cannot raise the credibility of a hypothesis referring to the class of circular fruit except by raising the credibility of a hypothesis referring to the class of fruit, the latter hypothesis being stronger than one referring to the class of green fruit or circular fruit.

To say that "p cannot raise the credibility of q except by raising the credibility of r" means that, while the credibility of q given p is higher than the prior credibility of q, the credibility of q given both p and not-r is not higher than the credibility of q given only not-r. "Green fruit or circular fruit" is not projectible because the credibility of "All circular fruit are radioactive," given both that all green fruit are radioactive and that not all fruit are radioactive, is not greater than its credibility given only that not all fruit are radioactive. By contrast, "dog" (which is equivalent to "fat dog or non-fat dog") is projectible because the credibility of "All non-fat dogs have spotted tongues," given both that all fat dogs have spotted tongues and that not all animals have spotted tongues, seems greater than its credibility given only that not all animals have spotted tongues.

We can tie these points together in terms of the following two definitions:

> *Definition.* The terms "F" and "G" are *evidentially disconnected* if and only if, for any term "H," the truth of "All F are H" cannot raise the credibility of "All G are H" (nor can the truth of the latter raise the credibility of the former) except by raising the credibility of some sentence that is stronger than "All things that are either F or G are H."[3]

On this definition, the terms "green" and "circular" are evidentially disconnected. So are the terms "green fruit" and "circular fruit," and the terms "red tomato" and "red ball." But "fat dog" and "non-fat dog" are evidentially connected. Also, any pair of terms are evidentially connected if one entails the other. Given this notion, we can define the projectibility of terms as follows:

---

[3]The definition will not work in the intended way if "H" is allowed to be equivalent to a term of the form "such that p" or some complication of this. For instance, if "H" is "green or circular and such that there are dogs," "All green things are H" entails (and raises the credibility of) "All circular things are H." Perhaps it can be assumed that such proposition-containing terms have been disqualified. (Alternatively, one may understand "raise the credibility of" in the definition to exclude entailment.)

"H" may need to be restricted in other ways as well. My hope is that the definitions offered here are essentially adequate, even if they should require some additional fine-tuning.

Definition. A term "*F*" is *projectible* if and only if it is not equivalent to the disjunction of two terms that are evidentially disconnected.

2. Which Terms Are Projectible?

Terms that are intuitively disjunctive, such as "grue" and "gricular," will not be projectible in the defined sense. This point holds independently of what language we use. In the Gricular language we can say that "gricular" is equivalent to the disjunction of the two terms "gricular and grincular" and "gricular and ngricular," and that no premise of the form "All things that are gricular and grincular are *I*" can increase the credibility of "All things that are gricular and ngricular are *I*" except perhaps by increasing the credibility of a relevantly stronger hypothesis.

More difficult to assess are intuitive conjunctions and negations. As regards the former, I would tentatively suggest that, at least in many examples, the conjunction of two (compatible) projectible terms will itself be projectible. However, the conjunction of a projectible term and a non-projectible term will often seem to be non-projectible, as in "fruit that is either green or circular."

It seems that the complement of a projectible term will often be non-projectible. "Non-green," for example, is equivalent to the disjunction of the two terms "red" and "non-red and non-green," which appear to be evidentially disconnected. Should we say, then, that typical English words containing negative prefixes are non-projectible? One might be tempted to suggest that a word like "dishonest" does not have the same status as "non-green" with respect to projectibility. Terms such as "fat and dishonest" and "non-fat and dishonest," the disjunction of which is equivalent to "dishonest," may not seem to be evidentially disconnected.

One difference that may be thought to hold between terms with standardized prefixes, such as "dishonest," and terms such as "non-green" is that the former are restricted to particular categories (e.g., to the category of intelligent beings). However, it is not implausible to hold that even the latter are so restricted.[4] Moreover, even if we consider the term "non-green body," which is explicitly restricted to a particular category, the intuition seems to be that this term is non-projectible.

If we take both "non-green" and "dishonest" as category restricted, one important difference between the two may be that "green" belongs to a range of mutually incompatible color words, whereas "honest" does not (at least on the face of it) belong to any such range of mutually incompatible words. The following seems intuitively compelling:

(1) If the complement of some color word is projectible, then so is the complement of any other color word.

---

[4] It might be held that "non-green" is restricted to the category of things with respect to which an ascription of "green" would be intelligible. See, e.g., Sommers 1967.

One can deny (1) only by showing that there is some relevant difference between the complements of the color words, which does not seem likely. From (1), it can be argued that the complement of no color word is projectible, for it seems plausible that:

> (2) For any three terms that are mutually incompatible, at most one of their complements is projectible.

Note, first, that (2) follows from

> (2') For any three terms that are mutually incompatible and exhaustive, at most one of their complements is projectible,

for if we have three mutually incompatible terms, we can always combine any two of them with a third term to form a mutually incompatible and exhaustive trio. To see the plausibility of (2'), consider, for example, the three mutually incompatible and exhaustive terms "red," "green," and "non-red and non-green." The complement of each of these is equivalent to the disjunction of the other two. Hence, if the complement of "green" is projectible, "red" must be evidentially connected to "non-red and non-green"; if the complement of "non-red and non-green" is projectible, "red" must be evidentially connected to "green." If both complements are projectible, "red" must be evidentially connected to both other terms. That is, for some "*H*," the truth of "All red things are *H*" raises the credibility of both "All green things are *H*" and "All things that are non-red and non-green are *H*," even if we are given the falsehood of the relevantly stronger sentence "All things (in the category of colored things) are *H*." This seems impossible in light of the fact that the red things, the green things, and the things that are non-red and non-green exhaust all the things there are (in that category).[5] It obviously follows from (1) and (2) that no complement of any color word is projectible. Insofar as no such argument appears to be available for "dishonest" (since "honest" does not belong to a mutually incompatible range of terms with respect to which a principle such as (1) is plausible), the projectibility of "dishonest" may remain an open question.

---

[5]This argument is less rigorous than one might wish. Clearly, however, one cannot derive (2) from a mere consideration of the standard probability calculus (since, in general, *p* may raise the credibility of *q* and raise the credibility of *r* without raising the credibility of the conjunction of *q* and *r*). The argument must depend upon intuitions about the evidential relations between terms. (2) should be compared to a principle that has been put forth in discussions of the distinction between positive and negative properties, namely,

> For any three properties that are mutually incompatible, at most one of their complements is positive.

See Sanford 1966, p. 203, and Hirsch 1989, p. 223.

3. *Projectible Terms and Hypotheses*

Assuming that the notion of a projectible term has now been somewhat clarified, I want to turn to a question about how this notion relates to that of a projectible hypothesis. We have seen examples of projectible hypotheses with both non-projectible subjects and predicates ("All grue things are either reflecters of light of type g and examined before t or blue and not so examined"). And there are examples of projectible hypotheses with non-projectible subjects and projectible predicates ("All things that are either emeralds or green are green," which is equivalent to "All emeralds are green"). Finally, there are many examples of projectible hypotheses with projectible subjects and non-projectible predicates ("All emeralds are either green or circular," which is entailed by "All emeralds are green"). So there appears on the face of it to be no definite connection between the projectibility of terms and the projectibility of hypotheses.

It should be borne in mind that when Goodman talks of a hypothesis being projectible he generally means that it is credible relative to the evidence we *normally* have.[6] Any hypothesis (of the sort under consideration) could presumably be rendered credible relative to some hypothetical evidence. Even "All emeralds are grue" might eventually become credible if all the emeralds observed before t were grue (i.e., green) and all the emeralds first observed after t were grue (i.e., blue). Certainly this point holds with respect to less extreme examples, such as "All green or circular fruit are radioactive"; we can easily describe hypothetical evidence relative to which this hypothesis would be projectible. The examples in the last paragraph serve to show that, even if we confine ourselves to the evidence we normally have, there is no general requirement that a projectible hypothesis have a projectible subject or a projectible predicate. So, whether or not we confine ourselves to the evidence we normally have, there is no straightforward connection between the projectibility of terms and the projectibility of hypotheses.

It seems plausible to suggest, however, that there is a connection between the projectibility of terms and another notion related to the projectibility of hypotheses. Let us say that a hypothesis is projectible *in the standard way* if it can be projected on the basis of any (sufficiently large) set of positive instances, given the absence of negative instances (where, as in Goodman, a positive instance of "All F are G" is an instance of "F and G," and a negative instance is an instance of "F and non-G"). One plausible idea is that if the subject term of a hypothesis is non-projectible, the hypothesis cannot be projectible in the standard way. For its subject term will then apply to two evidentially disconnected classes, so that positive instances of the hypothesis drawn from one class

---

[6]See Goodman 1973, pp. viii, 104.

will not support a projection with respect to the other class. Let me explain this further.

Projectibility, as Goodman says, is a matter of degree.[7] But it seems that a minimal condition for calling a universal hypothesis projectible is that it be more credible than any conflicting universal hypothesis. Specifically, in order for "All F are G" to be projectible, it must be more credible than any hypothesis of the form "All F that are H are non-G," where our evidence includes instances of "F and H."

Now, to say that "All F are G" is projectible in the standard way implies the following. Suppose that our evidence includes instances of "F and G" (the positive instances), no instances of "F and non-G" (no negative instances), instances of "F and H" (for some term "H"), and perhaps sundry instances of "non-G" that are not negative instances. Then, if "All F are G" is projectible in the standard way, it is, other things being equal, more credible than "All F that are H are non-G." The "other things being equal" clause is required because we are dealing with what Goodman calls "presumptive projectibility";[8] the greater credibility of "All F are G" presupposes the absence of overhypotheses (or other kinds of evidence) favoring "All F that are H are non-G." As an example of a hypothesis with a non-projectible subject term, consider "All green or circular fruit are radioactive." Suppose that our evidence includes positive instances drawn entirely from green non-circular radioactive fruit, though we have also observed circular fruit without testing them for radioactivity. And suppose that our evidence also includes sundry non-radioactive fruit, though none that are negative instances. It seems clear that, relative to this evidence, there is no presumption in favor of regarding the hypothesis as more credible than the conflicting hypothesis "All (green or circular fruit that are) circular non-green fruit are non-radioactive."

Having a projectible subject term seems, then, to be a necessary condition for a hypothesis to be projectible in the standard way.[9] In many examples, this condition seems sufficient; for instance, "All emeralds are green or circular" is projectible in the standard way, even though its predicate is non-projectible. In some cases the condition is evidently not sufficient; "All emeralds are grue" is not projectible in the standard way. The examples we have considered suggest, however, that if both the subject and predicate of a hypothesis are projectible, this is sufficient for the hypothesis to be projectible in the standard way (relative to evidence consisting of positive instances and no negative instances).

---

[7] See Goodman 1973, pp. 108ff. The account of a projectible hypothesis I am about to give is similar to Goodman's on p. 101 (except that I do not assume his theory of entrenchment).

[8] Goodman 1973, p. 108.

[9] Quine 1969a, p. 116, seems in effect to define a term as projectible when it can figure as the subject of a hypothesis that is projectible in the standard way.

Appendix 2

Similarity and Natural Properties

1. Quine's Similarity Condition

As I stated in section 3.3.a, Quine considers a similarity analysis of natural properties which says that a property P is natural if and only if it satisfies the following condition:

> For any x that lacks P, there is a y that has P such that, for any z that has P, the degree of dissimilarity between x and y is greater than that between y and z.[1]

I will henceforth call this condition (L). As we saw, Quine argues that (L) cannot be a sufficient condition of naturalness because it succumbs to the problem of imperfect community.

There is, I think, a rather fundamental mistake that Quine is making here, which I will come back to shortly. But let us first note a simpler point. (L) cannot really be the condition Quine meant to consider. For (L) does not merely appear to succumb to the problem of imperfect community. The simplest disjunctive property, such as that expressed by "green or circular," appears to satisfy (L). The set S of things that have either the property Green or the property Circular contains the subset U of things that have both properties. Anything in U will be similar to every member of S with respect to at least one of the properties. Hence, it appears that any non-member of S will be more dissimilar to some member of U than the latter is to any other member of S.

The condition that Quine really meant to consider is probably this:

> (M) For any x that lacks P, there is a y that has P such that, for any two things z and w that have P, the degree of dissimilarity between x and y is greater than that between z and w.

---

[1] Recall that throughout this discussion I assume that every property under consideration is such that some things have it and some things do not. Also, I generally assume that we are quantifying over actual and possible things.

(M), it appears, will not be satisfied by the property of being green or circular.

One might have thought to emend Quine's formulation in a different way, namely, by shifting the quantifiers in (L) in the following manner:

> (L') For any x that has P, there is a y that lacks P such that, for any z that has P, the degree of dissimilarity between x and y is greater than that between x and z.

(L') will indeed not be satisfied by a simple disjunctive property such as that expressed by "green or circular," since we are not free to restrict the choice of x to things that are both green and circular. However, it will be satisfied by any disjunctive property that entails a natural property, such as the property expressed by "green fruit or circular fruit." (L') does better than Quine's (L) in not being satisfied by typical disjunctions of compatible properties (which do not entail natural properties), but (L) does better in not being satisfied by disjunctions of incompatible properties, even when such disjunctions entail natural properties. For instance, the property expressed by "green fruit or red fruit" satisfies (L') but not (L). We need to go to (M) if we want a condition that appears to succumb only to the problem of imperfect community.

Quine assumes that an intuitively natural property such as Red will satisfy (M). This is so only if we suppose that there is an upper limit to the degree of dissimilarity between things having the property. For example, take as x some orange thing. Then one can choose as y some red thing that differs enormously from x in size, shape, and so on. But it still does not obviously follow that x and y will differ more than any two red things, for two red things may differ from each other in size and shape more than y does from x. In order for Red to satisfy (M), we must assume that there is an upper limit to how dissimilar two red things can be, and that, for the right choice of y, the difference between x and y will exceed that limit.[2] Perhaps this is an intuitively acceptable idealization.

As a solution to the problem of imperfect community, I suggested in section 3.3.a the condition

> (N) For any x and y, if x has P and y lacks P, there is a z such that z has P and, for any w, if w has P and w is at least as similar to y as z is, then w is more similar to x than y is.

2. Boundary Requirements

Robert Nozick seems to suggest another kind of connection between natural properties and similarity. In characterizing what constitutes a natural classification (which he also calls an "informative" and "illumi-

---

[2]So we are really assuming two things: first, that there is an upper limit to the dissimilarity between red things and, second, that, for any non-red thing, if there is an upper limit to the dissimilarity between it and red things, that limit exceeds the first one.

nating" classification), he says: "Two things are part of the same class
... when they are close enough and there is no third thing not in the
class which is closer to one of them than each and every other thing in
the class is."[3] There are evidently two requirements being imposed here
on the naturalness of a property P, namely,

(O) (a) For any two things x and y that have P, the degree of
similarity between x and y is high enough, and (b) for any x that
has P and y that lacks P, there is a z distinct from x that has P such
that the degree of similarity between x and y is not greater than that
between x and z.

This account appears to be defective, however. Assuming that every
natural property satisfies condition (Oa), the condition will also be satisfied
by any disjunction that entails a natural property. For instance, if the property expressed by "fruit" satisfies (Oa) then so does the property expressed
by "green fruit or circular fruit"; if the fruit are "close enough" then so
must be the green or circular fruit. As regards (Ob), Nozick says later in
that paragraph: "No boundaries can be drawn to delimit different classes
when the two points adjacent to a boundary will be as closely related as
any two points within the boundary." This seems to alter (Ob) and to suggest that (Ob) should read "the degree of similarity between x and y is *less*
than that between x and z." In any case, (Ob) is obviously not the condition Nozick was really looking for. First of all, it may be that P is such that
everything that has P has an exact duplicate distinct from it that has P. (This
will trivially be the case if we are quantifying over possible things.) But,
clearly, so long as P is an intrinsic property, even if P is intuitively disjunctive or negative, nothing that lacks P can be an exact duplicate of anything
that has P. So (Ob) will be trivially satisfied in this case. Even if we were to
exclude duplicates from consideration, it seems clear that any disjunction
of properties satisfying (Ob) must itself satisfy (Ob). Moreover, Nozick's
formulation seems to assume that only a finite number of things can have
a property. If we drop this assumption, we realize that (Ob) can be satisfied by a property P even if, for any specified small distance, we can find
two things closer than that distance such that one of them has P and the
other lacks P. This is surely not what Nozick intended.

Though it seems clear that (Oa) and (Ob) are not jointly sufficient
for naturalness, I think that what Nozick was trying to get at with condition (Ob) is important. It might be expressed as the following necessary condition on naturalness:

The Strong Boundary Requirement. There must not be a series of
things converging on a natural property.

Let us first say that two series converge on each other in the relevant
sense if the degree of dissimilarity between members of one series and

[3]Nozick 1981, p. 85.

members of the other becomes less and less as one moves to successive members, approaching zero as the limit.[4] Then, if S_1 is a series of non-P-bearers, S_1 will be said to converge on P if one can form a series S_2 of P-bearers such that the two series converge on each other.

This requirement may initially strike us as intuitively correct. Natural properties are often said to correspond to "joints" in the world. A "joint," one might suppose, must involve some form of discontinuity, a natural "break" in some sense. This may seem to preclude a situation in which a series of things outside a natural property converges upon the property.

The trouble is that many intuitively natural properties seem to fail to satisfy the strong boundary requirement. It seems quite certain that a color such as Red will not, because there is a series of orange things that converges on a series of red things. I think it would be implausible to respond to this by saying that, since there is an area of borderline cases between Red and Orange, any series of red things will end at some distance from where a series of orange things ends. We are here attempting to make sense of the idea of *objectively* natural properties and, as has often been said, vagueness is in language or thought, not in objective reality. In the present context, we must say that Red fails to satisfy the strong boundary requirement because any precisification of the term "red"—any choice we make of where to draw a precise boundary between "red" and "orange"—yields a property that fails to satisfy the requirement.

If Red fails to satisfy the requirement, then so do various intuitively natural shape properties, such as Spherical: a series of elliptically shaped objects will converge on Spherical. Indeed, if we allow possible things as well as actual ones, it seems that virtually no intuitively natural property will satisfy the requirement. It would seem, for example, that in the space of possible things, there must surely be a series of non-dogs that converges on a series of dogs.[5]

Why is it that the strong boundary requirement attracts us when even a little reflection seems to show that it is not satisfied by many of the properties we regard as natural? I believe that our intuitions in this area

---

[4]The relevant notion of "approaching zero" can be defined in terms of the standard four-termed similarity relation (without presupposing a similarity metric) as follows:

> Two series S_1 and S_2 converge on each other if and only if, for any objects x and y, if x is more similar to x than x is to y (i.e., x is not an exact duplicate of y), there is an object s_1 in S_1 and an object s_2 in S_2 such that, for any w in S_1 after s_1 and any z in S_2 after s_2, w is as similar to z as x is to y.

[5]Perhaps certain highly general properties, such as the property of being physical, satisfy the requirement. (Possibly, to call a property a "category" in one sense implies satisfaction of the requirement.) My point in the text is that the requirement seems inapplicable to the most standard examples of natural properties. Note that I interpret the requirement as referring to things at all times and places (and perhaps possible worlds). As I suggested in section 3.6.c, a "local" boundary condition may indeed have some bearing on degrees of naturalness, especially with respect to family resemblance properties.

are to some extent incoherent. (Intuitions about the property P*, considered in section 3.3.c, may be another illustration of this.) I find myself continuing to want to say that there is an upper limit to how similar non-red things can be to red things, though I realize on reflection that this must be nonsense. The fact that some of our intuitions in this area are faulty need not, however, push us to the extreme of egalitarianism. An inegalitarian can hold that our intuitions answer at least roughly to an objective distinction in the world, and that we can eventually work our way through the faulty intuitions.

The strong boundary requirement must be repudiated, but we may still wish to consider the following weaker requirement:

> *The Weak Boundary Requirement.* There must not be a series of natural properties converging on a natural property.

Perhaps the weak requirement would suffice to sustain the idea that there is a "break" in nature at the boundary of a natural property. However, there are several different ways to interpret this requirement, depending on how one defines the notion of a series of properties converging on a property. Let us say that two properties "touch" if they are incompatible and a series having one property converges on a series having the other. The requirement seems obviously wrong if it is understood to imply that no two natural properties can touch, since such presumably natural properties as Red and Orange (or Spherical and Elliptical) touch.

One might try to understand the requirement in a second way. Let us say that the "distance" between two properties P and Q is less than that between some specified pair of objects if for any x that has P there is a y that has Q such that the degree of dissimilarity between x and y is less than that between the specified pair, and for any x that has Q there is a y that has P such that the degree of dissimilarity between x and y is less than that between the specified pair. A series of properties, not containing a given property P, might be said to converge on P if the distance between members of the series and P becomes less and less as one moves to successive members, approaching zero as the limit.

If the weak requirement is understood in this sense, it appears again to be untenable. It seems virtually inevitable that a believer in natural properties will regard completely determinate properties, such as determinate shades of color, to be natural.[6] But determinate properties seem clearly to violate the second version of the weak boundary requirement. For example, any determinate shade of color will have a series of determinate shades converging on it in the sense explained.

The requirement might be interpreted in a third way, by adding to the previous definition of convergence the stipulation that a series of properties (not containing P) can be said to converge on P only if all of

---

[6]Armstrong, indeed, holds that these are the most natural properties; see Armstrong 1978, Volume 2, pp. 49, 117.

these properties are compatible with P. Evidently, determinate shades, which are not compatible, do not converge on each other in this sense. Interpreted in this third way, the weak requirement would serve, however, to exclude such properties as P^*, that is, the property of having a color between Red_{60} and $Orange_{40}$. If one considers this to be a natural property, there will be another such property shifted over a little closer to Red, and another shifted still closer, and so on, until one reaches Red. The weak boundary requirement disallows this. If the requirement is accepted, one can treat Red as natural only if one does not treat as natural such properties as P^*. Conversely, if we accept such natural properties as P^*, we must apparently repudiate any version of even the weak boundary requirement.

3. Imperfect Community Reconsidered

Once we realize that the strong boundary requirement is invalid, we should realize something else: Quine's account of the problem of imperfect community is incorrect. The problem, we recall, was supposed to arise with respect to such properties as I, which is the property of having at least two of the three properties Green, Circular, and Wooden. Quine claimed that any I-bearers z and w must share at least one of the properties, whereas, for any non-I-bearer x, one can choose an I-bearer y that is as dissimilar from x as one wants; hence, I, which is evidently not (perfectly) natural, satisfies (M). But suppose now that x is a non-I-bearer that is *almost* green and *almost* circular; and suppose that x is wooden. To choose an I-bearer farthest away from x, we can choose a non-wooden I-bearer y that differs greatly from x in material composition; but y will then have to be green and circular and hence can differ only slightly from x in both color and shape. Evidently there are I-bearers z and w that differ greatly in both material composition and shape. With respect to dimensions other than composition, shape, or color, we can make x and y, as well as z and w, as dissimilar as we like. It seems clear that the overall degree of dissimilarity between x and y need not be greater than that between z and w. So (M) is not satisfied by I, contrary to what Quine says.

Quine seems to be tacitly supposing that y can be chosen as far away from x as one pleases. That *might* have been the case if Green and Circular both satisfied the strong boundary requirement, for it might then have been the case that, say, any non-circular thing must be very dissimilar to any circular thing. Of course, that need not have been the case; even if Circular satisfied the strong boundary requirement, there might still have been non-circular things that are relatively close to being circular. So Quine's argument might collapse even if the strong boundary requirement holds. My point is that it collapses incontrovertibly, given that the strong boundary requirement does not hold.

Condition (M) seems, therefore, to be much stronger than Quine thinks.[7] There are, however, two reasons why we should not conclude that (M) is as strong as (N). First, my remarks here are not designed to show that (M) does not succumb to any possible example of the problem of imperfect community. They show only that (M) does not succumb to this problem in terms of the sort of example given by Quine. To construct a problem of imperfect community, we need three natural properties such that, for each one of them, nothing that lacks it can be said to be relatively close to having it. (The construction also depends on the three properties satisfying certain modal requirements, for example, that they be mutually compatible and that no conjunction of two entails the third.) If there are such properties, the imperfect community property constructed from them will seem to satisfy (M) without, presumably, being (perfectly) natural. Unless we can be a priori convinced that there are no such properties, (M) cannot provide an analysis of naturalness.

Furthermore, there is another problem for (M), which might be viewed as a kind of complication of the problem of imperfect community. I will call this the *problem of balls.* In geometry, a (closed) ball is a set of points that are at least as close to a given point x as is some other given point y. A property might be called a "similarity ball" if it is the property of being at least as similar to a given thing x as is some other given thing y (taking x and y as they are in the actual world).[8] For instance, let a be a certain square orange object and b a certain triangular orange object. Imagine that a and b do not differ in any respect other than shape. Let B be the similarity ball that consists in being as similar to a as b is. Some rectangular orange objects might qualify as having B; also some square red objects and some square yellow objects; also, perhaps, some rectangular red objects if their shapes and colors are sufficiently close to being square and orange. But no red object having the same triangular shape as b could qualify, for any such object would have to be more dissimilar to a than b is. It seems clear that B is not an intuitively (perfectly) natural property.[9]

I think it is also plausible to suppose that B satisfies (M). This seems to come out of the following sort of consideration. The maximal degree of dissimilarity among B-bearers must be in some sense double the "radius" of B, that is, double the dissimilarity between a and b. To make

<hr/>

[7]The same holds for (L). My earlier point was that if one thinks that the property I satisfies (L) then, by the same reasoning, even the simple disjunctive property of being either green or circular satisfies (L). In fact, neither property satisfies (L).

[8]That is, z has the property in the world w if the degree of similarity between z-in-w and x-in-actuality is as great as that between y-in-actuality and x-in-actuality. (This defines a similarity ball as indexed to the actual world; trivially, we could extend this definition to balls indexed to other worlds.)

[9]Cf. Quine 1969a, pp. 119–20.

this vivid, let us suppose that the degree of dissimilarity between a and some square red object c is the same as that between a and b, and also that the degree of dissimilarity between a and some square yellow object d is the same as that between a and b (where neither c nor d differs from a in any respect other than color). The details of these assumptions are unimportant, so long as they give us a reasonable picture of the general structure of B. Given these assumptions, the degree of dissimilarity between c and d might be taken to represent the maximal degree of dissimilarity among B-bearers. A representative non-B-bearer would be any object e having the same red color as c but differing slightly from c in shape. Evidently, the degree of dissimilarity between e and d must be greater than that between c and d. Thus, the degree of dissimilarity between a representative non-B-bearer and some B-bearer is greater than the maximal degree of dissimilarity between any B-bearers. (e is representative in this context because it is a non-B-bearer that is very close to B-bearers; if (M) is satisfied with respect to such a non-B-bearer, it should be satisfied with respect to any non-B-bearer.) (M), therefore, seems to be satisfied.

The following seems to show, however, that B does not satisfy (N). Let f be a non-B-bearer that has the same triangular shape as b and the same red color as c (and that does not differ from b or c in any respect other than color or shape). In order for (N) to be satisfied, the B-bearers closest to the non-B-bearer f must be closer to the B-bearer c than f is. But it seems that b is as close to f as any B-bearer can be, and b is evidently less close to c than f is.[10]

I am suggesting, then, that (M) but not (N) succumbs to the problem of balls.

4. (N) and Complementary Properties

I stated in section 3.3.d that if we accept condition (N) as definitive of naturalness, then it will follow that arbitrary disjunctions of natural properties are not natural, while arbitrary conjunctions of (compatible) natural properties are natural. In this section, I want to discuss the much more complicated question of whether the complement of a natural property can itself be natural.

[10]I take these considerations as supporting the view, widely held in the empirical literature, that similarity is not properly regarded as having a Euclidian metric. See, e.g., Garner 1947, pp. 100–102, where it is suggested that similarity may generally have a city-block metric, i.e., a metric in which distances between points are calculated by simply adding distances along different dimensions. I think it can be shown that in a city-block metric space, balls do not generally satisfy (N) but do generally satisfy (M). However, it is clear that in a Euclidian metric space, any set satisfying (M) must satisfy (N), and (closed) balls satisfy both. ((N) might be said to define a condition of convexity, but it must be noted that the ordinary notion of convexity is ambiguous with respect to a space, such as a city-block metric space, in which a pair of points can be connected by more than one straight line.) (My thanks to David Spring for help with this and the next section.)

As in the previous appendix, I assume that any negative term under consideration may be interpreted as restricted to some relevant category (for example, "non-green" may be restricted to visible bodies).[11] It may seem immediately obvious that a typical negative term will not satisfy (N) if negative terms are not category restricted; it is, however, not at all obvious whether such terms can satisfy (N) if they are category restricted.

In the previous appendix, I suggested that there might be a difference between such terms as "dishonest" and "non-green," for it may be that the first is projectible but not the second. I appealed to the principle that, if three terms are mutually incompatible, at most one of their complements can be projectible. I think it is possible to argue for roughly corresponding points with respect to the satisfaction of (N), and hence with respect to naturalness.

Let me first state a somewhat loose argument to show that it cannot be the case that the two properties Non-red and Non-orange both satisfy (N). A rough reformulation of (N) is

If x has P and y lacks P, anything that has P and that is sufficiently similar to y is more similar to x than y is.

Hence, if Non-red satisfies (N) then, if x is non-red and y is red, any non-red thing that is sufficiently similar to y is more similar to x than y is. In particular, if x is brown and y is red, any orange thing that is sufficiently similar to y is more similar to x than y is. That is,

(a) If an orange thing and a red thing are sufficiently similar to each other, the orange thing is more similar to any brown thing than the red thing is.

Arguing in a parallel fashion from the premise that Non-orange satisfies (N), we get the result:

(b) If an orange thing and a red thing are sufficiently similar to each other, the red thing is more similar to any brown thing than the orange thing is.

Since Red and Orange touch, we can get a red thing and an orange thing as close as we like. Let two such things be r and o. Assuming that Non-red satisfies (N), it follows from (a) that o is more similar to any brown thing than r is, but assuming that Non-orange satisfies (N), it follows from (b) that r is more similar to any brown thing than o is. Hence, it cannot be the case that both Non-red and Non-orange satisfy (N).

Generalizing on this we have the following principle:

Principle A. If the properties P, Q, and R are mutually incompatible and P and Q touch each other, then either Non-P or Non-Q fails to satisfy (N).

[11]See appendix 1.2.

I suppress certain complications in this argument.[12] Nevertheless, I think the argument does show that Principle A holds at least to a first approximation. The principle seems to hold for any properties P, Q, and R that one could readily specify in English, certainly for any ordinary properties, such as colors and shapes. (I conjecture that the principle holds at least where P, Q, and R all satisfy (N)).

Given Principle A, we can argue that complements of the standard colors fail to satisfy (N), since it seems obvious that these complements must relate to (N) in the same way. For example, it seems obvious that either the two properties Non-red and Non-orange both satisfy (N) or both fail to satisfy (N). Hence, by Principle A, they must both fail to satisfy (N). Note that there seems to be no comparable argument to show that Dishonest fails to satisfy (N). This result mirrors that of the previous appendix.

It is possible to argue more directly for the failure of many properties to satisfy (N). If P, Q, and R are mutually incompatible, let us say that P *separates* Q from R if the Q-bearers that are closest to a given P-bearer must be farther away than it is from any R-bearer. To put this a bit more precisely:

> *Definition.* P *separates* Q from R if and only if P, Q, and R are mutually incompatible and, for any P-bearer x and R-bearer y, there is a Q-bearer z such that, for any Q-bearer w, if w is at least as similar to x as z is, then w is less similar to y than x is.[13]

Orange evidently separates Red from Yellow. As an example in the domain of shape, Straight Triangle apparently separates Spherical Triangle from Straight Square, since it seems fairly clear that the spherical triangles closest to a given straight triangle must be farther away than it is from any straight square.

We now have the following principle:

> *Principle B.* If P separates Q from R, and P touches Q, then Non-P fails to satisfy (N).[14]

---

[12]The argument does not exclude the possibility that, however close we choose r and o, some non-orange thing will be closer to o than any red thing is or some non-red thing will be closer to r than any orange thing is. If such a possibility could be realized, (a) and (b) would not follow from the assumption that Non-red and Non-orange satisfy (N). And there are other, more exotic possibilities that my argument does not deal with. It seems clear, however, that such possibilities do not really apply to Red and Orange, or to any other property mentioned in this discussion.

[13]P may separate Q from R without separating R from Q. Symmetry may fail if instances of the properties are arranged as follows:

$Q\,P\,R\,P,$

in which case R-bearers that are close to a given P-bearer may be closer than it is to some Q-bearer.

[14]The qualifications mentioned for Principle A apply as well to Principle B: if the latter may admit of some exotic exceptions, it seems to hold at least with respect to all of the properties under discussion.

To see that this is so, let us consider Non-straight-triangle (i.e., the property of not being a straight triangle) as an illustration, on the assumption that Straight Triangle separates Spherical Triangle from Straight Square. Assuming that spherical triangles can be as close to straight as one wants, short of being straight triangles, it follows that Spherical Triangle touches Straight Triangle. In order for Non-straight-triangle to satisfy (N), if a non-straight-triangle is sufficiently close to a straight triangle, the former must be closer than the latter is to any non-straight-triangle. Hence, if a spherical triangle is sufficiently close to a straight triangle, the former must be closer than the latter is to any straight square. But, since Spherical Triangle touches Straight Triangle, there will be a spherical triangle and a straight triangle as close as one wants, and the former must be closer than the latter is to any straight square. This is incompatible with the assumption that Straight Triangle separates Spherical Triangle from Straight Square. It follows that Non-straight-triangle cannot satisfy (N).

It seems likely that whenever we can apply Principle A, we can also apply Principle B. To take another example, I think we can imagine a property W such that Dog and W touch and the three properties Dog, W, and Cat are mutually incompatible. Possibly, Wolf qualifies as W; if not, one can imagine a species even more closely related to Dog than Wolf is. It would then follow from Principle A that either Non-dog or Non-W fails to satisfy (N), and hence that neither does (unless there can be some reason to suppose that Dog is related to (N) differently from W). We can argue more directly from Principle B for Non-dog's not satisfying (N) by considering that, if W is a Wolflike property, Dog separates W from such properties as Half-Dog–Half-Cat or Dog Statue. With respect to a property such as Dishonest, it seems impossible to argue for its not satisfying (N) from either Principle A or B. I think it quite possible that both Honest and Dishonest do satisfy (N).

If we take (N) as definitive of naturalness, Principles A and B allow us to say that in most (though not in all) cases, if a property is natural, its complement is unnatural. In such cases, we may call the natural property the "positive" one and its complement the "negative" one. This would give us an explanation of the positive-negative distinction in terms of similarity.[15]

---

[15]On the present proposal, the positive-negative distinction may not apply to some (category-restricted) pairs of complementary properties, when both members of the pair seem to satisfy (N). Honest-Dishonest may be such a pair. (Two especially plausible examples of such pairs are Continuous-Discontinuous and Moves-Rests.)

It should be noted that the principle with respect to (N) that would correspond exactly to the one discussed in the previous appendix would be this:

> If three properties are mutually incompatible, at most one of their complements satisfies (N).

This principle does not seem to follow from Principles A and B, and I can see no way to establish it. With respect to most properties, however, there appears to be no difference in

5. The Problem of Conjunctive Entailment

The claim that (N) is sufficient for naturalness is threatened by the problem of P*, discussed in section 3.3.c, but that is a generic problem for any form of similarity analysis. I know of no non-generic problem for (N)'s sufficiency. One might have expected (N)'s necessity to be less precarious than its sufficiency, but there turns out to be a serious problem for the necessity claim.[16]

The general structure of the problem might be expressed as follows. Let us say that three properties are related by *conjunctive entailment* if they are mutually compatible, and neither one necessarily entails either of the others, but the conjunction of any two necessarily entails the third (where one property necessarily entails another if necessarily anything that has one has the other). Suppose that P, Q, and R are natural properties that conjunctively entail each other. Then there seems reason to expect that they may not satisfy (N). If x has P, Q, and R, and y has Non-P, Q, and Non-R, in order for P to satisfy (N), the P-bearers closest to y must be closer to x than y is. It seems that these closest P-bearers might include a z that has P, Non-Q, and Non-R (since there is no P-bearer that matches y in having Q and Non-R). Since y shares one of the properties with x, and z shares another one, it is not clear why z would be closer to x. Moreover, if we assume that z is closer to x, this may seem to generate a problem for Q's satisfaction of (N). One might expect the Q-bearers closest to z to include things like y that have Non-P and Non-R. But, then, for Q to satisfy (N), y must be closer to x than z is, contrary to what we had to assume for P to satisfy (N). The problem is further compounded if we try to imagine R also satisfying (N).

Consider, for example, the geometrical properties Closed, Four-Sided, and Four-Angled. These seem to be natural properties related by conjunctive entailment. Let x be a square and y a "punctured triangle," that is, the open, four-sided, three-angled figure that results from puncturing a hole in one side of a triangle. In order for Closed to satisfy (N), the closed figures closest to y must be closer to x than y is. It seems that triangles might be among these closest closed figures. However, in order for Four-Sided to satisfy (N), the four-sided figures closest to a given triangle must be closer than it is to x. It seems that punctured triangles would be among these closest four-sided figures. It therefore appears, to put it roughly, that for Closed to satisfy (N), triangles must be closer to squares than punctured triangles are, whereas the opposite

---

the application of this principle and the application of Principles A and B. Since I have shown in Hirsch 1989, p. 231, that condition (M) satisfies the following principle:

> If three properties are mutually incompatible and exhaustive, at most two of their complements satisfy (M),

assuming that (N) entails (M), we have that (N) satisfies this weaker principle too.

[16]This problem was brought to my attention by Andrew Strauss.

is required for Four-Sided to satisfy (N). And the problem is compounded if we try to imagine Four-Angled satisfying (N).

One possible response to this problem is to tough it out and insist that the correct assignments of similarity distances to geometrical figures would imply that all of the natural geometrical properties do satisfy (N). In support of this position, one should note that we certainly have no general argument to show that properties related by conjunctive entailment cannot possibly all satisfy (N). This can immediately be seen by considering the following three properties: being green and circular, being green and wooden, and being circular and wooden. These properties conjunctively entail each other, but one can quickly verify that there is no prima facie problem about their all satisfying (N). Although the geometrical example is far more complicated, it seems likely that, at least in principle, it is possible to assign similarity distances that would secure the satisfaction of (N) by all the intuitively natural geometrical properties. A proponent of the tough-it-out response might add that, even if such assignments have no independent plausibility, they should be accepted in behalf of an analysis that seems in many other respects illuminating.

My inclination, however, would be to try a different and more accommodating tack. This would be to isolate the cases of conjunctive entailment and treat them as exceptions—understandable exceptions—to the general rule that natural properties must satisfy (N). The idea would then be to qualify the analysis by saying that *P* is natural if and only if it satisfies the following condition:

> (N') For any *x* and *y*, if *x* has *P* and *y* lacks *P*, either (a) the condition specified in (N) is satisfied, or (b) there are properties *Q* and *R*, at least one of which is natural, such that *x* has both of them and *y* has only one of them, and *P*, *Q*, and *R* are related by conjunctive entailment.

The idea is to treat (N') as operating recursively. At the first level there are properties that are natural in virtue of satisfying (N). On the basis of these properties, other properties may qualify as natural under (N'). Note that we cannot simplify matters by deleting the clause "at least one of which is natural" from (N'b). Conjunctive entailment is ubiquitous among unnatural properties, so that the deleted version of (N'b) would be vacuously satisfied by virtually any unnatural property. (For instance, the three properties of being either green or circular, being either red or circular, and being either brown or circular are related by conjunctive entailment, which suggests that all such disjunctive properties would satisfy the deleted version.) Only if *Q* or *R* is natural in (N'b) do we permit a natural property *P* to fail to satisfy the condition specified in (N).

In the geometrical example, it seems quite plausible to treat Closed and Open as satisfying (N), and hence as natural at the first level. (This implies that a difference of closure counts more in similarity judgments than a difference between having n sides or angles and having $n + 1$, everything else being equal; this seems intuitively plausible.) Now, consider Four-Sided. Suppose x is a square and y is a punctured square (i.e., an open figure with five sides and four angles). Then it may be that the four-sided figures closest to y include some (e.g., punctured triangles) that are no closer to x than y is. But the failure of Four-Sided to satisfy (N) in this case would be permitted because there are the two properties Closed and Four-Angled, Closed is assumed natural, x has both of them and y has only one, and Four-Sided, Closed, and Four-Angled conjunctively entail each other. By contrast, if, keeping x as a square, we choose for y a figure that has neither Closed nor Four-Angled (e.g., a punctured pentagon), satisfaction of (N') requires that the four-sided figures closest to y be closer to x than y is. It seems that this requirement is met. This indicates how Four-Sided may qualify as natural under (N'). Note that in order for Four-Sided to qualify, it must satisfy the condition specified in (N) in many cases, even if not in all cases.

It should be emphasized that (N) is the core condition of the similarity analysis under consideration. (N') is merely a refinement of (N) introduced to deal with a quite special, if not marginal, range of cases. I am unable to feel any confidence that (N') fully deals with these cases, or that further refinements may not be needed to deal with other special cases.[17] But I do consider it quite plausible that property-naturalness is essentially equivalent to the satisfaction of (N) or some refinement of (N). It seems straightforwardly correct to say that P is natural if and only if P-bearers are in some sense more similar to each other than to other things. If we consider some intuitively natural property such as Four-Sided, it seems obvious that four-sided figures are in some sense especially similar to each other, that they are in some sense more similar to each other than to other figures. It seems clear that this is true in some sense in which it is not the case that bearers of disjunctive properties, or imperfect community properties, or similarity balls are especially similar to each other. I can see no hope of explaining what any of this means except by reference to (N) or some refinement of (N).

---

[17]One might attempt a refinement that somehow combines (N) and (M); but note that the problem of conjunctive entailment also threatens the necessity of (M).

Appendix 3

The Fine-Grained Doctrine

By the fine-grained doctrine I mean the five claims stated in section 6.3.a, the most important of which are the natural-constituents principle and the concepts-of-constituents principle. In formulating the doctrine, I deliberately left a number of questions open that I want to take up in this appendix.

1. Fine-Grained Propositions

One general question is how fine-grained are the "fine-grained propositions." The literature suggests a plethora of views about this. To say that p is fine-grained implies at least that there is a distinct proposition q such that p and q are necessarily equivalent (i.e., they hold in the same worlds). In principle, one could hold the extreme view that two sentences express the same fine-grained proposition so long as they are equivalent (as always, "equivalent" unqualified means "a priori necessarily equivalent"). This view, however, is almost never held, and is effectively excluded by the claim that fine-grained propositions are structured entities made up of constituents. Certainly, no one would regard equivalent sentences such as "Something is green" and "Something is either green and hard or green and not hard" as expressing propositions having the same constituents. At the other extreme is the view that two sentences express the same fine-grained proposition only if they are synonymous. Many authors seem to hold an intermediary view, though it is difficult to spell out clearly what this is. I will formulate a couple of possibilities presently.

The same sorts of questions about degrees of fine-grainedness apply to the notion of fine-grained properties. I will turn to that notion in section 4 of this appendix.

In order to fix the fine-grainedness of propositions, an immediately crucial question is this: Do the ultimate constituent properties of a proposition have to be unanalyzable? Perhaps this question will be somewhat more tractable if we initially confine the notion of analyzability to language or concepts. A word is analyzable if it is equivalent to an expression whose (non-logical) words are in some sense more basic than the analysandum word. (The notion of analysis is discussed further in the next section.) Let us say that the word "*F*" is *propositionally ultimate* if the property expressed by "*F*" is an ultimate constituent of any proposition expressed by a sentence containing "*F*." Our question is whether an analyzable word can be propositionally ultimate.

A basic tenet of Russell's logical atomism was to answer this question in the negative. (This answer is part of what makes the doctrine "atomism.") By contrast, the natural-constituents principle does not exclude an analyzable word from being propositionally ultimate so long as the word expresses a natural property of natural things.

Our intuitions seem to move in two directions with regard to this question. On the one hand, we want to say that ultimate constituents of propositions should answer to the metaphysically ultimate ingredients of reality, and unanalyzable words would seem to be the best candidates for representing such ingredients. On the other hand, there is the intuition, associated with the "paradox of analysis," that a proposition unanalyzed is distinct from a proposition under analysis. Suppose that I learn to recognize a particular melody, which I call "M." (I am treating "M" as a general word that applies to many melody instances.) It may be a priori necessary that M is the melody consisting of the succession of notes N_1, N_2, . . . N_n. Then one would presumably want to say that "M" is analyzable in terms of these notes. But I may have no idea that this is so. Indeed, it seems that I might not even have any concepts of particular notes. It would surely seem correct to say that, at least in one sense, the proposition that M was played is not identical with the proposition that the melody consisting of the succession N_1, N_2, . . . N_n, was played. In this sense, M seems to be an ultimate constituent property of the proposition that M was played.

We evidently have conflicting intuitions about whether the proposition that M was played is identical with the proposition that the melody consisting of the succession N_1, N_2, . . . N_n was played. It seems doubtful that this conflict can be resolved any better than by saying that there are more and less fine-grained senses of "proposition." The atomists often associated (true) propositions with "facts," where the latter were evidently fine-grained to some degree. Perhaps one is inclined to say that the fact that M was played is identical with the fact that the melody consisting of the succession N_1, N_2, . . . N_n was played. However, the *thought* that M was played does not seem to be identical with the thought that the melody consisting of the succession N_1, N_2, . . . N_n was played. Propositions in the sense of facts seem to be less fine-grained than propositions in the sense of thoughts.

I am not suggesting that "facts" are fine-grained to the lowest degree—i.e., that equivalent sentences express the same fact—or that "thoughts" are fine-grained to the highest degree—i.e., that only synonymous sentences can express the same thought. The idea would rather be roughly as follows. Let the *isomorphic case* be one in which a sentence "S_1" (relative to a certain context of utterance) expresses a proposition isomorphically and a sentence "S_2" (relative to a certain context of utterance) also expresses a proposition isomorphically, and the words in "S_1" can be put in one-to-one correspondence with the words in "S_2" such that corresponding logical words are identical, corresponding general words express the same property, and corresponding singular terms are coreferential. I will assume that in the isomorphic case "S_1" and "S_2" express the same proposition.[1] In the general case, "S_1" and "S_2" express the same proposition if and only if a certain operation converts "S_1" and "S_2" into the isomorphic case. As a first approximation, we get propositions in the more fine-grained sense of "thoughts" if we specify the relevant operation as "replacing expressions by their synonyms," and we get propositions in the less fine-grained sense of "facts" if we specify it as "replacing expressions either by their synonyms or by their analyses."[2]

It would seem to follow from these criteria of identity for "thoughts" and "facts" that a general word is propositionally ultimate with respect to "thoughts" so long as it is not synonymous with any complex expression—that is, so long as it is a semantic primitive—but to be propositionally ultimate with respect to "facts," a word must be unanalyzable.[3] (Note that if there could be a pair of non-synonymous semantic primitives that express the same property, replacing one by the other in a sentence yields a non-synonymous sentence expressing the same "thought" as well as the same "fact.")

The burden on a proponent of the fine-grained doctrine is to find a level of fine-grainedness for which the doctrine holds. Suppose that the doctrine is taken to be about facts in the previous sense. The concepts-of-constituents principle seems virtually impossible to defend on this interpretation. It seems that one can think a proposition without having

---

[1]This sketch of propositional identity probably fits Kripke's view of definite descriptions more easily than Donnelan's, but it could be altered in obvious ways to accommodate various treatments of singular propositions. My concern here is primarily with non-singular propositions. See Kripke 1977.

[2]I do not mean to suggest that "thoughts" and "facts" in the senses indicated are the only fine-grained items a sentence might be said to express. Perhaps there are also "meanings" and "concepts," which have additional kinds of fine-grainedness.

[3]As usual, when I speak of words having complex synonyms, I should be understood to include the case in which the words can be defined only within a context; a parallel qualification applies to the analyzability of words. Salmon 1986, p. 138, implies that a word is propositionally ultimate if it is not synonymous with any complex expression.

any concepts of the constituents of the proposition under analysis, as the example of M and the notes shows.

I think we must therefore assume that the fine-grained doctrine deals with propositions in the more fine-grained sense of thoughts. Henceforth, "proposition" will be understood in this sense. The doctrine, as formulated, does not say that *every* natural property can be an ultimate constituent of a proposition. However, if a property like M can be an ultimate constituent, the most obvious idea would be that any natural property can enjoy this status. Consider the conjunctive property of being both green and circular. The criteria of property-naturalness discussed in chapter 3 seem to indicate that this property is at least as natural as M. It seems, therefore, that this property can be an ultimate constituent of a proposition. Let "conj" be equivalent to "green and circular." If we suppose that there are no sources of concept dependence beyond those implied by the concepts-of-constituents principle, it would follow that one could possibly have the concept "conj" without having the concept "green" (or concepts from which the concept "green" is constructible), but one could not possibly have the concept "gricular" under these circumstances. This contrast between "gricular" and "conj" may initially seem surprising, but it can be made to seem more plausible if one imagines a situation in which the properties Green and Circular typically go together. The most extreme possibility is one in which, for any natural thing, the thing is green if and only if it is circular.[4] I think it strikes us that, in this kind of situation, people might possibly form a "gestalt" concept "conj" without necessarily distinguishing the analytical ingredients of this concept. This is indeed different from the case of "gricular," for it makes no sense to talk about a "gestalt disjunctive" concept (or about properties that always "go together disjunctively").

I want to emphasize that I do not mean to foreclose the possibility of there being constraints on ultimate constituents beyond those implied by the natural-constituents principle, or sources of concept dependence beyond those implied by the concepts-of-constituents principle.[5] These possibilities do not immediately threaten the general argument put forth in chapter 6 to derive concept-dependence claims from the fine-grained doctrine. The more critical question for that argument is whether the constraints on ultimate constituents, and the sources of concept-dependence, implied by the fine-grained doctrine can be sustained. Certainly my remarks in the last paragraph are not likely to satisfy a skeptic who wants to know why an unnatural property like Gricular cannot be an ultimate constituent, or why it should be impossible to have the concept "gricular," albeit not as a "gestalt" concept, without having the concept "green."

---

[4]Or, perhaps, for any natural thing other than a mere bit of matter, the thing is green if and only if it is circular.

[5]A possible example of the latter, touched on in section 6.3.d, is the apparent dependence of the concept of any property on the concept of the property's complement.

2. Analysis

The notion of analysis has figured in the previous discussion and has also shown up in several places throughout the book. In this section I want to make a few tentative suggestions about what is involved in giving an analysis.

I suggested in section 6.2.c that a necessary condition for a successful analysis is that no analysans concept depends on the analysandum concept. It seems plausible to suggest, further, that a sufficient condition for a successful analysis is that, besides the necessary condition being satisfied, it is also the case that the analysandum concept depends on each analysans concept. In the example of M and the notes, however, this second condition is not satisfied. What, it may be asked, makes this a successful analysis? That is, what makes the note concepts analytically more basic than the melody concept?

As a preliminary, let us say that a complex term "E" constitutes a *natural definition* of a word "F" if and only if, first, "E" is equivalent to "F"; second, no word in "E" expresses an unnatural property or denotes an unnatural thing; and, third, "E" does not contain any superfluous words (i.e., words the deletion of which would yield an expression equivalent to "E"). (Note that the third condition implies that "E" does not contain a word equivalent to "F.") It seems that in many examples, a natural definition of a word will also qualify as a correct analysis of the word. Although a word may perhaps have several different and equally correct analyses, I think that, in at least one important sense of the notion, analyses must go uniquely in one direction, from the less basic to the more basic. Hence, there cannot be a case in which one word figures in a correct analysis of a second word while the latter word also figures in a correct analysis of the former. A general principle that is suggested, then, is that one word figures in a correct analysis of a second word if the former belongs to a natural definition of the latter but not vice versa.

This principle may seem to explain why M is correctly analyzable in terms of the notes. Assuming that "M," "N_1," "N_2," . . . "N_n" all express natural properties, it may be suggested that we have a natural definition of "M" in terms of the note concepts but not vice versa. (I assume that each note concept represents an intrinsic property of one of M's notes; we want to analyze the concept "M" in terms of a succession of notes having the required intrinsic properties.) This principle seems relevant to other examples of intuitively complex concepts. A few paragraphs back, it was suggested that it might be possible for people to have the concept "conj" without having the concept "green." It would still seem correct to say that the concept "conj" is analyzable in terms of "green" and "circular." A tempting explanation of this is that "green" and "circular" belong to a natural definition of "conj" but not vice versa.

Appendix 3

These remarks need to be complicated in a certain way, however. We can, in fact, define "green" in terms of "conj" as follows: "green" is equivalent to "something that has the most determinate color P such that it is necessary that anything which is conj has P." Likewise, we might have the following definition of "N_i" in terms of "M": "(instance of) N_i" is equivalent to "something that has the most determinate intrinsic property P such that it is necessary that the i_{th} note of any token of M has P." These do seem to qualify as natural definitions insofar as they contain no words that express unnatural properties or denote unnatural things. However, these definitions require such higher-order terms as "color" and "determinate intrinsic property," that is, terms that express properties of properties, whereas natural definitions in the reverse direction—that is, "conj" in terms of "green" and "M" in terms of "N_i"—require no such higher-order terms. It appears that it counts against a natural definition's being the proper direction of analysis if the definition employs such higher-order terms.

With respect to M, another point might be made: The notes are parts of the melody. That may seem in itself sufficient to make the note concepts more basic than the melody concept. In general, it seems that, other things being equal, a natural definition of a word is favored as the proper direction of analysis if the definition describes the internal constitution of things denoted by the word.

In the previous remarks, I have indicated three conditions, each of which seems, in conjunction with the non-circularity condition, to be sufficient for a successful analysis, at least in many typical examples. If the word "F" is equivalent to the complex term "G," and the non-circularity condition is satisfied, then "G" will often constitute a proper analysis of "F" if one of the following conditions is satisfied:

(i) It is impossible to have the concept "F" without having the concepts signified by the words in "G."

(ii) "G" constitutes a natural definition of "F" (at a certain logical level), but "F" does not belong to a natural definition of any word in "G" (at that logical level).

(iii) The words in "G" express natural properties and relations of natural parts of the things denoted by "F."

I am sure that these conditions would have to be qualified in various ways before they can be strictly sufficient. Even as they stand, however, they seem to express three related ways, rooted in metaphysics, in which a concept might be less basic, less simple, than other concepts in terms of which it is analyzed.

It should be noted that, in this account, equivalent words have the same analysis, even if they are not synonymous. This seems correct at least in many examples. In a later section of this appendix, however, I will introduce the notion of an "analytic expansion" of a word, such that equivalent words that are not synonymous may have different analytic expansions.

Suppose that we have available a distinction between analyzable and unanalyzable words. It seems that on that basis we ought to be able to explain a distinction between simple and complex (coarse-grained) properties. The rough idea would be that a property is simple if and only if it could possibly be expressed by an unanalyzable word.[6] Moreover, a property might be said to be conjunctive (disjunctive, negative) if and only if it is not simple and it could possibly be expressed by the conjunction (disjunction, negation) of unanalyzable words.

3. A Kripkean Problem for the Fine-Grained Doctrine

In an earlier discussion I mentioned that, according to Kripke, it might turn out that there are two kinds of tigers that have nothing to do with each other, that is, that Tiger, rather than being a natural property, is the disjunction of two natural properties.[7] It seems difficult to reconcile this with the fine-grained doctrine. Let us suppose that Tiger turns out to be unnatural and to be the disjunction of the natural properties T_1 and T_2. It would then follow from the natural-constituents principle that, if p is a proposition expressed by a sentence containing the word "tiger," the property Tiger is not an ultimate constituent of p. What, then, could be the ultimate constituents of p? If we try to say that T_1 and T_2 are, this conflicts with the concepts-of-constituents principle. For it would then follow from that principle that anyone who thinks p must have concepts representing T_1 and T_2. This is surely wrong; it seems that to think p, one must have the concept "tiger," but surely one need have no concepts representing any particular kinds of tigers.[8]

The edge of this objection can immediately be softened by considering the extent to which Kripke's overall view about natural kind terms appears to be congenial with the natural-constituents principle. Clearly, one of Kripke's key ideas is that there is a sense in which terms such as "tiger" *aim for* natural properties. If it turns out that there is no such natural property as Tiger, this is evidently, for Kripke, a kind of misfiring of our linguistic intentions and practices. So we might try to say, at least, that the natural-constituents principle holds, barring misfires. If the whole fine-grained doctrine can be said to hold for propositions that are expressed non-defectively (i.e., without misfire), this may suffice to

---

[6]On some views, a natural-kind word like "tiger" might be considered unanalyzable (see the Kripkean view discussed in the next section). But I do not think we want to say that the property Tiger is simple. Perhaps the definition of simplicity can be relativized to special kinds of words, e.g., to words that (enable us to) pick their references out essentially (cf. section 3.5.b, p. 69). The idea would then be that a property is simple only if it could possibly be expressed by an unanalyzable word that picks out the property essentially.

[7]Cf. section 3.5.b, p. 69.

[8]I discuss this as a problem for the fine-grained doctrine, but it also appears to be a problem for the basic intuition that concepts of unnatural properties must depend on concepts of natural properties, from which the former are constructible.

formulate a suitably qualified version of the overall argument presented in chapter 6.

To defend the fine-grained doctrine without qualification, however, the most obvious move would be to deny what Kripke says about "tiger." Kripke himself says that in some examples we may "drop" a term if it turns out not to express a natural property.[9] It may be possible to claim that this holds for all examples. On this view, it is a priori that Tiger is not an unnatural property (i.e., that if there is such a property as Tiger, it is natural).

There are other ways that the Kripkean problem might be dealt with. Kripke's discussion implies two points about "tiger": first, that "tiger" (or, more accurately, the abstract expression "the property Tiger") refers rigidly to a certain property and, second, that rigid reference in this case is not fixed by a description. It is possible to accept the first point while rejecting the second. In some literature, it has been held that the reference of "tiger" is rigidly fixed by a description involving the stereotype of a tiger. The stereotype need not be unpacked; it can be represented simply as "the tiger-appearance" (which may be understood to embrace various typical forms of tiger behavior). I write "the tiger-appearance" instead of "the ordinary appearance of a tiger" to emphasize the point that one can have a concept of *the ordinary appearance of a tiger* before one has a full-blown concept of tigers. Hence, one might be able to employ "the tiger-appearance" in a non-circular analysis of "tiger." An analysis might be formulated in terms of the following biconditional:

x is a tiger if and only if *x* belongs to the species most of whose members around here in actuality have the tiger-appearance.[10]

Here it is assumed that the actuality operator serves to rigidify a description. If we agree with Kripke that Tiger can turn out to be unnatural, then we have to emend the biconditional by replacing "the species" by "a species" or something roughly to that effect.

It does not seem to me implausible to accept the biconditional (or some variation of it) to be a priori necessary. Kripke would presumably reject this. However, he does treat other terms, such as "heat" and "yellow," as having their references rigidly fixed by descriptions similar to the one in the biconditional.[11] I can see no intuitive basis for sharply distinguishing between those terms and "tiger."

[9]Kripke 1980, p. 136.

[10]This corresponds roughly to Putnam's account in Putnam 1975. It would probably be better to replace "around here" by "in that (anaphorically determined) place" because, if one were transported to Twin Earth, one's use of "tiger" would not automatically come to refer to the different species that is there called "tiger."

[11]On "heat," see Kripke 1980, p. 136; on "yellow," see p. 140, note 71. Kripke may not welcome the actuality operator as a rigidifying device, but that does not seem to be the central issue here.

If the biconditional is held not just to be a priori necessary but also to express a synonymy relation, then it would follow that the proposition that some specified thing is a tiger (let us call this a "tiger-proposition") is identical with the proposition that it belongs to a species most of whose members around here in actuality have the tiger-appearence (let us call this a "tiger-appearance-proposition"). It would then follow that Tiger is not an ultimate constituent of any tiger-proposition. Moreover, even if Tiger turns out to be the disjunction of T_1 and T_2, the latter properties would not be constituents of tiger-propositions, since they are obviously not constituents of tiger-appearance-propositions (the constituents of tiger-appearance-propositions are the property of having the tiger-appearance, the property of belonging to a species, etc.). The possible unnaturalness of Tiger would therefore present no immediate problem for the fine-grained doctrine.

However, it does not seem, on the face of it, plausible to hold that the biconditional is a synonymy relation, at least not if synonymy requires obviousness of equivalence, for the biconditional seems at best to be a typically non-obvious piece of analysis. It might be suggested that, even though the biconditional is not a synonymy relation, tiger-propositions are anyway identical with tiger-appearance propositions. An argument for this might derive from the claim, which does seem plausible to me, that one cannot possibly understand sentences containing "tiger" without having a concept of the tiger-appearance. This concept-dependence claim could easily be explained on the basis of the concepts-of-constituents principle, on the assumption that tiger-propositions are identical with tiger-appearance-propositions. Nevertheless, it is difficult to see how to defend the assumption of propositional identity if the biconditional is not a synonymy relation, for we have noted in the first section of this appendix that identity under analysis is in general not a sufficient basis for propositional identity. Certainly, if we accept the principle that words are propositionally ultimate so long as they are not synonymous with complex expressions, and we assume that the biconditional does not express a synonymy relation, then it appears that "tiger" must be propositionally ultimate and Tiger must be an ultimate constituent of tiger-propositions.

There is an intermediary position that might be adopted. It might be held that Tiger is an ultimate constituent of tiger-propositions (and "tiger" is propositionally ultimate) if and only if Tiger is a natural property. If Tiger turns out to be unnatural, there is a kind of misfiring, a kind of defectiveness in our use of the word "tiger" and sentences containing this word. In such cases, there may be a "default" rule to determine which proposition, if any, a defective utterance expresses. The default rule might be roughly this: If the sentence "S" contains a word "F" that expresses an unnatural property and that is not synonymous with any complex expression, then "S" expresses a proposition p such that p is expressible by a sentence that results from replacing "F" by an analysis, and p is such that the people who employ "S" are able to think p, that is, they have the requisite concepts representing p's constituents. (Some additional stipulation is apparently needed to choose between different levels of analysis; perhaps one takes the least detailed analysis.) If the biconditional constitutes a correct analysis of "tiger" then, if Tiger turns out to be an unnatural property, tiger-propositions turn out (by default) to be identical with tiger-appearance-propositions.[12]

Obviously, I make no attempt here to settle these delicate points of propositional identity. My aim is only to indicate how the fine-grained doctrine might be sustained in the face of the Kripkean problem. I have suggested several options for accomplishing this.

4. Fine-Grained Properties

In chapter 6 I generally assumed that the constituent properties of fine-grained propositions are themselves coarse-grained. I now want to examine this assumption.[13]

It is worth trying to clarify first what the connection is between the naturalness of coarse-grained and fine-grained properties. Only the former was treated in chapter 3. The simplest extension of that discussion would be that a fine-grained property is natural if and only if it is necessarily equivalent to a natural coarse-grained property. But, if we were to allow that fine-grained properties can be ultimate constituents, the simple extension seems to give rise to the following sort of problem. Let GH be the fine-grained property expressed by "either green and hard or green and not hard." Then GH is presumably distinct from Green. If we say that GH is natural (because necessarily equivalent to Green), and if we allow fine-grained properties to be ultimate constituents of propositions, it seems that the fine-grained doctrine does not exclude GH from possibly being an ultimate constituent of a proposition. However, this possibility seems absurd. There is the proposition that something is green, and the second proposition that something is either green and hard or green and not hard, but surely there is no third proposition consisting of the existential operator and the ultimate property-constituent GH.

One way of responding to this problem is to maintain that fine-grained properties cannot be ultimate constituents. This need not be viewed as an arbitrary stipulation. Rather, the point may be that, strictly speaking, no property has an inherent fine-grained structure. When we

---

[12]The suggestion in this paragraph, if accepted, would qualify the principle IC3 of section 6.4.a, which implies that any general word expressing an unnatural property must be synonymous with an expression built up of general words expressing natural properties; IC3 might still hold for non-defective cases.

[13]Here again (as in the last section), I present a question in terms of the fine-grained doctrine, but the question also applies directly to the intuitive claim that concepts of unnatural properties depend on concepts of natural properties: Which sort of properties do such claims involve?

make fine-grained distinctions between properties, what we are in effect really doing is distinguishing different ways in which a given property can be logically built up within different propositions. But the constituent properties of propositions (whether ultimate or non-ultimate) are themselves nothing but coarse-grained thing-conditions.[14]

This account represents, I think, the theoretically most straightforward interpretation of the fine-grained doctrine. However, in terms of the aspiration in chapter 6 of employing the doctrine in defense of concept-dependence claims, the account suffers from a certain limitation. Suppose that the species K is contingently the only species to have one of the natural properties T or U. Let "C" be a word equivalent to "something that belongs to a species that in this (actual) world has either T or U." Then, "C" expresses the coarse-grained natural property K. Hence, on the view that constituent properties are coarse-grained, there is apparently no reason why "C" could not be propositionally ultimate, and apparently no reason why having the concept "C" need depend on having a concept that represents T. This seems intuitively wrong; it seems that "C" ought to be lumped together with "gricular" as disjunctive in the sense relevant to disqualifying both of them from being propositionally ultimate.

A defender of the view that constituent properties are coarse-grained may answer that all that is shown by the example of "C," at most, is that there are constraints on ultimate constituents, or sources of concept dependence, beyond those implied by the fine-grained doctrine. The doctrine seems to deal effectively with the most central examples of intuitively strange words, even if certain other examples, such as perhaps the example of "C," lie beyond its scope.

It would be preferable, however, other things being equal, if the scope of the doctrine could be enlarged. Suppose that we adopted an interpretation of the doctrine in which constituent properties are assumed to be fine-grained. We may then hope to find some basis to regard the fine-grained property expressed by "C" as unnatural. This would give us an explanation for why it intuitively seems that "C" could not be propositionally ultimate.

What could be a basis for regarding the fine-grained property expressed by "C" as unnatural, though the coarse-grained property expressed by "C" is natural? Let me suggest an approach to this. In what follows, it will be convenient to assume that, when a word is analyzed, the analysans does not contain any superfluous words. To determine whether the fine-grained property expressed by the (simple or complex) term "F" is natural, we first derive an *analytic expansion* of "F." This is accomplished by replacing words in "F," wherever possible, by synonymous complex expressions or by analysans, continuing this process until we arrive at unanalyzable words that are not synonymous with any com-

---

[14]Bealer's view is close to that of the present paragraph; see Bealer 1982, chapter 8.

plex expressions. (Note that "*F*" will not have a unique analytic expansion, if for no other reason than, trivially, because the synonyms and analysans can be couched in a number of languages.) Now, my suggestion is that the fine-grained property in question might be said to be natural if and only if no analytic expansion of "*F*" contains either superfluous words, or negative constructions, or disjunctive constructions. The requirement about superfluous words is enough to render GH unnatural, as well as, for example, the fine-grained property of being red and red.[15] More fundamentally, the fine-grained property expressed by "C" is unnatural because any analytic expansion of "C" contains negative or disjunctive constructions. The discussion of coarse-grained naturalness in chapter 3 (and in appendix 2) revealed that applying disjunctive or negative constructions to natural properties typically yields unnatural properties. On the present suggestion, it is a blanket rule with respect to natural fine-grained properties that they must not involve disjunctive or negative constructions.[16]

Let us assume that, if "*F*" cannot be analytically expanded any further, in the sense explained, then "*F*" itself counts as a degenerate analytic expansion of "*F*," as does the result of replacing any word in "*F*" by a synonymous word. We can then suggest that "*F*" and "*G*" express the same fine-grained property if and only if any analytic expansion of "*F*" is an analytic expansion of "*G*."[17] On this view, a fine-grained property has an inherent structure independent of the structure of propositions. A given fine-grained property, if it is natural, may be an ultimate constituent or a non-ultimate constituent, depending on whether its inherent structure shows up in the structure of a proposition. For instance, the fine-grained property expressed by "M" is an ultimate constituent of the proposition expressed by "M was played" and a non-ultimate constituent of the distinct proposition expressed by "The melody consisting of the succession $N_1, N_2, \ldots N_n$ was played."

A point worth emphasizing is that, on the account just sketched, fine-grained naturalness presupposes coarse-grained naturalness. This is because the notion of a natural fine-grained property was partly explained in terms of the notion of analysis, which was in turn partly explained (in section 2 of this appendix) in terms of the notion of a natural coarse-grained property discussed in chapter 3. So, at bottom, we have the notion of a natural coarse-grained property.[18] Indeed, any fine-grained

---

[15]Note that whereas, on the earlier account of analysis, "green" and "GH" have the same (null) analysis, they have different analytic expansions.

[16]This rule should probably be complicated in various ways (e.g., by specifying degrees of fine-grained naturalness), but it may suffice for my immediate purposes.

[17]I am imagining that "*F*" and "*G*" contain no singular terms; otherwise, some qualifications may be required.

[18]I do not rule out the possibility of developing these ideas in a different direction. One might, for example, take the notion of analysis as itself unanalyzable and perhaps build up everything from there. The sort of approach indicated in the text seems more intuitively promising.

property can be associated with a set-theoretical construction in which logical operators are applied to certain natural coarse-grained properties, that is, the properties expressed by the unanalyzable words in an analytic expansion. One should, however, repeat at the fine-grained level the distinction made in chapter 3 between "ontological inegalitarians" and "elitists." The former will say that only natural fine-grained properties are genuine universals, the unnatural properties being mere set-theoretical constructions. The elitist acknowledges no such ontological difference between natural and unnatural properties.

The interpretation of the fine-grained doctrine in terms of fine-grained constituent properties has the advantage of treating examples like "C" in what seems to be the intuitively right way. One would have to examine other kinds of examples to see whether this interpretation is uniformly as successful as the interpretation in terms of coarse-grained properties.[19] The former suffers, however, from another kind of limitation, in that the intuitive motivation for the specified notion of a natural fine-grained property is obscure. In chapter 3, the notion of property-naturalness was guided by the idea that only in some cases does sharing a property seem to make things "really similar" or make them "really have something in common." But, surely, things that share GH, or that share C, really have something in common and are really similar. What is the force of saying, then, that these properties are "unnatural"?

I shall not attempt to decide between the two ways of interpreting the fine-grained doctrine. Both ways are probably worth developing further. In the discussions in Chapters 6 and 7, what I say is intended to be applicable to both views.

---

[19]The interpretation in terms of fine-grained properties may also help to deal with the Kripkean problem discussed in the previous section. One can say that, even if the coarse-grained property expressed by "tiger" turns out to be unnatural, the fine-grained property expressed by the word is natural, and it is the latter that is the ultimate constituent of tiger-propositions.

References

Achinstein, P. (1983). *The Nature of Explanation* (Oxford University Press, New York).

Armstrong, D.M. (1978). *Universals and Scientific Realism*, Volumes 1 and 2 (Cambridge University Press, London).

Bambrough, R. (1966). "Universals and Family Resemblances," reprinted in Pitcher, G., ed., *Wittgenstein* (Anchor Books, New York).

Bealer, G. (1982). *Quality and Concept* (Oxford University Press, New York).

Burge, T. (1979). "Individualism and the Mental," in French, P.E., Uehling, T.E., and Wettstein, H.K., eds., *Midwest Studies in Philosophy*, Volume 4 (University of Minnesota Press, Minneapolis).

Butler, J. (1736). "Of Personal Identity," Appendix 1 of *The Analogy of Religion*; reprinted in Perry 1975.

Carnap, R. (1956). "Empiricism, Semantics, and Ontology," in *Meaning and Necessity*, 2d edition (University of Chicago Press, Chicago).

Chisholm, R. (1976). *Person and Object* (Open Court, LaSalle, Ill.).

Davidson, D. (1975). "Thought and Talk," in Guttenplan, S., ed., *Mind and Language* (Oxford University Press, London).

Davidson, D. (1977). "Reality without Reference," *Dialectica* 31, 247–53; reprinted in *Inquiries into Truth and Interpretation*.

Davidson, D. (1984). *Inquiries into Truth and Interpretation* (Oxford University Press, Oxford).

Field, H. (1975). "Conventionalism and Instrumentalism in Semantics," *Nous* 9(4), 375–405.

Field, H. (1982). "Realism and Relativism," *Journal of Philosophy* 79(10), 553–67.

Fodor, J. (1975). *The Language of Thought* (Thomas Y. Crowell, New York).

Fodor, J. (1981). "The Present Status of the Innateness Controversy," in *Representations* (MIT Press, Cambridge, Mass.).

Frege, G. (1980). *Philosophical and Mathematical Correspondence*, Gabriel, G., et al., ed. (Chicago University Press, Chicago).

Garner, W.R. (1947). *The Processing of Information and Structure* (Lawrence Erlbaum, Potomac, Maryland).

Goldman, A. (1987). "Cognitive Science and Metaphysics," *Journal of Philosophy* 94(10), 537–44.

Goodman, N. (1972). *Problems and Projects* (Bobbs-Merril, New York).

Goodman, N. (1973). *Fact, Fiction, and Forecast*, 3d edition (Bobbs-Merrill, New York).

Goodman, N. (1977). *The Structure of Appearance*, 3d edition (D. Reidel Publishing, Dordrecht, Holland).

Goodman, N. (1978). *Ways of Worldmaking* (Hackett, Indianapolis).

Goodman, N., and Quine, W.V. (1947). "Steps toward a Constructive Nominalism," *Journal of Symbolic Logic* 12, 105–22; reprinted in *Problems and Projects*.

Hampshire, S. (1959). *Thought and Action* (Chatto & Windus, London).

Harman, G. (1975). "Language, Thought, and Communication," in Gunderson, K., ed., *Minnesota Studies in the Philosophy of Science*, Volume 7 (University of Minnesota Press, Minneapolis).

Harman, G. (1978). "Is There Mental Representation?" in Savage, C.W., ed., *Perception and Cognition: Issues in the Philosophy of Psychology* (University of Minnesota Press, Minneapolis).

Hirsch, E. (1982). *The Concept of Identity* (Oxford University Press, New York).

Hirsch, E. (1986). "Metaphysical Necessity and Conceptual Truth," in French, P.A, Uehling, T.E., and Wettstein, H.K., eds., *Midwest Studies in Philosophy*, Volume 11 (University of Minessota Press, Minneapolis).

Hirsch, E. (1989). "Negativity and Complexity: Some Logical Considerations," *Synthese* 81, 217–41.

James, W. (1890). *The Principles of Psychology*, Volume 1 (Holt, New York).

James, W. (1907). *Pragmatism* (Longmans, Green, and Co., New York).

Kaplan, D. (1989). "Demonstratives," in Almog, J., Perry, J., and Wettstein, H.K., eds., *Themes from Kaplan* (Oxford University Press, New York).

Kohler, W. (1947). *Gestalt Psychology* (Liveright, New York).

Kripke, S. (1971). "Identity and Necessity," in Munitz, M.K., ed., *Identity and Individuation* (NYU Press, New York).

Kripke, S. (1977). "Speaker's Reference and Semantic Reference," in French, P.A, Uehling, T.E., and Wettstein, H.K., eds., *Midwest Studies in Philosophy*, Volume 2 (University of Minessota Press, Minneapolis).

Kripke, S. (1980). *Naming and Necessity* (Harvard University Press, Cambridge, Mass.).

Kripke, S. (1982). *Wittgenstein on Rules and Private Languages* (Harvard University Press, Cambridge, Mass.).

Lewis, C.I. (1929). *Mind and the World Order* (Dover, New York).

Lewis, D. (1973). *Counterfactuals* (Harvard University Press, Cambridge, Mass.).

Lewis, D. (1983a). "Extrinsic Properties," *Philosophical Studies* 44(2), 197–200.

Lewis, D. (1983b). "New Work for a Theory of Universals," *Australasian Journal of Philosophy* 61(4), 343–77.

Lewis, D. (1983c). *Philosophical Papers*, Volume 1 (Oxford University Press, New York).

Lewis, D. (1984). "Putnam's Paradox," *Australasian Journal of Philosophy* 62(3), 221–36.

Lewis, D. (1986). *On the Plurality of Worlds* (Basil Blackwell, New York).

Lewis, D., and Lewis, S. (1970). "Holes," *Australasian Journal of Philosophy* 48(2), 206–212.

Nagel, T. (1979). *Mortal Questions* (Cambridge University Press, Cambridge).

Nozick, R. (1981). *Philosophical Explanations* (Harvard University Press, Cambridge, Mass.).

Perry, J., ed. (1975). *Personal Identity* (University of California Press, Berkeley).

Plato, *Phaedrus*.

Putnam, H. (1975). "The Meaning of 'Meaning,'" in Gunderson, K., ed., *Minnesota Studies in the Philosophy of Science*, Volume 7 (University of Minnesota Press, Minneapolis).

Putnam, H. (1981a). *Reason, Truth, and History* (Cambridge University Press, Cambridge).

Putnam, H. (1981b). "Reductionism and the Nature of Psychology " in Haugeland, J., ed., *Mind Design* (Bradford Books, Montgomery, Vt.).

Putnam, H. (1987). *The Many Faces of Realism* (Open Court, LaSalle, Ill.).

Quine, W.V. (1954). "Reduction to a Dyadic Predicate," *Journal of Symbolic Logic* 19(3), 180–82.

Quine, W.V. (1961). *From a Logical Point of View* (Harvard University Press, Cambridge, Mass.).

Quine, W.V. (1969a). "Natural Kinds," in Quine 1969b.

Quine, W.V. (1969b). *Ontological Relativity and Other Essays* (Columbia University Press, New York).

Quine, W.V. (1969c). *Set Theory and Its Logic*, revised edition (Harvard University Press, Cambridge, Mass.).

Quine, W.V. (1972). *Methods of Logic*, 3d edition (Holt, Rinehart and Winston, New York).

Quine, W.V. (1973). *The Roots of Reference* (Open Court, LaSalle, Ill.).

Quine, W.V., and Ullian, J.S. (1970). *The Web of Belief* (Random House, New York).

Rawls, J. (1971). *A Theory of Justice* (Harvard University Press, Cambridge, Mass.).

Reid, T. (1785). "Of the Nature and Origin of Our Notion of Personal Identity," in *Essays on the Intellectual Powers of Man*, essay III, chapter III, section II; reprinted in Perry 1975.

Rosch, E. (1977a). "Human Categorization," in Warren, N., ed., *Studies in Cross-Cultural Psychology*, Volume 1 (Academy Press, London).

Rosch, E. (1977b). "Linguistic Relativity," in Johnson-Laird, P.N., and Wason, P.C., eds., *Thinking: Readings in Cognitive Science* (Cambridge University Press, New York).

Russell, B. (1918). "The Philosophy of Logical Atomism," *The Monist* 28, 495–527; reprinted in Marsh, R.C., ed., *Logic and Knowledge* (G. Allen, London, 1956).

Russell, B. (1948). *Human Knowledge, Its Scope and Limits* (Simon & Schuster, New York).

Ryle, G. (1931). "Systematically Misleading Expressions," *Proceedings of the Aristotelian Society*, 1931–32; reprinted in Flew, A., ed., *Logic and Language*, Volume 1 (Basil Blackwell, Oxford, 1951).

Salmon, N. (1986). *Frege's Puzzle* (MIT Press, Cambridge, Mass.).

Sanford, D.H. (1966). "Negative Terms," *Analysis* 27(6), 201–205.

Schiffer, S. (1987). *The Remnants of Meaning* (MIT Press, Cambridge, Mass.).

Shoemaker, S. (1963). *Self-Knowledge and Self-Identity* (Cornell University Press, Ithaca, N.Y.).

Shoemaker, S. (1969). "Comments On Chisholm," in Care, N.S., and Grimm, R.H., eds., *Perception and Personal Identity* (Case Western Reserve University, Cleveland).

Shoemaker, S. (1975). "On Projecting the Unprojectible," *Philosophical Review* 94(2), 178–219; reprinted in Shoemaker 1984.

Shoemaker, S. (1979). "Identity, Properties, and Causality," in French, P.A, Uehling, T.E., and Wettstein, H.K., eds., *Midwest Studies in Philosophy*, Volume 4 (University of Minnesota Press, Minneapolis); reprinted in Shoemaker 1984.

Shoemaker, S. (1980). "Causality and Properties," in Inwagen, P., ed., *Time and Cause* (D. Reidel Publishing, Dordrecht, Holland); reprinted in Shoemaker 1984.

Shoemaker, S. (1984). *Identity, Cause, and Mind* (Cambridge University Press, London).

Shoemaker, S. (1988). "On What There Are," *Philosophical Topics* 16(1), 201–223.

Sommers, F. (1967). "Types and Ontology," in Strawson, P.F., ed., *Philosophical Logic* (Oxford University Press, London).

Stalnaker, R.C. (1987). *Inquiry* (MIT Press, Cambridge, Mass.).

Strawson, P.F. (1966). *The Bounds of Sense* (Methuen, London).

Tversky, A. (1977). "Features of Similarity," *Psychological Review* 84(4), 327–52.

Ullian, J.S. (1961). "More on 'Grue' and Grue," *Philosophical Review* 70, 383–89.

Urmson, J.O. (1956). *Philosophical Analysis* (Oxford University Press, Oxford).

Van Cleve, J. (1986). "Mereological Essentialism, Mereological Conjunctivism, and Identity through Time," in French, P.A., Uehling, T.E., and Wettstein, H.K., eds., *Midwest Studies in Philosophy*, Volume 11 (University of Minnesota Press, Minneapolis).

van Fraassen, B. (1980). *The Scientific Image* (Oxford University Press, Oxford).

van Inwagen, P. (1981). "The Doctrine of Arbitrary Undetached Parts," *Pacific Philosophical Quarterly* 62(2), 123–137.

Wallace, J. (1977). "Only in the Context of a Sentence Do Words Have Any Meaning," in French, P.A., Uehling, T.E., and Wettstein, H.K., eds., *Midwest Studies in Philosophy*, Volume 2 (University of Minnesota Press, Minneapolis).

Wiggins, D. (1967). *Identity and Spatio-temporal Continuity* (Basil Blackwell, Oxford).

Wiggins, D. (1980). *Sameness and Substance* (Harvard University Press, Cambridge, Mass.).

Index

Printed in the United States
18544LVS00002B/132